The Homeless Transient in the Great Depression: New York State, 1929–1941

JOAN M. CROUSE

STATE UNIVERSITY OF NEW YORK PRESS

Published by
State University of New York Press, Albany

For information, address State University of New York
Press, State University Plaza, Albany, N.Y., 12246

Library of Congress Cataloging in Publication Data

Crouse, Joan M., 1948–
  The homeless transient in the Great Depression.

    Revision of thesis (doctoral)—State University
of New York at Buffalo
    Bibliography: p.
    Includes index.
    1. Transients, Relief of—New York (State)—History—
20th century. 2. Homelessness—New York (State)—
History—20th century. 3. Domicile in public welfare—
New York (State)—History—20th century. 4. Transients,
Relief of—Government policy—United States. I. Title.
HV4506.N7C76   1986   362.5'8'09747   86-14451
ISBN 0-88706-311-X
ISBN 0-88706-312-8 (pbk.)

10 9 8 7 6 5 4 3 2 1

To My Family
For Rallying To The Cause

Contents

List of Illustrations

Acknowledgments

WRITING a book and seeing it through publication is a humbling experience, for it is only then that the author fully realizes how indebted she is to others for their expertise, assistance, and moral support. This has been just such an experience and the thanks are many.

My indebtedness begins with the original committee that oversaw the writing of my doctoral dissertation at the State University of New York at Buffalo. In the acknowledgment to that manuscript, I expressed my appreciation to Selig Adler, Milton Plesur, and David Gerber for their guidance, advice, and support. As the present study began with that original work, I thank them again. In the intervening years, the committee chairman, Professor Adler, passed away. With him went an invaluable source of inspiration and encouragement. Both his red pen and his kind words have been sorely missed.

Since that time, many more friends, colleagues, and committed professionals have lent their assistance to this project. I appreciate all of the assistance I have received from the numerous librarians, archivists, curators, and support staff who have made seemingly impossible tasks seem routine. Among their number are those who serve at Lockwood Library, State University of New York at Buffalo; the New York State Library and Archives; the Buffalo and Erie County Historical Society Library; the libraries at the University of Rochester and Syracuse University; the Rochester Public Library; and the Corning Public Library. Special thanks go to David Klaassen, curator of the Social Welfare History Archives Center, University of Minnesota, for his genuine interest in finding the most elusive records and the personal attention he gave this project; to

Judith Johnson, archivist for the Salvation Army Archives and Research Center, for her equal commitment to searching beyond the card catalogs and reference shelves to find just what was needed; and to the researchers and staff of the National Archives who kept the "trucks" rolling to the Research Room.

To my colleagues at Hilbert College, I also am indebted. Carmen Notaro read the complete manuscript, offering valuable suggestions and comment, and assisted in the indexing process. Members of the English Department, Edward Holmes, Jocelyn Hughes, Michael Degnan, Charles Ernst, Sister Alberta Surowiec, and Marc Smith, all assisted in proofreading. The Faculty Development Committee provided much needed funds for travel expenses. I also appreciate the secretarial and copying services provided for my use by the college.

Finally, my gratitude comes home to my family. This has been truly a time when all came together to give unselfishly. My mother and father, Marion and Milton Langenfeld, provided the moral support, while my sister, Carol Kern, went well beyond the call by typing the entire manuscript and offering perceptive comments along the way. My husband, Warren Crouse, has been there every step of the way. He has assisted me professionally, often putting aside his own doctoral research to accompany me on research trips, to run to the library for that missing citation, or simply to steer me away from digressions, and as a friend who stuck by sharing my joys and lifting my spirits when they so needed it. I thank my daughter Marla for patience and understanding beyond her years.

J.M. Crouse

Introduction

In the tradition of American legends, the "man on the move" has generally been a larger than life national hero. The pilgrim braving the merciless ocean, the pioneer following new horizons, and the cowboy in constant pursuit of the sunset, are all symbols of American individualism, determination, cunning, and, above all, success. Each such hero was in effect a "migrant" or a "transient," but, in the ways of legend building, the more romantic terms "pioneer," "frontiersman," and "adventurer" have always been preferable to the more pejorative, but more accurate, former labels.

When romanticized through these heroes, geographic mobility takes on a certain intrinsic worth and becomes entwined with other American traditions, values, and myths, thereby gaining additional validity from them. The American Dream, for example, relies heavily on the success stories of the restless men and women who settled the country and won the West. Even though their efforts took them far from the safety of their home communities and put their very lives in danger, their achievements gave substance to the myth that in America success was and is always possible somewhere beyond the horizon. Similarly, when Horace Greeley exhorted the poor of the East to "Go West," he gave added credence to the belief that, in this land of abundance, opportunities were ripe for those willing to seek them out. With the introduction of the "frontier thesis," historian Frederick Jackson Turner gave this westward migration credit for the very development of the peculiar American character and our unique form of democracy. While Turner's thesis has been modified significantly, the traditions it reflected are not subject to as easy revision. The belief that in America when one

1

becomes discontented he need only pull up stakes and move on to something better is an integral part of the American Dream. Thus, in our tradition migration has not only satisfied the individual hungers of the pioneers of the past and present, but has also satisfied needs in the American psyche.

The idea of a country on the move has fit conveniently well with our economic system, as well as with our ideals. Mobile labor built our railroads, bridges, and roads; it mined our natural resources; it tilled, cultivated, and harvested the Great Plains; and it has and still does fill in seasonally whenever industry or agriculture beckon. With the course of industrialization, and its reliance on a readily accessible surplus labor force, the legitimization of the concept of mobility has proven to be an asset for economic development. This reality was recognized as early as the eighteenth century by Adam Smith when he wrote in *The Wealth of Nations* that a free circulation of labor was essential to the free market system.

Laden thus with well established values and confident of his integral part in the industrial economy, the man on the move has been able to assume a small piece of the hero character as he relives in his own way his pioneer heritage. Both the ideal and the economy it served so well, however, were and are carefully balanced mechanisms. They run well as long as each segment of the economy balances out the others and the transient laborer is able to reap some rewards. In periods of economic depression, when the surplus of labor swells to such a state that it is no longer considered a beneficial pool and becomes instead a horde of unproductive and unconsuming unemployed, the balance is destroyed and the system stalls. During these hard times the man on the move no longer looks like a hero as he stands in soup lines, begs at back doors, scavenges through garbage dumps, and sleeps in make-shift shelters, on park benches, or in the dank basements of police stations. Instead of being lauded as a sign of America's greatness he is seen as a threat to the health and financial well-being of local communities, and his status often plunges well below the questionable "transient" category down to that of "tramp" or "bum." In the words of one contemporary depression-weary social worker, such men became "pioneers without a frontier."[1]

In times of economic scarcity the concepts of pioneer and adventurer are luxuries that we cannot afford. Instead of remembering the place of the transients in our history, our dreams, and our economy, we turn defensively to other less romantic but very apt propriate traditions from deep in our past. During the very years when America was jubilantly proclaiming the virtues of her wide expanses and the freedom of each and every American to journey where he would in search of promised successes, there quietly accumulated all the legal and attitudinal devices necessary to prevent that very movement. In times of economic distress its benefits became detriments. From the earliest days of colonial America attitudes contrary to those ballyhooed in the American Dream existed and were nurtured. Attitudes such as community exclusiveness and a fear of wandering strangers, first imported from England, were firmly entrenched in the American system through the adaptation of harsh vagrancy laws that branded poor wanderers as criminals and strict settlement and removal laws, modeled on the English Poor Law of 1601, that limited the right of transients to impose their presence and needs upon communities other than their own. The laws were so specific and exclusive that communities were able to build statutory walls around themselves that were as effective as if they were made of brick. Legally, unwanted transients could not only be denied relief in times of need, but, if considered undesirable, they could be forcibly removed from the vicinity.

What we are seeing here is that there are two sets of values that determine the American response to the individual on the move. There is, first of all, the well-publicized version that is the stuff of our legends and ideals. In a vast and bountiful country like the United States, so the story goes, any individual seeking to better himself need only move on to find his dream. Concurrently, in this version America is made up of friendly communities always ready to open their doors to the industrious traveler because of the mutual advantages to be accrued. This is the interpretation of the American experience that is romanticized in our history and praised as part of our continuing heritage. It has been buttressed by the aphorisms of Poor Richard, the example of Abe Lincoln, the stories of Daniel Boone, and the Horatio Alger myth, and it continues to receive a good deal of patriotic attention. However, there are other values that are equally strong and equally American that are not so well publicized precisely because they do not complement the above model. The American legal system contains within it well used statutes to limit the mobility of Americans. This is not to deny that America has been, and still is, a geographically mobile country. However, the individual who ventured off to improve himself, through at least the first half of the twentieth century, often did so at a substantial risk. If he were to succeed in his quest he never had to realize the consequences of that risk. If, however, he found himself in need during the course of his travels, whether due to his own shortcomings or to external economic conditions, he would have quickly learned of the second set of attitudes and the laws to enforce them.

In other words, we have two ways of perceiving and dealing with migrant people. In times of prosperity they are happy reminders of the past and welcome labor in the industrial system. In times of economic depression they are surplus people, looking little like American heroes. They are demanding of the community by their idle presence. Instead of enriching it through their talents, they present a competitive economic threat, and, as such, they are guarded against. This latter response is precisely how indigent transients were perceived during the Great Depression.

The Great Depression dwarfed the experiences of the nineteenth century by any standard of comparison. The extent of the economic collapse and the dislocation it caused were unparalleled in our history. As home mortgages were lost, as dust storms and foreclosures pushed farmers off the land, and as unemployment urged people to move on looking for opportunity elsewhere as their forefathers had done, the number of transients increased from a healthy flow to a deluge. The number of people noted by newspaper articles as sleeping on park benches or in "hoovervilles" shifted from a few good human interest stories, like those told by *The New York Times* under captions such as "54 Men Hail Arrest in Subway" and "Jobless Women in Parks,"[2] to a phenomenon involving an estimated 200,000 to 400,000 people in what *Business Week* called "one of the greatest interstate migrations since the gold rush."[3] As the numbers increased, state and community defense mechanisms against them tightened. In times when the needs of the resident unemployed taxed the local community beyond endurance, the welcome that could be afforded to the nonresident stranger was naturally limited. In such a predicament most communities relied on those devices at hand, namely, residency and vagrancy laws, to protect their limited tax funds for the "worthy" residents and to "move-on" the unwanted stranger.

On the federal level, aid to the wandering poor was sporadic and incomplete. The Hoover administration, with its staunch belief in the values of volunteerism and self-help, did little to acknowledge the government's responsibility to aid these victims of the depression. The only visible assistance offered was in the form of a pamphlet distributed to local communities to help them cope with the problem.[4] Thus, the nonresident poor had to await Franklin D. Roosevelt and the promises of the New Deal for any substantial government aid. With the passage of the Federal Emergency Relief Act in May 1933, the government provided funding for a Federal Transient Program.[5] With this program there began a brief two-year experiment in government responsibility that involved forty-four states and, at peak, over three hundred thousand individual transients[6] Despite the success attributed to the federal program by administration and observers alike, an order to stop intake was issued in September 1935, and a quick dismantling of the program began. In a time of foreseeable economic recovery, and with increasing pressure from the business community, the New Deal philosophy was being directed away from direct relief emergency measures into the more conservative policy of work relief. The time, however, was not practical for absorbing unemployed transients along with the resident unemployed into work programs; thus, the state and local governments were again faced with the dilemma of how to cope with the transient.

The center stage for this study, by reason of Washington's default, will be the state. Since the federal government responded only temporarily to the needs of the transient, it was the state that was left to formulate and implement policy to deal with transient relief. The "welcome" received by transients in the state of California has already been vividly described by both contemporaries and historians from Carey McWilliams' classic *Factories in the Field*, to the more recent *California and the Dust Bowl Migration* by Walter Stein. The brutality of border patrols and roving vigilante gangs, as well as the injustices of exclusion laws and unreasonable settlement laws, are already familiar. But all transients did not make the pilgrimage westward. Instead, these modern day pioneers criss-crossed the country making a jumble out of Turner's "safety valve" thesis, roaming from South to West, West to East, and from South to North in search of fleeting economic opportunity. Unfortunately, concern for the hostility met by transients in California has long overshadowed interest in contrasting experiences in other states. Instead of lamenting again over the well-publicized tragedies of John Steinbeck's fictional Joad family of *The Grapes of Wrath* and the many others they represented, it is time to move on to examine the experience of transients in other states and to relate that experience to broader historical and contemporary issues. The purpose of this study is to examine a state that was looked at by contemporary social workers and concerned observers alike as a model of social responsibility and to see just how the transient fared in that environment. The state they referred to and which this study will examine is New York State.

The story of the migrants is told in the setting of New York before, during, and after the federal government's involvement in transient relief. Immediately, almost prophetically, before the depression, the state had revamped its old poor law creating a more "modern" public welfare law. It was, therefore, ready with new machinery to meet the transient problem in the early years of the depression. This fortuitous timing allows us to study how the state perceived its modern welfare duties at a time when the federal government's perception remained rooted in the past. When Washington finally did assume responsiblity for the transient in 1933 through specific programs and financial reimbursement to the states, New York cooperated vigorously and did so until the dissolution of the program in 1935. This intermediate phase provides an excellent opportunity to study an early example of state and federal cooperation in public relief. From 1935 to 1940 New York, like other states, willingly or not, inherited responsibility for the transient. This last period is especially interesting because it offers a unique opportunity for investigating how the state and the local communities reconciled their concepts of social responsibility with the added burden of the transient, without philosophic or financial aid from Washington. The study ends in 1941 with the report of the House of Representatives Select Committee to Investigate the Migration of Destitute Citizens. While the committee's report went into great detail as to the enormity of the situation during the depression years, its findings were somewhat anticlimactic as most people accepted the common belief that wartime mobilization was rapidly absorbing the surplus population. While this assessment was only partially true, and the solution was temporary at best, the migrant was once again relegated to the "forgotten man" category not to be seriously reexamined until the present generation.

Besides correcting the mistaken impression that the mid-section of the country got up and moved west in the 1930s, an examination of New York's adjustment to a problem of this magnitude offers added insight into a decade of our history noted for its great social upheavals. FDR and his New Deal are given credit, or condemnation, for beginning this country on the road to the welfare state; yet, when one looks at what was happening prior to and even during the New Deal on the state level, questions arise as to just who was in the forefront in the development of social welfare—the federal government or the state. Thus, while this study is concerned with asking the question of how well New York accepted its social responsibility, the answer to this limited question has broad implications. Was the federal government merely playing catch-up to the grassroots level of social welfare? While the rhetoric of the New Deal spoke of the "forgotten man," were the states already dealing effectively with him?

This perspective from the state level provides a necessary counterbalance in a history that is dominated by the charisma and overwhelming presence of FDR and a precedent-shattering federal government encroaching at will into previously forbidden waters. It is important for historians to resist this natural attraction and change focus to the grassroots level to complete the history of the New Deal. James Patterson broke this ground in 1969 with *The New Deal and the States* and then called upon fellow scholars to "turn from the excitement of Pennsylvania Avenue to the more prosaic events of Albany, Atlanta, and Sante Fe."[7] He challenged the profession to take a new measure of the New Deal, to set it in a new context and see it from a new perspective. Work has been underway since.

In addition to its contribution to New Deal history, the study of transient relief in the 1930s also has contemporary relevance. As with most histories of social welfare policy and practice, past example—the failures and successes of our predecessors—can provide present day policy makers with valuable information to aid them in the hard decisions they face. The same questions asked in the 1930s regarding the extent of the state's responsibility and the long-range consequences of welfare are still being asked today. Does welfare encourage idleness? Does it debilitate our society and our economy? After almost fifty years of expanding the federal cloak over an increasing segment of our population, we are now experiencing a backlash against the whole concept of federal responsibility for the social welfare of the individual. As federal emphasis is now definitely focused on returning responsibility to the state governments through a "New Federalism," we cannot help but question if the consequences to the individual of this move will parallel those experienced by the transient in the 1930s. We must question whether the states are in any better position to absorb the needy than they were almost fifty years ago.

Before proceeding with our investigation, some clarifications are necessary. The first deals with terminology. In the early days of the depression, before real note was taken of their particular plight, transients were often mistakenly referred to as hobos. As their numbers increased and people were forced to notice that they were in fact a distinct new breed, the label *transient* was applied. Friendly journalists wrote about the transient problem, Congress investigated transient relief, and the government established the Federal Transient Program. After the termination of that program, the term transient took on a certain stigma, so a new label was adopted — *migrant*. The literature now spoke about the plight of the migrant, and Congress held hearings on the interstate migration of destitute citizens. By the end of the decade the terms migrant and transient were being used almost interchangeably even by old friends. For our purposes, however, the term migrant has a slightly too large context that may lead to confusion between the subjects of this study and seasonal or casual laborers who are commonly referred to as migratory labor. Therefore, we will continue to use the original label of transient to distinguish those persons who were, for one reason or another, away from their place of legal residence, and were usually in transit in search of a job or a community in which to relocate.

Second, it is important to note that all depression transients were not Joads, that is, displaced and indigent agricultural families. The image created by Steinbeck's sensitive prose and reinforced on the screen by Henry Fonda and Jane Darwell of devastated Oklahoma farm land and dispossessed Oakies trekking westward is overpowering. Yet the migration that Steinbeck wrote about was a phenomenon of the second half of the depression decade, reaching its peak, in fact, well after the termination of the Federal Transient Program. This Dust Bowl exodus was preceded in the early to mid-thirties by the equally significant, if less publicized, uprooting of industrial, urban America, an uprooting that was to continue in the shadow of the publicity spawned by the Oakies well into the next dacade. It is this transient who was most represented in the Northeast and makes up the bulk of the population examined by this study.

Third, it will become readily apparent before the reader proceeds too far into the text that the story being told has a very white complexion and masculine population. This is definitely a product of the contemporary situation and not the author's predilections.

While transiency knew no racial or sexual bounds, the vast majority of the transient population was white, male, and relatively young. As we will see, there were more transient women than the statistics allow. This was the direct result of standard policy on the part of all relief-dispensing agencies to return unattached women to their homes. Those who did not want to be returned avoided the agencies. and, consequently, were not counted by the statisticians. Blacks, on the other hand, often found the same agencies discriminating and either chose not to apply or were rejected at intake. There was also a thin line between transiency and vagrancy and the homeless black man found it wise to keep a low profile and not to challenge officials to make a decision. Consequently, the material available on women and blacks is limited. Whenever possible, however, their stories will be told.

Finally, both time and geographic boundaries are, by necessity, treated liberally. The title of this study indicates that the focus will be on New York State during the depression, yet we are dealing with attitudes toward and perceptions of the "stranger" that are rooted deeply in our past, and a "clientele" that knows no state boundaries. The transient who summers in the Midwest may winter in a Northern city. The man found in Buffalo one day may hop a freight and be in Cleveland the next. Whether we catch up with him in Chicago or Rochester, Syracuse or Detroit, his story will be basically the same. To realize the impact of long-held attitudes and perceptions on the transient we will listen whenever and wherever he can be found, regardless of state boundaries. Likewise, to realize the impact of long-held attitudes toward the transient, we will look back through the nineteenth century, to colonial experience, and further yet, to English precedent. It is to these precedents from deep in our past that we now turn.

§ 1 §

Precedents From The Past

WHEN the indigent transient crossed the border into the Empire State during the hungry years of the Great Depression, the people he met there, like Americans everywhere, represented a complex mixture of values, traditions, and ideals which were the product of generations of American experience and centuries of English heritage. For the transient, the values that were most important in this encounter were those that would help to determine the welcome to be accorded him by the state, the community, and the individual. What went into that welcome was an explosive mixture of English and American laws, customs, and attitudes.

The first element in the social, cultural, and legal concoction that determined the "appropriate" attitude toward the wandering poor came from our English heritage. To begin with, centuries of harsh and repressive English vagrancy laws had encouraged a very definite fear of wandering strangers. Working against the very social and economic forces that were preparing the mobile surplus labor pool that was to feed England's industrial revolution, the landowning class was formulating laws as early as the fourteenth century to keep their labor immobile by branding wandering laborers as criminal and subjecting them to corporal punishment.[1]

As the problem persisted, subsequent laws became more inclusive and prescribed punishment progressively more severe. Under Henry VII authorization was given for a search through the realm for "idle vagabonds and suspected persons living suspiciously." Those apprehended were to be punished by three days in the stocks on bread and water. During the reign of Henry VIII the increase in

11

vagabondage and begging led to a more severe punishment for wandering able-bodied beggars. They were

> to be taken to the nearest market town, or other place most convenient, and there to be tied to the end of a cart naked and be beaten with whips throughout the town until their bodies are bloody, after which they are to return to the place where they were born, or where they last dwelt by the space of three years.

Under Edward VI the severity of punishment was increased. Because "idleness and vagabundrye" were believed to be the "mother and roote of all theftes robberyes and all evill actes and other mischiefs," the law provided that any person found loitering or wandering and not looking for work should be arrested as a vagabond, marked with a *V* on the breast with a hot iron, and given as a slave to whoever apprehended him. If he were to run away, the law provided that for the first offense an *S* was to be similarly branded on his forehead. The second such digression warranted death.[2]

For the next three centuries the old devices of detection and punishment were rewritten in the laws and new devices were added, including banishment to "the New found Land, the East and West Indies, Fraunce, Germanie, Spayne, and the Lowe Countries," and, during the American Revolution, impressment into the Royal Army or Navy.[3]

Despite the innovative punishments devised, the problem continued. To compensate, local officials resorted to alternative methods that were more realistic, but equally ineffective, for the treatment of vagrancy. One such alternative was to threaten vagrants with arrest to frighten or *warn* them out of town. Another was to arrest but not punish the transient. The official merely sent the apprehended vagrant on his way with a *pass* to the next parish where he would be again *passed-on*, from parish to parish, until presumably he reached the place of his birth or last legal residence. Since many knew where neither was, the passing and warning systems only added to the overall problem of the wandering poor.

What is particularly significant about the laws and local practices regarding vagrants is both their severity and the almost indiscriminate classification of a diverse aggregate of individuals, ranging from hardened criminals to honest laborers seeking employment, uprooted peasants, and individuals merely "unable to give a good account of themselves," under the common category of vagrant or vagabond. The cumulative effect of loosely labelling indigent strangers as criminals and subjecting them to degrading punishments such as public floggings, branding, and even execution, was to impose upon all poor strangers an unwarranted stigma and to reinforce in the minds of the populace an inbred fear of unattached strangers.

In addition to vagrancy laws, our English heritage provided a second even more influential precedent — the Elizabethan Poor Law. Passed in 1601, the poor law was meant to consolidate in law a very laudable recognition of local responsibility for the poor that had been developing on the grassroots level since the fourteenth century. The law imposed a compulsory tax on all inhabitants of every town, borough, and parish for the purpose of relieving the poor who had resided in their locale for at least three years.[4] While the local communities accepted responsibility for their own poor, they demanded in return assurances that their generosity would not be taxed by outsiders. Such assurance came in 1662 with the enactment of a statute entitled, An Act for the Better Relief of the Poor of This Kingdom, but more commonly known as the Law of Settlement and Removal. To prevent the poor from flocking to those "parishes where there is the best stock, the largest commons or wastes . . . and the most woods," and thereby to protect those parishes from having their bounty devoured by "strangers," the law provided that,

> upon complaint made by the churchwardens or overseers of the poor of any parish to any justice of the peace within 40 days after any such person or persons coming to settle as aforesaid in any tenement under the yearly value of ten pounds, for any two justices of the peace . . . to remove and convey such person or persons to such parish where he or they last legally settled.[5]

In other words, *settlement*, or the legal recognition of belonging, could be secured by forty days undisturbed residence, but, at the same time, anyone not able to pay a yearly rent of ten pounds was subject to *removal*, that is, physical expulsion, by force if necessary.

The result of An Act for the Better Relief of the Poor of This Kingdom has been aptly described by British historians Sidney and Beatrice Webb:

> From and after 1662, for more than a century and a quarter, any person (not belonging to a class of property owners numbering fewer than one-tenth of the population), who either, to take a situation, or merely on a visit to relations or friends, or for any other reason whatever, however lawful or laudable, came into a

parish in which he had not a settlement, was liable—however good his character and conduct, without any application for relief or for any other gift or favour, and even after he had secured remunerative employment—unless he could give sufficient security that he would never become chargeable to the parish, to the satisfaction of the Justices—to be summarily removed in custody, together with his wife and children, under ignominious and horribly uncomfortable conditions, to whatever parish, however distant, might be believed to be the place where, according to an extremely complicated and always uncertain code of law, he had his legal settlement.[6]

The law, therefore, put the wage earner, visitor, or seeker of employment in the same category as vagabonds and beggars and subjected them to removal, despite the fact that they had committed no crime and had not asked for any relief. For some persons so removed, this experience could become not only an inconvenience but a living nightmare. If their settlement was in doubt, they could find themselves removed endlessly back and forth across the realm, from parish to parish, while the courts attempted to determine who was actually responsible for them. To understand the effect of passing-on one need only remember the vagabond orphan Jo conjured up by the sensitive and socially aware conscience of Charles Dickens. When told once again to move on, Jo cried out in total desperation: "I've always been a-moving and a-moving on, ever since I was born. Where can I possibly move to, sir, more nor I do move!"[7] Jo and many more like him, who were guilty of no crime other than poverty and rootlessness, were stigmatized, nonetheless, as criminals.

The cumulative effect of the statutes and practices surveyed thus far reveals a very negative attitude toward the indigent stranger who had the misfortune to be in a community to which he did not belong. The vagrancy act labelled such wanderers criminals, be they highwaymen, or merely laborers looking for better wages in a new environment. The treatment accorded them by law was that used on the worst of felons, including whipping, branding, enslavement, and under certain circumstances, death. Thus, destitution became equated with crime, if one did not commit the "crime" of poverty in his own community.

England was to temper her poor laws with the passage of time. By the nineteenth century many of the harshest provisions were corrected through the amendment process. By that time, however, the

English colonies were already the United States, and they had long before included the English poor law system and past practice as part of their cultural baggage and had adopted them as part of the American way.

Throughout the colonial period the movement of strangers was carefully monitored through the use of vagrancy devices imitative of the English experience, while colonial settlement and removal laws determined what the local responsibility for the poor was and how it should be restricted. As early as 1629 Captain John Endicott was instructed by the Governor and Company of Massachusetts Bay Colony that "noe idle drone bee permitted to live amongst us." Three years later the General Court of Massachusetts ordered constables "to take knowledge . . . of common coasters," and to turn them over to the court.[8] These early instructions were followed throughout the seventeenth and eighteenth centuries by local ordinances and colonial laws restricting the right of citizens to entertain guests, requiring transients to register with local officials upon entering any town and/or post security, and even, in some localities, requiring a prior guarantee of employment.[9]

Colonial poor laws proceeded in pace. Rhode Island adopted local responsbility in its first colonial legislative session when the representatives voted to collect money for the poor, "according to the provisions of the law of England." The colony of Virginia adopted the English parish system of local relief in 1641, and Connecticut provided in its first general poor law of 1673 that "every town shall maintain their own poor." By 1770 all the British colonies, except Georgia, had adopted similar laws.[10]

It is laudable that the colonies recognized as early as they did the responsiblity to care for the needy. They did not do so, however, without carefully defining who would be included in their largess and, in the process, effectively protecting themselves against the indigent stranger. As the title of New York's 1683 poor law, An Act for Defraying the publique & necessary Charge of each respective Citty, towne and County throughout this Province & for maintaining the poor, and preventing vagabonds, indicates, vagabondry was still a major concern.[11] Consequently, all of the colonies adopted specific requirements that had to be fulfilled before one gained legal settlement and with it the right to public assistance under their poor laws. As in England, residency requirements were a popular means for determining settlement and, consequently, for limiting the burden of public relief. To receive assistance in New York required forty days' residence; in Massachusetts, three months; in North Carolina, one year; and so forth. At any time the prospective inhabitant could be eliminated from consideration in most colonies by the practice of warning out.[12]

Further assurances against burdensome strangers were included in various colonial laws. To prevent "vagabonds and idle persons" from entering New York, for example, the colony's earliest poor law provided that persons who "hath not visible estate, or hath not a manual craft" must post security for two years in order to reside in the colony. Those who could provide the above had to post such assurances within eight days after arrival. Such provisions were followed by a removal clause that specified that those unable to post such security or assurances be removed by the constable to the county from whence they came.[13] Other colonies added their own particular variations. To gain inhabitance in some New England towns, for example, required the vote of the residents or selectmen of the town, after the newcomer had been thoroughly examined as to economic standing, property, moral character, and religious views. In Connecticut it was specified by law in 1660 that a person could not to be admitted unless "known to be of an honest conversation."[14]

Thus, despite the long held belief that the colonies constituted a new world of opportunity that beckoned with open arms to all the discontented and oppressed people of the Western world, that welcome had in fact been severely limited by the eighteenth century through the adaptation of English laws and practices to the American experience. The colonists imported all of the English features that stigmatized the stranger as criminal or dangerous and then adapted them to the colonial experience. Furthermore, the vagrancy and poor laws were "improved" upon by innovative additions that further limited those people deemed acceptable to the whole. The result was that the exclusive laws of old England became even more stringent in the new world of America.

As time passed the model of the staid Puritan gave way to the lonely pioneer folk hero, the Daniel Boones and Davy Crocketts, who seemed too large for the confines of one community. Movement and freedom became ideals as attention was diverted from the rigor of holy missions to the adventure of engaging the world's mightiest power in battle in the name of liberty during the American Revolution and in the conquering of a mighty continent in the westward movement. While the man on the move had stolen the historical spotlight, the values restricting that very freedom of movement, as accrued from English precedent and colonial experience, continued as an undercurrent running through those glamorous years of our history, ever ready to emerge when the ideal became inconsistent with reality.

When the colonies became states, the patriots were eager to do away with those British laws and customs that were reminiscent of their past "bondage." Old laws, political forms, social structures, and religious priorities were either discarded or adapted to the circumstances of the new nation. In so shedding their past, however, the people could not divest themselves of all of the inbred values and attitudes that were part of their English heritage — they were still Englishmen in this respect. For this reason, and because of the practical necessity of returning quickly to day-to-day operations, there were many carryovers in the transition from colony to nation. Among such survivals were the familiar vagrancy and poor laws. As the states wrote their new constitutions these laws were recodified with little or no change, and as the country expanded they were carried westward to become part of our frontier heritage.[15] Thus, the laws and attitudes formulated generations and even centuries before in medieval England, imported to and adjusted in the colonies, were now passed to the new democracies of the American West and to the future, there to remain for the most part through the first half of the twentieth century.

Logistically, the decentralized system of poor relief as represented by the English system of local responsibility suited the new circumstances, especially in the territories and western states where the local government was that closest to the people, and the concept of local responsibility was fully compatible with local reality. The states and territories, however, were part of a larger whole — a federated government. In Great Britain, the poor law was administered and financed on the local level, but the law itself was a mandate of Parliament and thus represented a national commitment to the relief of the poor. In the federal system of the United States, however, where each state is responsible for its own domestic policy, each wrote and administered its own poor law without a corresponding national commitment or federal directive. Thus, the model was fundamentally altered when adopted individually by the states within the federation.

There were two glaring problems evident in the transference of English law to the American scene. First, in the process of adaptation, the national government was effectively excluded and, consequently, absolved of all responsibility for the poor. Unlike the English model, the national government remained uninvolved as the states rewrote their colonial poor laws. Care of the poor was strictly a state and local issue with which the federal government should not, and later emphatically would not, interfere. This is how we define local responsibility as adapted from the English precedent. This is not to say that the English system did not suffer from local variations or uneven standards. These problems did, in fact, characterize much of England's poor law history and contributed to the passage of the 1832 Poor Law Reform Act, which is again an example of the commitment of the government to the issue of poor relief and its ability to intercede on the national level. In the United States there was an equal assumption of responsibility for the poor, but it was done on the state level; consequently, whenever reform was needed, the avenue of federal intervention was closed. The important point for our consideration is that with the absence of national legislation there was a corresponding absence of federal recognition of any jurisdiction in the realm of public welfare or relief. This set the precedent of noninvolvement that proved to be so difficult to break in the twentieth century. The states had assumed local responsibility for the poor through their legislation, thereby absolving the federal government not only at this time but setting the precedent upon which future presidents would rely as they resisted the assumption of that responsibility at later dates. Thus in the process of converting English law and precedent to the American situation, the concept of local responsibility took on a new meaning and new consequences.

The second problem resulting from the adaptation of the British system by the individual states rather than the national government was the chaos caused by the lack of uniformity in state laws. With each state free to set its own qualifying terms for gaining or losing settlement, each adopted those qualifications it felt were most convenient to its needs. With little or no regard for overall national coordination, numerous variations occurred. Residency requirements, for example, ranged from five years in Maine to one year in New York, while, depending upon the state, a person could be removed for being a "vicious character," of "bad fame and reputation," "not a suitable inhabitant," or for having "no visible means of support." In Maryland, classification as a "poor person" was enough to warrant removal.[16] The situation resulting from these diverse laws was one of utter confusion that was to plague both the individual seeking aid and interstate relations until the mid-twentieth century. It was not until 1969 that the Supreme Court of the United States declared residency requirements for relief unconstitutional, thereby making settlement a moot point.[17]

At the same time that the states were writing the poor law into their statutes, intellectual currents from both England and América were challenging the very concept of public aid to *any* poor. In such a climate the attitude toward the indigent transient was to be further disparaged. Intellectual challenges to the concepts of the poor law came first from England where the classic economists began the onslaught. As early as 1776 Adam Smith had criticized the poor laws for checking the mobility of labor and thereby inhibiting the free market system. While he also sympathized with the victims and stressed the inconsistency of the law with the traditions of English freedom, his doctrines of the free market with mobile labor were better remembered in the nineteenth century. There they combined with the markedly less sympathetic criticism of Thomas Malthus. In his *An Essay on the Principle of Population* Malthus advanced the idea that the poor were responsible for their own poverty, and, therefore, the public had no duty to relieve them. In fact, public relief was an evil that must be curtailed because it artificially sustained a surplus population which threatened a limited food supply. The Malthusian belief that the poor constituted a dangerous surplus population was given further "scientific" credence in the latter part of the nineteenth century by the adaptation of Charles Darwin's explosive doctrine of evolution to society itself by Herbert Spencer. Society, Spencer explained, was governed by the same evolutionary laws of the "survival of the fittest" as were the animal species studied by Darwin. In the process of improving the species the weak and poor were naturally eliminated. Simply stated, the same scientific laws that governed animals governed human beings: "If they are sufficiently complete to live they *do* live, and it is well that they should live. If they are not sufficiently complete to live, they die, and it is best they should die."[18] It is but a short step from that premise to the belief that it was against nature to sustain the unfit poor through public aid and to the conclusion that such meddling with nature would be detrimental to the species. As a result of such theories, it became increasingly popular in England to see poverty as an individual flaw, one that must not be pampered through generous aid, but one that must be dealt with severely.

Nineteenth-century America was ripe for the ideas coming from England regarding poverty. England was, after all, still our cultural and intellectual motherland, and faithful Americans continued to look to her for much that was new and fashionable. The idea that poverty was the fault of the individual was particularly appropriate to the American scene and was eagerly received. After all, especially in the United States, land of unlimited opportunities, why should any able-bodied person be wanting if not for some personal flaw? This chauvinistic optimism, born of the spirit of the American Revolution and nurtured by generations of Jeffersonian and Jacksonian democracy, now justified by the latest economic and scientific theory from Victorian England, set the stage for the intellectual condemnation of the able-bodied poor, resident and wandering, that was to mature in nineteenth-century America.

To make poverty a crime one must make a work a virtue. This was effectively accomplished in America by the secularization of the Puritan ethic. To the Puritans, idleness was a sin because God had given to each person talents that He expected would be improved upon. Therefore, hard work and diligence were religious duties, and, while one could never be sure, earthly success could be a welcome sign of God's saving grace. As the Puritan ministers and their exhortations for the saintly life lost their influence over the flock, the values of hard work and success remained. In the process they were increasingly nationalized into what Max Weber called the "Protestant ethic," or, in more secular terms, what we know as the "American dream." What were primarily religious virtues to be rewarded in eternity gradually became moral virtues guaranteed to improve one's character and situation in life.[19] Industry and frugality thus became the tools of earthly success as the ethic or dream assured that if one were to work hard and follow a virtuous life he would indeed succeed. If one doubted this formula for success, he need only look about him to see the glowing example of its truth in the proliferation of successful self-made men such as John D. Rockefeller and Andrew Carnegie, or turn to any of the more than one hundred success stories penned for inspiration and profit by novelist Horatio Alger. If all else failed, success was still waiting beyond the horizon through Frederick Jackson Turner's safety valve.

Adding to the growing belief that success was possible to any American with the right virtues was the ready adoption of Herbert Spencer's rationalization for the apparent cruelty reserved for those who failed. Very simply, the rich were winners of nature's game of survival of the fittest, and the poor were the losers. Nothing could, or should, be done to change this harsh, but necessary, screening process. This is the type of Social Darwinism that was preached at

Yale University by Herbert Spencer's chief American disciple, Professor William Graham Sumner. In his lectures Sumner tied together the theories of Spencer, as imported from England, and the Protestant ethic of America. The result was, according to historian Richard Hofstadter, the assumption that "the industrious, temperate, and frugal man of the Protestant ideal was the equivalent of the 'strong' or 'fittest' in the struggle for existence."[20]

With this logic we come full circle from English precedent to American practice. In this wedding of the Protestant ethic and Social Darwinism comes a philosophy that fully complements the American economic and social scene of the nineteenth century. Nature dictates that the fittest is the hard working, virtuous, self-made man. In other words, nature's measure of success, just as America's, is material well-being. Consequently, nature's sign of failure is poverty. The poor, therefore, are failures of both nature and the American Dream. The transient poor were never even in the game.

In each of the American values discussed thus far the center of attention in the struggle between success and failure has been the individual. Next to democracy the belief in individualism is probably the most cherished value in America. It has influenced, and continues to do so, our politics, economy, and society. As explained by historian Charles Beard, individualism "placed the individual at the center of interest and made individual enterprise the primary source of invention, progress, wealth, and national greatness." As a concept it is the culmination of English and American thought and the unique experience of America. From Darwin, Beard explained, we learned that individual animals struggled for existence; from Sumner we learned that "all civilizations had come from free individual initiative, that all hope of progress and improvement lay in giving the fullest liberty to individuals;" and from Turner we learned that "the secret of America's uniqueness" was to be credited to the "stoutest of all alleged individualists—the man of the frontier."[21] This is the message that was taught in political science classes at Columbia University by John William Burgess, in economics classes by John Bates Clark at the same school, in the editorials of *The Nation* by E. L. Godkin, in the history classes of Frederick Jackson Turner at the University of Wisconsin and at Harvard, and in schools and homes throughout the nation.

By the reasoning of all that went into the American mind in the nineteenth century, it follows that the man on the move should indeed be a hero. He was an individual seeking success in a land ripe with opportunities. Any successes he did achieve were, under this reasoning, rightly credited to his superiority. This is the vision conjured up by the American ideal. However, there is another side to the story. What of the individual who fails? For him society has no praise and, in many cases, no sympathy. If an individual was able-bodied yet poor, then the fault was his own. All the values and beliefs of the American ideal pointed to this obvious conclusion. The Protestant ethic preached success to the individual, the self-made man illustrated the possibilities open to him, the frontier offered a safety valve through which he could find success in the West, and Social Darwinism sanctioned a fierce competition among individuals to achieve his success. In other words, it was part of the American way to champion the loner, the pioneer, the man on the move, but only if he did not stop during his travels to ask for help. Then he automatically was labelled a transient or vagrant, and was treated accordingly.

As the country moved into the twentieth century leaving behind the Jeffersonian ideal of a rural utopia in favor of an urbanized, industrialized nation, the inappropriateness of the poor laws became increasingly evident. The phenomenal urbanization which occurred in the first half of the twentieth century has been the subject of a good deal of contemporary and historical writing. Through the eyewitness accounts of Jacob Riis, the creative imaginations of the novelists Theodore Dreiser and Upton Sinclair, and the output of numerous social historians, there has been painted a compelling picture of the problems created as countless migrants from the rural environs met with a teeming flow of immigrants from abroad in cities physically unprepared for this human deluge. In addition to this, the mass migration of black Americans north to meet the needs of a wartime economy in the mid- to late-teens added an explosive element of racism to the mix. In enumerating these problems, critics have thoroughly discussed overcrowding, substandard housing, corrupt political bosses, sweatshop working conditions, and so forth, but they have generally overlooked the hidden dangers resulting from the poor law system. This is most likely because the critics, as well as the migrants themselves, assumed that geographic mobility was a given freedom in America, a part of our heritage. Yet, there still existed poor laws and vagrancy statutes that put transient Americans in a precarious position. In an industrial situation migrants who left the farm for the city gave up the security of rural life which at least provided sustenance. In the city they became dependent on wages and, subsequently, on the boom and bust cycle of the economy. A modern industrial society, theoretically, should be able to cope with the periodic downturns of the business cycle, if it can provide a relief system for the unemployed during hard times. But what happens when the public relief system is rooted in sixteenth-century England? In such cases the archaic settlement laws provide the protection intended for the taxpayer, but they do so at the expense of those very people whose labor is needed to revive and sustain the economic system. These people now find themselves unsettled and undeserving of aid because they left their place of settlement to come to the urban areas to feed the industrial machine. Virtually anyone who moved from his place of birth, no matter how long ago, who did not fulfill specific state settlement requirements, was not legally eligible for relief.

By the end of the 1920s all of the intellectual trends and practical realities discussed thus far were thoroughly woven together into the fabric of the American ideal. America saw herself as a nation of individuals, each and every one of whom was free to achieve all that he was capable of becoming. Individuals who failed still had to shoulder the burden of their own guilt, but, due to the optimistic spirit that prevailed, the Malthusian theory that poverty could never be ended was replaced by the belief that through the greatness of America even this timeless scourge would soon be gone. Ironically, this optimism was being voiced on the very eve of America's greatest economic disaster yet, the Great Depression, and immediately preceding the greatest deluge of transients ever experienced.

Thus the stage has been set for the arrival of the indigent transient of the Great Depression. Before the interaction between community and transient can begin, however, we must take a few more moments to narrow that stage from the national to the state level. Now that we know what the American attitude was toward the transient poor, let us look more closely to see how New York State conformed to the national model.

⟨ 2 ⟩

New York State on the
Eve of the Depression:
Attitudes and Policy

ON the very eve of the Great Depression, almost in anticipation of what was to come, New York State enacted a public welfare law which, according to contemporary reformers and the social workers who promoted it, was a model of humanitarian reform, a departure from the Elizabethan past, and a step onto the threshold of the future. In their praises, commentators credited the Public Welfare Law of 1929 with removing the stigma of poverty from the poor, modernizing the antiquated machinery of the old poor law, and revolutionizing the whole concept of public relief. In regard to the indigent transient, the law was seen as a landmark in the acceptance of state responsibility for all poor — resident and nonresident alike.

On the surface this assessment was correct. The 1929 law, as we shall see, changed the terminology of the poor law and humanized many of its services. However, the spirit of this law, as interpreted by its supporters, came into direct conflict with attitudes and past practices dating as far back as fourteenth-century England, and with a very active application of those precedents in the history of New York State. The law itself was, in fact, but one step in an ongoing conflict between such deeply rooted attitudes that rejected the able-bodied poor and/or the indigent transient and the steadily encroaching development of what has come to be known as the welfare state. Upon closer examination, the 1929 law proves to be but a compromise in that conflict that masks an uneasy tension about all able-bodied poor. To understand this conflict, let us retrace the history of the transient in New York State and the evolution of the laws intended to deal with him.

From the earliest days of the Dutch colony of New Netherland to the passage of the Public Welfare Law of 1929, the stranger was looked upon with suspicion and was carefully guarded against. By the time that Peter Stuyvesant surrendered the colony to the English in 1664, the settlers had become well acquainted with the problem of transiency and had already experimented with a number of devices meant to curb it. Centrally located between the English colonies of New England and the Tidewater South, the Dutch province provided a convenient sanctuary for bond servants fleeing from their indentures in the English colonies and thus gave the province its first transiency problem. In response to constant complaints about these transients, "who frequently carry their passports under foot," the director-general of the province issued a proclamation in 1642 forbidding any householder to entertain a "stranger" for more than one night without notifying him directly. Later, when the province was threatened by "rovers and vagabonds," who, according to observers, were plundering citizens under the guise of harmless travelers, all citizens were prohibited from conversing with, harboring, concealing, or provisioning strangers, upon penalty of being declared an enemy of the province and being banished.[1]

The Dutch were not the only ones faced with a transiency problem in this early period. Just as English settlers fled the confines of their settlements, so too did the Dutch. A convenient place for refugees and law breakers fleeing from New Netherland was the English settlements on Long Island where they combined with other undesirables banished from the surrounding English colonies to plague the already impoverished settlers there. In defense against this peculiar influx, the inhabitants of Long Island resorted to a number of legal and extralegal devices reminiscent of the response of local governments in England when they faced similar situations. They organized military companies to protect their towns, issued strict local settlement laws, and regulated and/or proscribed the entertainment of strangers by the inhabitants.[2]

Under the proprietorship of the Duke of York, British legal precedents and practices modeled on both English and colonial experiences were spread to mainland New York. In the first colonywide poor law of New York (1683) the English concept of local responsibility was firmly established through a system of tax-supported local poor relief. In formulating the legal language of the law, the colony's indebtedness to English practice was explicitly recognized:

> Whereas itt is the Custome & practice of his Majestys Realm of England, and all the adjacent Colonys in America that very respective County Citty towne parrish & precinct doth take care & provide for the poor who do inhabit in their respective precincts, . . .

so too would the colony named after the future King of England. After briefly establishing the principle of local responsibility, the law then went on to elaborate its primary function, which was to specify means by which this largess would be protected from unwelcome strangers. It provided that all persons who

> shall come to Inhabit within this province or any part or place thereof, and hath nott a Visible Estate, or hath nott a manual craft or occupacon shall befor hee bee admitted an Inhabitant give sifficient Security thatt hee shall not bee a burthen or charge to the respective places hee shall come to in habitt in which Security shall Continue for two years.

It further provided for the forceful removal of anyone who could not give such security. Strangers who could contribute their skills to the growing communities could avoid the posting of security by making application to the local authorities within eight days of their arrival. Stipulations added in 1721 requiring ship captains to post security for all of the improverished strangers they imported into the colony, entertainment laws requiring householders to report to the authorities the "quality, condition and circumstance" of strangers visiting in their homes, and the enforcement of strict punishments including being "stripp't from the wast upward" for thirty-one lashes for a man and twenty-five for a woman, emphasize the determination of the colonial leaders to prohibit transiency among the needy poor.[3]

During its remaining years as a colony, New York expanded upon the restrictive and exclusive features of the poor law. A revised law in 1773 repeated almost verbatim the English settlement law of over one hundred years earlier. A forty-day residency requirement for settlement was established. Any person living in a tenement valued at under five pounds yearly could, if deemed likely to become chargeable to the local unit, be removed at any time during those forty days to his last place of legal settlement. In compliance with these laws, persons considered suspect could be removed from the locality in a manner reserved for hardened criminals, despite the fact that they had committed no crime.[4] The result of the law was a trail of poor homeless persons, who had been adjudged by local officials to be a possible burden on the tax funds, trekking across the colony, from town to town, as they attempted to retrace their steps as the law dictated.

In 1776 the colony of New York joined with her sister colonies in declaring her independence from Great Britain. After the successful conclusion of the ensuing Revolution, the citizens of New York State celebrated their independence by divesting themselves of many of the remnants of British control. They saw no need, however, to discard the poor law system. The first state law for the Settlement of Relief of the Poor (1784) thus proved to be basically a repetition of the law of 1773. The only changes that occurred when the poor law was again rewritten in 1788 served to increase the restrictive features of settlement and removal.[5]

In examining these laws it is apparent that their primary purpose was not how to best service the poor, but, rather, how to limit public relief to those who truly "belonged" to the state or to the local community. The very logistical order in which the laws were written is evidence of this. The first paragraph generally dealt with how to distinguish who was worthy to receive public aid, the second consideration was how to eliminate those who were not worthy, and then finally, as if an abbreviated afterthought, provision was made for caring for the poor. The effect of such statutes was to carry over and intensify the most exclusive features of the colonial law, regardless of the change of government or the revolutionary change of spirit that accompanied independence.

The inauguration of George Washington as the first president of the United States on April 30, 1789, in Federal Hall at Wall and Broad Streets, New York City, turned the eyes of the nation to New York and to the dawning of a new era. As far as the transient poor were concerned, however, life went on as usual. The end of the Critical Period did little to change the poor law concept inherited from the past and embodied in the statute of 1788. Little concern was given to revising the poor laws to keep pace with the growing population and economy of the state or the principles embodied in the new federal Constitution. Thus, when a new poor law was passed in 1801, it merely repeated the 1788 law. The same provisions for obtaining settlement and for removing persons "likely to become chargeable" were once again accompanied by entertainment laws, a certification system, and the ultimate recourse to corporal punishment.[6]

Up to this point in time, it is quite apparent that New Yorkers, along with their countrymen, spared very little sympathy for society's downtrodden, especially if their residency was in question. In both colonial and state poor laws the chief concern was to limit the number of persons eligible for relief and to guarantee that only those who belonged to the colony or state received such aid. It is equally apparent that the traditions and attitudes set centuries ago in England were having a pronounced effect on the state. Despite the impetus for change marshalled in by the revolution and the stimulus of nation building, the influence of the past was still very strongly felt.

The stranglehold of the past, however, was not to go unchallenged. From the beginning of the Jacksonian Era down to the eve of the Civil War, a nationwide humanitarian spirit swept across America challenging its priorities. During this time, New York kept pace with and often preceded her sister states in seeking the outcasts of society in an attempt to aid and/or rehabilitate them. A combination of humanitarian concern, an interest in cost efficiency, and a good deal of public pressure, prompted the state legislature in 1823 to instruct the secretary of state, J.V.N. Yates, to study and report back to them on the expenses and operation of the state's poor laws, in order to compare them to those of other states, and to suggest improvements. The state thus began the first comprehensive survey of poor relief in the country.

In conducting his survey, Yates had asked various local officials across the state to express their opinions on just where the current laws had failed. In response he received numerous complaints about the existing settlements and removal schemes, especially in regard to the expensive litigation they involved. From Albany came the complaint that, in at least several known cases, "the cost of prosecuting a single appeal, amounts to a sum more than equal to the annual support of all the poor of the town." The supervisor of Austerlitz found that such expensive court costs often deterred officials from seeking removals. Thus, he argued, it was often decidedly cheaper to keep the pauper, even for a lifetime, than to prosecute for a just removal. In addition to cost, the respondents also criticized the cruelty of the system. "There is so much of barbarity in the disposition of the poor," wrote the Albany respondent, "that I am astonished when I reflect that in a country boasting of its free institutions, a custom so abhorrent to the best feelings of our nature, should have so long obtained." He, and others, referred with condemnation to the custom of removing persons from constable to constable, from one corner of the state to the other, often while in feeble health or during inclement weather, merely to avoid responsibility for them. The supervisor of Franklin graphically illustrated the often inhumane results of the system with the story of an old, deranged man who, upon becoming sick while traveling through town, had been secretly "dumped" in Massachusetts, "the Lord knows where" to avoid additional expenses.[7]

Most of the respondents concurred with contemporary reformist thought calling for the abolition of the existing laws and their replacement with a more simplified and less costly system. From Austerlitz came the suggestion that settlement be determined solely by a certain number of years residence. Amsterdam's supervisor felt that both mercy and cost demanded that paupers be cared for in the county where they became unable to support themselves, rather than being "carried from constable to constable like *felons*." The common request was for more exact and less confusing laws.[8]

For those whose eligibility for relief would be established by the simplified laws, most respondents concurred with the contemporary belief that mandatory poorhouse confinement was the best recourse. Within its protective walls the worthy poor could be cared for. For the impoverished but able-bodied, the poorhouse would provide the corrective influence of hard labor.* The substitution of mandatory

---

*The poorhouse concept reinforced a very marked distinction between worthy and unworthy poor that was to be of crucial importance to the transient. It had long been held that, barring emergencies such as war, pestilence, or widespread unemployment, all able-bodied persons could and should be self-supporting. If not, then, according to the belief of the day, some "flaw" in that person's character was responsible for his poverty, and, consequently, that of his family. Ignorance, idleness, imprudent marriages, lotteries, prostitution, and intemperence were some of the most

confinement in place of outdoor relief, that is, poor relief in the privacy of one's own home, was also believed to deter potential applicants who could, with some ingenuity and perseverance, care for themselves rather than submitting to the humiliation of the poorhouse.

Yates agreed with the majority opinion on most issues, including the need to abolish the existing settlement and removal laws and to create a poorhouse system. As a result of the subsequent report he submitted, the legislature revised the poor law in November 1824, establishing the poorhouse as the chief means of relief and designating the county as the unit chiefly responsible for that relief. The law directed specific counties to purchase land to erect poorhouses, to be paid for by county taxes, to which "any poor person in any city or town of the same county shall apply for relief." In concurrence with additional recommendations from Yates, the legislature abolished the removal of paupers from one county to another and provided for the care of such transient paupers in the county where they became destitute. This provision alleviated a good deal of needless travel and hardship. To eliminate the clandestine dumping of paupers from one county into another with the intention of thereby avoiding financial responsibility, the law designated a one hundred dollar fine or six months imprisonment for such activity.[9]

In 1827 the law was further clarified in the Revised Statutes of 1827. All property qualifications were dropped from the settlement laws and replaced by a simple one-year residency requirement for a person of full age. Inmates of poorhouses, however, were specifically excluded from gaining settlement in this manner. The earlier prohibition against the removal of indigent transients from one county to another was extended to a prohibition of such removal even from towns and cities within the same county. All persons worthy of

---

frequently mentioned sources of such flaws. While sympathy could be spared for worthy persons, whose poverty was due to external uncontrollable forces, little was available for those whose poverty was their own "fault." This distinction is important to the transients because, more often than not, such people were healthy enough to travel from place to place. By implication, then, such people must contain a flaw within their being, thereby making them doubly unworthy of aid. For an interesting expression of such beliefs see: The Society for the Prevention of Pauperism in the City of New York, "A Report on the Subject of Pauperism," *The First Annual Report*, New York, 1818.

public aid were to be cared for in the poorhouse, resident and nonresident, wherever such a facility was available. While the law reinforced the generosity accorded indigents already in the state, it by no means was meant to encourage persons to immigrate to New York. Section 64 of the act made this clear by providing a penalty of seventy-five dollars plus costs for bringing "any poor or indigent person, or lunatic" into the state and leaving him there.[10]

The intention of the courts to uphold this last provision to its utmost was illustrated in the case of *Winfield vs. Mapes*. In this case, involving the removal of a pauper from Pennsylvania to New York by public welfare officials, the court ruled that even when a person who at one time had New York State settlement and then left the state was duly returned to New York by public officials from another state, where settlement had not been gained, the penalty for dumping was still applicable. In other words, just because New York adjusted its treatment of interstate transients, this did not mean that the state would accept the burden of refugees from the laws of other states.[11]

The whole attitude upon which past poor laws had been based seemed to be challenged by the encroachments on local responsibility represented in the acts of 1824 and 1827. Before we become too preoccupied with the significance of the changes, however, it is important to look to another section of the Revised Statutes of 1827, which, for the most part, harked back to fourteenth-century England. Title II of the statute continued to group together disparate groups under the label "vagrant" and to punish them all accordingly. All "beggars and vagrants," that is,

> all idle persons who, not having visible means to maintain themselves, live without employment; all persons wandering abroad and lodging in taverns, groceries, beer-houses, outhouses, marketplaces, sheds or barns, or in the open air, and not giving a good account of themselves; all persons wandering abroad and begging, or who go about from door to door, or place themselves in the streets, highways, passages, or other public places, to beg or receive alms,

were to be committed for up to six months at hard labor in the poorhouse.[12] While the punishment of six months at labor was an improvement over public floggings, ear croppings, branding, and so forth, the formula of inflicting punishment on the vagrant, instead of looking for the cause of vagrancy, still persisted.

More important, perhaps, are the qualifications that this statute put upon the previously reported changes. If all "idle persons" with "no visible means to maintain themselves" continued to be regarded as criminals deserving punishment, then the humanity expressed in those sections outlawing removal was in actuality reserved for the worthy poor, that is, the sick, maimed, feebleminded, and so forth. Yates made this distinction quite clear in his recommendations to the legislature when he advised that no male, in good health, between the ages of eighteen and fifty be allowed to receive any pauper aid. Therefore, even with the new legislation, the treatment accorded the able-bodied transient would have remained basically unchanged The obvious conflicts within the statutes themselves mirror the ongoing tug-of-war between the hold of the past and the present impulse toward reform. Despite the humanitarian interest of this era and the legal changes it prompted, able-bodied transients were still unacceptable by law.

In the day-to-day practices and experiences of the local level, conditions and attitudes also remained basically unchanged. An examination of attitudes across the state, conducted by historians David Schneider and Albert Deutsch, revealed little if any change in the long established animosity toward the nonsettled poor. Each locality faced the problem in its own way, but uppermost was the question: "How can we get rid of the transient at the least cost and trouble to the community?" The general practice was to give the transient a night's lodging, a meal or two, and then pass him on. Except for the inclusion of the meal, the formula had not changed since the days of medieval England.[13]

Further indications of a suspicious and often antagonistic attitude toward strangers can also be found in the annals of those very agencies responsible for relieving the distress of the poor. Such attitudes, for example, were unashamedly espoused in the constitution and annual reports of the very influential New York Association for Improving the Condition of the Poor. The specific instructions to *"withhold all relief from unknown persons"* were emphatically underscored in the association's "Visitor's Manual." The association repeatedly voiced the fear that indiscriminate giving to nonresidents, the establishment of soup kitchens, bread lines, and other give-away meals and free lodging; and the creation of make-work jobs for the unemployed, would attract thousands of vagrants to their city. What it preferred was a program to help induce the unemployed to migrate, or, at the very least, a preventative program such as existed in Boston, Massachusetts. Migrants were deterred from coming to that city by the publication and wide distribution of an official manifesto recommending that they "avoid disappointment and the loss of time and money" by staying away.[14]

Partially due to the inequities evident in law and practice, but more in reaction to the complaints of local governments which, despite the local practice of passing-on, were still obliged to meet the increasing cost of caring for resident and nonresident disabled poor, the state legislature passed a law in 1873 known as the State Pauper Act. By definition a state pauper was any poor person who was "blind, lame, old, impotent, or decrepit, or in any other way disabled or enfeebled, so as to be unable by work to maintain himself, who shall apply for aid . . . and who shall not have resided sixty days in any county of this State within one year, preceding his time of need." Such persons were to be provided for, at state expense, in institutions specifically contracted for as state almshouses. Should anyone choose not to remain in the almshouse, preferring to be sent to a state or country where they have settlement or friends, he could be removed if "the interest of the State and the welfare of the pauper will be promoted thereby." How this should be determined was not specified.[15]

The law of 1873 was a landmark in the development of state responsibility for the nonsettled poor. For the first time the state government accepted the obligation to care for the transient as a permanent function. The distinction between worthy and unworthy poor, however, was not tampered with. The law very specifically limited such help to the disabled. Roaming, unsettled, able-bodied persons, therefore, were still subject to the settlement, removal, and vagrancy laws. Furthermore, the care to be given to the state pauper was poorhouse care, even after both public and private investigations scathingly criticized conditions within these houses.* Once again, the state had initiated change, but it could not go beyond the philosophical restraints it inherited from the past.

---

*In 1856 a special committee was appointed by the state legislature to investigate conditions in the poorhouses. What they found were "badly constructed, ill-

Thus far we have been speaking about the passage of laws, but the evidence has afforded us only brief glimpses of how they were implemented. The directive of the state legislation to the State Board of Charities to provide them with annual reports on the operation of the poor law finally allows us the opportunity to look more closely at the law in practice.[17]

Between the passage of the law and the turn of the century the reports show that 40,885 state poor persons were admitted to almshouses. Out of that number 11,199 were discharged, 87 were adopted, 1,948 absconded, 249 were transferred to state hospitals, 860 died, and 75 remained as of October 1, 1900. The remaining 26,466 cases were sent "out of State to friends or places of legal settlement." By 1916 the figures were 32,622 out of 53,432 as the total number removed since 1873.[18] From these figures it is obvious that the legal recourse to remove state paupers was applied frequently. The cold statistics, however, do not explain whether the removals were indeed done upon the request of the state pauper as the law required nor whether they were done in the "best interests" of both the pauper and the state. A clearer appreciation of the large proportion of removals, over 50 percent, is better supplied by the text of the reports.

Throughout the reports there is a continuous emphasis on the benefits the state gained by removing these paupers. Almost every report costed-out the difference between maintaining the poor in state institutions and removing them. Taking into consideration the longer life expectancy that would result from the improved shelter and diet provided in the almshouse, the board generally concluded that it was a financial benefit to the state to remove rather than support the state poor. As they explained in 1899, "unless these aliens and non-residents are returned promptly, they are likely to become permanent dependents upon the charity of the State," and thus constitute an undue burden upon the state. Besides being economical,

---

arranged, ill-warmed, and ill ventilated" overcrowded "noxious" shelters, where inmates were herded together indiscriminately, regardless of age or sex. "Common domestic animals," they concluded, "are usually more humanly provided for than the paupers in some of these institutions; where the misfortune of poverty is visited with greater deprivations of comfortable food, lodging, clothing, warmth and ventilation than constitute the usual penalty of crime. The evidence taken by the committee exhibits such a record of filth, nakedness, licentiousness, general bad morals, and disregard of religion and the most common religious observances, as well as the gross neglect of the most ordinary comforts and decencies of life, as if published in detail would disgrace the State and shock humanity."[16]

removal also provided "a moral lesson to be pointed in this refusal on the part of our own State authorities to accept the refuse and debris of other states and countries." The very use of such terms as "refuse" and "debris" speaks for itself as a measure of the board's opinion of their charges. In all, the common attitude expressed in the reports was that

> no moneys of the State are expended with greater economic and other beneficial results than in the removal, to their former homes, of these enfeebled and helpless poor persons, who find temporary lodgment in its institutions of charity, and who in no wise have legitimate permanent claim upon its benefactors.[19]

This statement is a curious interpretation of a law that specifically established the rights of state paupers.

Despite the apparent willingness of the legislature to accept the burden of state paupers, the reports show the board considered them to be a burden upon the state and saw its duty to be their removal. Nowhere in the reports is there any indication that the procedures involved in affecting such "beneficial" removals were predicated upon the wish of the state pauper to be removed. The law specifically stated that if the pauper so preferred to be removed, he could request transportation elsewhere. The emphasis of the reports, however, seems to be on the desire of the state to effect removals, and the statistics confirm that that desire was being fulfilled. While it is impossible to determine if the letter of the law was broken in any of these numerous removal cases, it is evident by the attitudes expressed in these reports that the spirit of the law was at least severely bent in its implementation.

While the State Board of Charities handled indigent interstate transients quite summarily, its diligence in no way eliminated the influx of such persons into the state. In the years following the Civil War the economic and social changes prompted by industrialization and urbanization increased the problems of poor relief. New York, a state already possessing a natural magnetism, became even more inviting to transients as industrial expansion and growing cities promised great new opportunities for the adventurous, and improved transportation facilities provided the means of mobility. The problems created by this natural migration were further aggravated by the attempts of other states to rid themselves of their undesirables by "dumping" them over the New York State border.

Between 1870 and 1879 an estimated seven thousand paupers were so passed from Massachusetts to New York, despite the fact that they had no settlement there or, in some cases, had never even set foot in the state before being passed across its border.[20]

Economic panics in the 1870s and 1890s further complicated the situation as massive numbers of unemployed added to the ranks of the dispossessed and transient population. The resulting fear of economic unknowns and needy strangers added to the stigma attached to the transient. Beginning in the 1870s, for example, there was introduced into popular expression and the collective imagination — the *tramp*. This new American character or stereotype was not the comical, heart-of-gold, little man as portrayed to the delight of the movie-goers years later by Charlie Chaplin. This character was a danger that lurked in dark shadows, that stood threateningly on the family's back doorstep, that lured young boys to its idle and perverse way of life.

This new American boogeyman was, in part, the product of the panic of 1873 which threw many able-bodied men into the ranks of the unemployed and, in part, the by-product of the philosophic distinction made by scientific charity workers between the worthy and unworthy poor. In his study of tramps and reformers in Gilded Age New York, Paul Ringenback has made a convincing case that charity workers failed in the 70s and 80s to see the wandering poor as victims of the economic crisis, choosing rather to see them as voluntary tramps, victims only of some personal flaw. In New York City charity workers branded tramps degenerate, warned the population to resist the temptation to disperse indiscriminate assistance to them, and, under the leadership of Mrs. Josephine Shaw Lowell, advocated repressive anti-tramp legislation that would subject tramps and vagrants, that is, the able-bodied unemployed, to incarceration and hard labor to cure the flaw and make them once again productive members of society.[21] Showing its commitment to the method, Westchester County in 1886 instructed its superintendents of the poor to construct water traps, large tank-like constructions filled with at least six feet of water, into which tramps would be lowered. The unfortunate prisoner would then be "compelled to bail or be submerged." This unique work-test device fortunately never came to fruition. A term at hard labor was substituted.[22] The attitudes that made such a scheme even thinkable did not abate until well into the Progressive Era of the twentieth century.

In 1894 a long overdue reorganization of state administrative machinery was accomplished by the adoption of a new state constitution. Following closely upon this impetus to reorganize came a new poor law that was designed to consolidate and simplify a system that had become a legal quagmire due to constant amending and judicial interpretation. In nine articles, the 1896 law, entitled An Act in Relation to the Poor, clarified much of the confusion that had accumulated since the legislature had implemented the Yates recommendations seven decades earlier.[23] The law, however, was important for reasons other than the implementation of administrative reform. It was important as a reflection of current trends and attitudes rife within the state. By 1896 the grassroots reform impulse, later to be labelled progressivism, was beginning to eat away at the supposedly more efficient aspects of "scientific" charity.

One target of progressive reform was the poorhouse. In reaction to the indiscriminate herding of persons together in these institutions, the law provided for the immediate removal of idiots, lunatics, and infectious persons from the houses. Also, discretionary power was given to local relief officials to determine what other individuals would be better served by noninstitutional care. Section 23 provided further that any person who was too "sick, lame or otherwise disabled" to be removed to a poorhouse was to be cared for at home.[24] While some of the inhumanity of the poorhouse was thus mitigated by the law, both the legislators and the public were not willing to drop the distinction between those who deserved relief by virtue of their residence and those who were outsiders. The pull of the past was still very strong. Settlement laws continued in effect, and, despite the element of choice allowed for in the care of resident paupers, the state poor were still to be cared for in specially designated state almshouses. Should they be unappreciative of such care and flee before discharge, the law provided that if they were found anywhere in the state soliciting public or private aid, they would be subject to three months hard labor in the workhouse. The message very clearly was: We will care for you, but it will be on our terms, that is, the almshouse or nothing.[25]

The state further exhibited its humanity by prohibiting the heartless removal of paupers from place to place within the state. State poor, however, were specifically excluded from this provision. That is a very significant exception. Resident poor persons were to be spared the humiliation and trauma of removal, but the state poor were not. In a special section dedicated to their needs, soldiers, sailors, and mariners, specifically those who had served in the Mexican or Civil Wars, were to be rewarded for their service by home relief rather than almshouse care, that is, if they qualified by a one-year state residency; if not, then apparently any special consideration due them was not applicable. In addition to these very obvious attempts to limit the increasing largess of the state to resident poor, it remained a misdemeanor to dump nonresident and foreign poor into the state.[26]

The law of 1896, in effect, did increase the rights of state paupers significantly by excluding the qualifying provision that they be disabled to receive aid. The distinction between worthy and unworthy poor had finally been dropped, at least by the letter of the law. But, at the same time, the legislators left open the option of removal by repeating the provisions that state paupers could be removed, upon their request, if it was in the best interest of the individual and the state.[27] If the deletion of the disability requirement was enacted in practice, as well as in law, then the natural consequence should have been an increase in the number of persons cared for in the state and a decrease in out-of-state removals. A survey of the statistics provided in the annual reports of the State Board of Charities for a five year period before, during, and after passage of this law, 1894–1898, should give some indication of how effective its changes really were. (See Table 1, page 39).

Looking at the number of persons removed, the figures remain fairly stable. The number of removals was down by 82 persons in the year after the law, but by 1898 it was up by 21 persons over the 1896 level. Nevertheless, the trend was downward; fewer persons were removed after the law was passed, which is perhaps indicative of an acceptance of the care of able-bodied paupers in the state. The decrease, however, is minimal. Furthermore, the statistics must be weighed against the economic climate of the time. The years 1894 and 1895 were years of a severe economic crisis that resulted in mass unemployment and distress in New York State. During this time the number of needy, resident and nonresident, increased; thus, the number of removals should automatically have been high. Therefore, when a slight drop occurred in 1897, it would most likely reflect economic improvement rather than changed attitudes. In fact, should the law have been interpreted as a directive to aid the able-bodied, the number of removals should have been reduced

TABLE 1.

Year	Number of Removals	Number of Persons Supported in State
1894	1488	2052
1895	1673	2262
1896	1437	2187
1897	1355	2074
1898	1458	1913

(Compiled from the *Annual Reports of the State Board of Charities, 1894–98*).

drastically to reflect both the improved economic conditions and the additional persons eligible for aid. Instead, by 1898 the figures were back up, almost to the 1894 level.

The same logic holds true for the figures regarding the total number of persons supported from 1894 to 1898. The early years should naturally be inflated due to the economic conditions; similarly, the later years should show a natural drop in the numbers supported because the need was reduced. However, the change in the law increasing the number actually eligible for care would at least make up the difference between good times and bad. In other words, the number of persons cared for should go up even though the economic crisis ended, but it does not. Instead, 349 persons less were cared for in 1898, two years after the law, than in 1895, the year before the law.

The statistical reports at least increase one's suspicions about the possibility of any substantial change after 1896. The comments of the board reinforce this doubt. In the annual report for 1896 the board explained that chapter 225 made "no material changes . . . in respect to these classes, [state paupers] and has been put into operation without interruption." They anticipated no need to enlarge their facilities as a result of the law.[28] There is no evidence in the statistics or the reports to indicate whether the removals were indeed enacted in the best interests of the individual and the state. The State Board of Charities reports make it seem dubious. The only conclusion that can be drawn from this empirical and subjective data is that life went on as usual for the state poor, regardless of changes in the law.

Between the years 1896 and 1929, the existing poor law showed glaring inadequacies. To begin with, it was ideologically outdated. During this period New York was experiencing full-fledged progressivism under the able leadership of men of the calibre of Charles E. Hughes, Theodore Roosevelt, and Alfred E. Smith in Albany, and through the zeal of muckrakers and social workers on the grassroots level. In such a climate emphasis was on reform, modernization, and efficiency. The poor law, even in its revised state, was a prime candidate for a progressive overhaul. In addition to progressivism, the period was also marked by temporary, but nonetheless severe, economic crises that tested the poor law and again found it wanting in very practical ways. During the depressed years of 1907-08, 1914-15, and 1920-22, massive unemployment increased the number of persons needing relief, resident and nonresident alike, to a point well beyond what the present system could manage. The inadequacies of the poor law resulted in the spilling over of the needy from overcrowded municipal lodging houses into the streets of many of the large cities across the state. For example, in New York City, during the crisis years of 1914-1915, municipal lodging houses, annexes, and even the emergency opening of Ellis Island, were not enough to shelter the homeless. A similar situation in Buffalo resulted in an overflow from the Erie Lodging House that landed the homeless once again on the floors of the police stations. By January 1915 the situation had deteriorated so badly that the city opened up Broadway auditorium for the homeless. Those still unattended were sent to the penitentiary. During the 1907 crisis, the accelerated tramp problem prompted many to consider adopting a labor colony system as had been advocated in England by a man well acquainted with downtrodden transients, the father of the Salvation Army, General William Booth. The plan to absorb vagrants into mandatory labor camps was very attractive to the state legislature. A plan for such a camp in Dutchess County was passed, but the projected costs of its construction and maintenance caused the plan to be abandoned.[29] Finally, the existing law was found to be wanting legally. In times of both depression and prosperity, the courts of New York were crowded with cases involving disputes between local authorities over settlement and removal. Even with the clarification of the 1896 law, local authorities were intent upon using the courts as a means to lessen their responsibilities.[30]

Cognizant of all these inadequacies, the State Charities Aid Association began in 1925 a carefully orchestrated, impressively professional, and ultimately successful lobbying effort with the legislature and public alike for the adoption of a new progressive state welfare law.[31] As part of the campaign a number of press releases, leaflets, and pamphlets were prepared and disseminated. In one such pamphlet, *Patchwork or Progress*, the state's poor law was likened to a dilapidated house that could no longer be repaired or "patched." As with the house of analogy, the poor law also needed a complete overhauling to bring it into the twentieth century. According to the pamphlet, the old laws were "rigid, cumbersome, unworkable, and inapplicable to present day conditions." In its stead what was needed was a "progressive, modern statute — *A Public Welfare Law*."[32] To many contemporary observers this was just what the law passed on April 12, 1929 provided.

The revised poor law made its first symbolic break with the past in its title and definition of terms. The law of 1929 was entitled the Public Welfare Law, rather than the poor law. Symbolically, this took the onus of poverty off those treated under its provisions and changed the emphasis of relief from charity to public duty. The first article of the law continued the spirit of change by revising the terminology which had for centuries stigmatized the poor: *almshouses* became county, city, or town *homes*; *superintendents of the poor* became *county commissioners of public welfare*; and *overseers became public welfare officers.*[33]   The State Board of Charities, now renamed the State Board of Social Welfare as part of the spirit of change, added that "these changes in title were not made merely in a desire to adopt new names, but represent a new viewpoint of the functions of the organizations, their methods of and their relation to the public and their beneficiaries."[34] This change in nomenclature was indeed a symbolic landmark, but it remains to be seen if a change in name by legal fiat did indeed correspond to a change of heart in the implementation of the law.

Administratively, the law modernized the public welfare system by streamlining it. The state was divided into well defined public welfare districts to which specific duties were assigned. Sections were included in the law for dealing with the specialized concerns of the blind, children, veterans, and the elderly. Finally, much of the contradiction and confusion caused by generations of amendments was eliminated by the repeal of legal remnants from as far back as the eighteenth century. All of this was done in an effort to modernize and make more efficient the administration of public relief within the state.

Another significant change was the new emphasis of the law on serving a clientele. Article IX, entitled "Relief and Service," was a complete break with the past. The article dealt specifically with how to *care* for the poor; this was never deemed necessary before. Now the legislators instructed the public welfare officials to "administer such care and treatment as may restore such persons to a condition of self-support, and shall further give such advice to those liable to become destitute as may prevent the necessity of their becoming public charges." This talk of service, prevention, and implied re-habilitation was dramatically opposed to the earlier emphasis on poorhouse confinement as a form of punishment meant to deter ap-plicants rather than to serve them. This new spirit was even more evident in the next paragraph. "As far as possible families shall be kept together, and they shall not be separated for reasons of poverty alone. Whenever practicable, relief and service shall be given a poor person in his own home." Again the emphasis was on service and on caring for the client by no longer allowing the family unit to be rent. Furthermore, after over one hundred years, the priority of relief was once again placed on indoor aid in the privacy and comfort of one's own home, rather than in the much criticized poorhouses.[35]

In another effort to make the law more efficient, the settlement and removal laws were clarified so that it no longer took a Phila-delphia lawyer and numerous long and costly court sessions to in-terpret its finer points. The law was made more specific, the steps to qualify were outlined precisely, and the procedures for disputing claims were carefully laid out. Any person of full age who was a "resident and an inhabitant" of a town or city for one full year, and his family, was to gain a settlement which would be valid until he gained another settlement elsewhere or left the state for one year. No time to fulfill this requirement could be accrued while any member of the family was receiving relief from either a public or private agency. Subsequent sections of the law defined that the settlement of a wife was to follow that of her husband, with special provisions in the event of death, divorce, or desertion. In the case of minors the law provided that their settlement follow that of their parents. Provisions for emancipation from parents and the course to follow in the event of the death of either or both parents, or divorce, separation, or desertion were also included. These laws were very specific to avoid future complicated litigation. Further sections excluded settlement by birth or residence in public or private charitable institutions, or settlement by residence of less than five years by persons inflicted with tuberculosis in specific counties housing sanatoriums.[36]

It was all of these aspects of the law in 1929 that led Schneider and Deutsch to conclude that the best part of the law was its progressive spirit. "Where the old law was characterized by a negative approach, providing for relief in severely restrictive language, and was concerned primarily with keeping the 'undeserving' from obtaining any relief at all," they explained, "the new law carefully avoided harsh and humiliating terms and recognized in principle a far wider scope of public responsiblity than had ever appeared in the statute books before." Even while they admitted that the law contained large loopholes with phraseology such as "as far as possible" and "in so far as funds are available," and that old attitudes would only change slowly, despite the law, they believed that the public welfare law marked a significant turn of events, raised the standard of care, and would have been successful in making a complete break from the past if it had not been for the Great Depression.[37] In their own study, its passage was the climactic moment to which all of the past history of the state poor had led.

While the changes outlined above are momentous in the chain of events that we have been tracing from as far back as medieval England, a closer look at the law shows that remnants of the old system still abounded. As Edith Abbott, Dean of the School of Social Service Administration of the University of Chicago, wrote a decade later: "The New York Public Welfare Law, although in many ways a drastic revision of the old poor law, still retains the seventeenth-century poor law principles: (1) local responsibility, (2) family responsibility, and (3) settlement (or a residence requirement for eligibility for public aid.)"[38] The old settlement and removal concepts, while dressed up with new concern for the individual and long stripped of their primitive aspects, were still there.

The only significant change in the settlement law was the effort to include all possible future claims within its legal language, that is, to make provisions to cover all possible relationships that otherwise would result in litigation. Thus, where the law of 1896 stated that a wife's settlement followed that of her husband, this law went beyond that to outline all possible exceptions, that is, divorce, separation, and desertion. The same intention was behind the laws determining the settlement of minors. Other than this, and the exclusion of tubercular patients in specific counties, the only changes in the law were minor ones of phraseology. Thus the law defining settlement was basically unaltered.

In dealing with removal the new law actually was a step back from 1896. In the earlier law the removal of any poor person *across* the state, *except for state poor*, was strictly prohibited. Persons were to be cared for in the locality where they became disabled. The law of 1929, on the other hand, specified that:

> When a person cared for in the public welfare district where he is found shall have a settlement in some other public welfare district within the state, the public welfare official responsible for his support may send for and remove such person and care for him in his own public welfare district, or elsewhere, when it shall seem for the best interest of such persons that he be removed.

Thus, intrastate removal was once again acceptable, even though it was qualified by the "in the best interest" clause. Again the question arises of who was to determine the best interest? Not only was removal now acceptable, but so also was forced removal:

> If such a person shall refuse to be so removed, the commissioner of the public welfare district responsible for his support may apply to the county judge of his county for the issuance of an order to the sheriff of the county, or to some other person or persons, for the removal of the person to the public welfare district legally responsible for his support.

Therefore, if it was in the "best interest" of both, a pauper could be forcibly removed. What was illegal in 1896, intrastate removal, was now sanctioned even if force were necessary.[39]

The next article that showed little positive change over the 1896 poor law related specifically to "State Non-Resident and Alien Poor." This section basically repeated the same definition of the state poor: "Any person who had no settlement in any public welfare district in this state for sixty days during the year prior to an application for public relief and care." Such persons were to continue to be supported at state expense in public homes with which the state would make special contracts. The only changes here were in the name of the institutions from almshouses to public homes, and the provision that their care would be equal to that of any other persons in need. The 1929 law also eliminated the punishment for leaving the public home that had been contained in the 1896 law. Everything else in regard to the state poor remained fundamentally unchanged. The state remained generous in its willingness and readiness to care for nonresident or unsettled poor, especially in comparison to other states, but they were still to be institutionalized.

Therefore, at the same time that the law was being praised for taking the resident poor out of the living tombs that the poorhouses had become, the state poor continued to be relegated there.[40]

A similar situation existed in the section of the law dealing with the removal of nonsettled poor. Both laws, 1896 and 1929, had provisions for the removal of nonresident and alien poor to other states and counties. Basically they were the same. Any inmate, if it was in his best interest, could be removed from New York at state expense. However, there was one important difference. In 1896 the provision of such removal stated that if any inmate expressed a preference to be removed, he could be accommodated. In 1929 the matter of preference was not mentioned. Instead section 73 of the law read simply:

> When any person who is an inmate of any public home or is otherwise cared for at the expense of the state or of any public welfare district belongs to or has friends willing to support him in any other state or county, the superintendent of state and alien poor may cause his removal to such state or county, provided, in the judgment of the superintendent, the interests of the state and the welfare of such person will be thereby promoted.[41]

Again the question is who was to decide? One need only remember the priorities set earlier by the State Board of Charities to anticipate how "best interest" was to be determined. Unfortunately, it is virtually impossible to test whether this rewording of the law increased the number of removals or not because the Great Depression was soon to upset all previous means of measurement.

This then is the law that contemporaries looked upon as enlightened—a model for the future. It is perhaps unfair to examine the law only in those sections pertaining to settlement, removal, and the state poor, and then to further judge its deficiencies by comparison with today's welfare state. The law, for example, did do a great deal for specific classes of individuals, children, the elderly, veterans, the insane, and other groups, by singling them out for specific treatment; and, while it did not catapult the state into the future, it did lay the groundwork for change. These qualifications aside, we must look at this law with its positive and negative points as the only legal machinery available when the Great Depression struck six and one-half months later. Therefore, it is important to remember both the changes that were made and the shadows of the old poor law that still lay on the statute books when we turn to an examination of the state during this unprecedented economic crisis.

From this survey it is apparent that, while the forward moving progress of the state to the eventual acceptance of responsibility for all persons in need was proceeding by 1929, at the same time, the experiences of the past provided a countervailing force holding it back from a total commitment. Beginning with the earliest colonial experiences of the Dutch and English, there was a marked antagonism toward the impoverished wanderer. Entertainment laws, settlement and removal provisions, and vagrancy statutes all made it clear that the first priority of the law was to prevent persons "likely to be chargeable" from joining their communities. Attitudes toward those not belonging did not change when the colonies became states; instead, they were bolstered by settlement laws that erected even higher barriers against gaining a place in the community. During the nineteenth century, the state did initiate a number of laws that appeared to mark a break from the past. Following the Yates report, the legislature simplified settlement, ended removal, and put relief on a countywide basis; however, the indigent transient, as well as the resident poor, had to first qualify by some disability, as all able-bodied men ages eighteen to fifty were excluded. The same was true of the State Pauper Act of 1873. The state recognized a responsibility to care for unsettled poor, *if* they suffered from some disability. By 1896 the poor law was once again sanctioning the removal of the state poor if it was at their request and in their best interest. The State Board of Charities reports illustrate well what that meant. Even the Public Welfare Law of 1929, for all its contemporary praise, was only a symbolic break with the past. The old concepts of settlement and removal remained an integral part of the "modern" law, and a distinct suspicion of the stranger continued to lurk in its legal terminology.

Thus the state public welfare system appeared on the eve of the Great Depression. In this ambiguous position, caught between the forward motion of its new law and the tenacity of deeply rooted fears and suspicions, New York State stood ready to meet the unprecedented influx of needy transients uprooted by the greatest economic upheaval yet experienced.

⟨ 3 ⟩

Immediate Impact
of the Depression:
The State Reacts, 1929–33

THE stock market crash of 1929 and the resulting economic crisis took the unsuspecting playful America of the Roaring Twenties by surprise. Comforting words from Washington assured the stunned population that the crisis was only temporary and that the antidote to this present inconvenience was a large dose of national confidence. It was not long, however, before the signs of a long economic pall became apparent. Jobs were lost and new ones were frighteningly scarce; savings dwindled and then ran out; mortgages were foreclosed and family homes were lost; the hospitality of friends and relatives was strained by weeks and then months of distress. One by one individuals and then entire families were taking to the road leaving behind home, roots, and community ties in search of new positions and new lives elsewhere. As their numbers increased from a handful here and there to a steadily swelling body of wandering homeless persons, the deep-rooted nature of the depression became all that much harder to ignore and confidence became less and less possible.

It was difficult to determine in the early years of the depression exactly how many homeless there were in America, and even more difficult to estimate how many of these were nonresidents or transient. Early signs indicated that there was a "new army of transients moving across the country." A formal attempt to provide a reliable

47

count of their numbers was undertaken in January 1933 when the National Committee on Care of Transient and Homeless (NCCTH) coordinated a nationwide census in 809 cities, representing all forty-eight states and the District of Columbia, of all homeless persons being sheltered or cared for by the participating private and/or public agencies on the three census days—January 9, 10, and 11th. The final census figures showed a homeless population of 370,403. When estimates of the number of uncounted, those sleeping in speakeasies, hallways, and outdoors, were added to the total, the final estimate of America's homeless population rose to 1,225,000 which was still considered to be a conservative figure. Approximately 50 percent of this number were believed to be transient.[1]

Many of these uprooted persons set out hopefully with the belief that in America all one needed to do when times got rough was to move on, or, in the pioneer lore of the past, to seek a better life somewhere beyond the horizon. This was their tradition—the American Dream. But the dream was not working. There was no place for them to move on to, no safety valve, no new frontier. Instead of finding the opportunities they sought, they met with hostile communities already hard pressed to care for their own, exclusive settlement laws to prevent their staying, and a liberal use of the passing-on system. In addition, states were rapidly increasing their residency requirements and beginning to include in their statues specific instructions on how settlement could be *lost*.* In other words, these new pioneers met the full force of the apparatus that had been constructed by generations of state and local governments to protect their own communities from undesirables. In this greatest of industrial economic crises, they met head-on the archaic poor laws imported from England and "improved" on by generations of American practice.

But these people were not the vagrants and vagabonds, tramps and thieves that the laws had been written to guard against; these were the inheritors of optimistic America, its sons and daughters. Due to the unprecedented economic crisis, they were now forced to

---

*In 1931 alone, California raised its requirements from one to three years, Colorado went from sixty days to six months, and North Carolina followed suit by requiring three years to gain legal settlement and with it the right to relief. States, including New York, also began to include in their statutes specific instructions as to how settlement could be lost. In New York only one year's absence was necessary to lose all of the benefits that came with settlement.[2]

mingle with the hobos of old, temporarily adopting their life style, but as long as courage and morale could be maintained, not their culture.

It was not until mid-decade that a definitive statistical profile of the depression transient was finally drawn. At that time, the findings of Works Progress Administration (WPA) researcher John Webb confirmed the common assumption held all along by most concerned social workers. "Except for the fact that they were non-residents," Webb explained, "there seems little reason for considering transients as a distinct and separate group."[3]* When sociologist Nels Anderson compared these wanderers to the Rickety Bills, Toledo Sams, and Kleen Heel Sams that he had studied a decade earlier, he found a significant difference between the two. Unlike hobos, the depression migrants did not consider travel an end in itself; rather, they were traveling in search of new homes, and, if accepted by the community, they would strive to be active and productive citizens.[5] Anderson and Webb agreed that these transients were simply victims of an economic crisis that threatened everyone. Still later Henry Hill Collins, Jr. effectively pointed this out in his emotion-packed volume, *America's Own Refugees*: "Many a reader of this book, now comfortablly lounging in his favorite chair, well fed, well dressed, well housed is a potential candidate for migration." "Present affluence," he warned, "is no herald of future security."[6]

Each of these commentators, along with scores of social workers, public welfare officials and concerned citizens, appreciated the fact that the transient was no different than the proverbial "you and me." In fact, most agreed that the transients were generally superior to the sedentary population because they chose to look for work, no matter what the hazards, rather than staying at home and living upon the charity of others. General Pelham D. Glassford,** for

---

*Similar findings resulted when Webb studied migrant families and migratory casual laborers. The common conclusion he reached in all three of his studies was that these people were not, as misconception held, irresponsible, degraded, or "addicted to wandering." Instead, their social statistics, attitudes, etc. corresponded closely to the general relief population, and it was his opinion, which he readily contributed to the Secretary of Labor, that they should be treated in the same manner as the general relief population. He recommended that all settlement laws be abolished and relief be made available to them regardless of residency.[4]

**Glassford's interest in the transient had been aroused by his official dealings as police chief of Washington, D.C. during the encampment of the Bonus Army in that city in 1932 (see pp. 52-53).

one, concluded from his personal study of young transient men and boys that it was the more ambitious who took to the road. "Those without ambition, content to remain in their communities unemployed, idle and hanging around street corners and pool rooms . . . are not in any way comparable with the young men who are traveling the road today."[7]

Since the terms of migration had undergone such a dramatic change with the uprooting effect of the depression, and since the composition of the group had accordingly come to include those like "us," a corresponding change in attitude was imperative. Unfortunately, as we have seen, the attitudes ascribed to homeless wanderers were well etched in the American mind long before the onset of the depression. Any change or loosening of these preconceived notions was tenaciously resisted throughout the depression. The association between "me" and "thee" was still an unpleaseant one that few people cared to make. As a result, communities already overburdened by their own impoverished unemployed and fearful of the tattered strangers appearing on their streets reverted more and more to their traditional exclusiveness.

Even when, and if, the helplessness and need of the individual elicited some sympathy, the poor law system prevented his receiving thing approaching adequate relief. Settlement laws clearly defined where each person "belonged" and removal laws provided the means to get him there. The transient problem, however, had long ago transcended this simplistic medieval scheme. Even before the depression, the increased mobility afforded Americans by a transportation revolution that first gave them intercontinental railroad service and then provided individual motorized vehicles for an even greater range of mobility, made settlement and removal laws unworkable, if not totally illogical. To further complicate the situation, there was a great variance between the settlement laws of the individual states. In some states an absence of as little as six months was all that was necessary to lose settlement, while others demanded up to five years residence to gain it.[8] Theoretically, and in actuality, many persons could and did lose all relief rights by being caught between such provisions. As a result, the wandering unemployed found themselves passed from town to town and across state and county lines in accordance with archaic laws designed centuries before to control disorderly servants and unwanted vagrants. The only way to begin to solve these existing inadequacies and at the same time to respond intelligently to an unprecedented economic crisis was to impose a nationwide system to cover the entire issue of public relief. In other words, it was necessary to incorporate the federal government into the welfare scheme from which it had been omitted long ago when the individual states first adopted the English poor law system.

On the federal level ever increasing pleas for such a scheme fell on deaf ears. The Hoover administration, in its staunch belief in the value of self-help, did little to acknowledge Washington's responsibility to aid the depression-weary citizenry, wandering or otherwise. Instead of looking to the government for a solution to the crisis, the president advised Americans to look within for the answer. "Economic depression," he explained "can not be cured by legislative action or executive pronouncement. Economic wounds must be healed by the action of the cells of the economic body — the producers and consumers themselves."[9] This self-repairing process was to begin by individual cooperation and, when necessary, be bolstered by the aid of private charities, public local welfare departments, and, only if absolutely necessary, the state governments.

Consistent with these beliefs, Hoover continued to oppose all suggestions and appeals for a federal dole. Instead, he offered the citizenry what he felt it needed most: encouragement that they would weather the storm and advice on how it could be done on the individual, state, and local levels. To that end he created, in late 1930, the President's Committee for Employment which was renamed the following year the President's Organization on Unemployment Relief. To this committee he assigned the task of collecting and disseminating information and advice to local communities to aid them in shouldering their burden — alone. Numerous pamphlets published by the Russell Sage Foundation, such as, Joanne C. Colcord's *Community Planning in Unemployment Emergencies* and *Emergency Relief in Times of Unemployment* by Philip Klein, were distributed as an elixir to hard-pressed communities, sent along with the good wishes of the president.[10]

The transient problem was handled in like manner. The U.S. Department of Commerce, under the auspices of the same presidential organization, published and distributed literature advising communities on how to care for transients. Twenty thousand copies of a National Association of Travelers Aid Societies' pamphlet entitled *A Community Plan for Service to Transients* were offered to local communities "in the belief that it may serve as a helpful guide in dealing with the problem of transient families." As with other advice literature, the pamphlet offered a blueprint which "was a composite of the best features of many plans of communities that have attempted to make an intelligent and practical approach to the problem of service or care of transients."[11] Similarly, the Family Welfare Association of America was requested to prepare a companion volume based on a survey of the "actual experiences in a few carefully selected communities" that were successfully coping with the transient problem. The resulting pamphlet, *Community Planning for Homeless Men and Boys*, by Robert S. Wilson of the University of Kansas, offered the programs of sixteen cities as models. [12] Unfortunately, none of these documents, for all their good intentions, could do much to ameliorate the plight of thousands of destitute individuals. Given the magnitude of the depression and lack of financial assistance from the government, it was highly unlikely that the beleaguered communities would have the time or inclination to study the government's advice or the wherewithal to imitate the models offered. For the subject of all of this attention, the transient, the models provided no relief. The communities through which he passed simply did not want him.

Even the nation's capital refused the transient a welcome. The hostility toward unwanted strangers reported in communities around the country paled in comparison to that exhibited by the Hoover White House as orders were given in the summer of 1932 to rout the tattered Bonus Army of unemployed, often homeless, World War I veterans who had bivoucked in Washington awaiting word on legislation then before Congress to extend to them much needed but premature bonuses for their services in the war. When Congress refused their petition, those who had homes to return to left. The thousands who did not remained in their make-shift homes on Anacostia Flats. Fearing a communist plot, the administration ordered their removal. Before fixed bayonets, tear gas, and tanks the veterans were "escorted" from the city with their shanty town in flames behind them. When asked, "What next?" most simply replied, "I do not know." "We have no home," "I have lost my settlement," "We lost our house and savings," "Our people are all poor and unemployed," "There are no funds for relief in our town," and so on. Thousands left with no homes to return to and no direction in which to turn. [13]

This tattered and impoverished army of some twenty thousand men, women and children provides us with the best visual identification of transient America that is available. On this one occasion transients from across the nation set their sights on a single destination — Washington. They came by car, by rail, and by foot, setting out as individuals but soon blending into a whole. They were not tramps, they were not bums, they were not communist agitators. They were America's unemployed. They were good family men. They had been steady employees, skilled in their trades, successful in their professions, white collar and blue. Many had been homeowners. All had faithfully served their country. Then came the depression. For many of them Washington had been their last hope, yet, much to their horror and surprise, Washington had refused them. Again they were on their own — going their separate ways.

While Herbert Hoover was warning from the White House that economic depression could not be cured by legislative action, and that any such effort would make a "tyrant" of the government,[14] Governor Franklin D. Roosevelt of New York State was preparing just such an intrusion of the state government into the yet uncharted waters of social welfare. Not only was FDR claiming state responsibility for the welfare of the citizenry, but he was also insisting that this recognition marked the difference between "the civilization of yesterday and the civilization of today."[15] This change in attitude was a practical departure by a practical man. New York as an industrial state was suffering sorely from the depression, and it could not find solace in the platitudes offered by the White House. With factories closing at an alarming rate, and industrial jobs and wages falling off at a corresponding pace, the state could not wait for the inevitable better days that Hoover predicted. Almost 3,500 factories in the Empire State had closed their doors between 1929 and 1933. As a result industrial employment fell from 1,105,963 to 733,457 and wages from $1,650,389,000 to $754,367,000.[16] Soup kitchens, milk stations and overcrowded lodging houses were becoming a way of life. Despite the valiant efforts of private charities and public relief, the expansion of public works, and innovative stop-gap measures such as apple vending and man-a-block programs, conditions continued to deteriorate. Without governmental aid or direction, local resources were being rapidly depleted. As Hoover stood firm on the federal level, staunchly protecting the old values, it became more and more apparent on the local level that those values were no longer viable. The immediacy of the situation called for bold new action.

FDR, unlike Hoover, recognized the need for experimentation, change, and immediate action. After the localities had proven that they were physically and financially incapable of handling the steadily increasing burdens of unemployment relief, Roosevelt called the legislature into special session to bring the machinery of the state to bear. As early as August 28, 1931, with unemployment in the state approaching one million, FDR addressed the assembled legislators with words of expediency and practical logic. The government, he explained "is not the master but the creature of the people;" as such, its duty is that of "servant to its master." One duty of the state, recognized by all civilized nations, he explained, was the assistance it afforded to disabled persons unable to help themselves. In modern society, he argued, this duty is extended: "In broad terms I assert that modern society, acting through its government, owes the definite obligation to prevent the starvation and dire want of any of its fellow men and women who try to maintain themselves but cannot." By this he meant not only those incapacitated by "accident or old age," but, "the same responsibility of the State undoubtedly applies when widespread conditions render large numbers of men and women incapable of supporting either themselves or their families because of circumstances beyond their control which make it impossible for them to find remunerative labor." These persons deserved government aid "not as a matter of charity but as a matter of social duty."[17] Having redefined the social responsibility of government in a modern industrial age, he went on to recommend a program to meet such responsibility. He proposed the creation of a Temporary Emergency Relief Administration (TERA) and the appropriation to that commission of $20,000,000 to meet the needs of the coming year. The money was to be raised by increasing by one-half the personal income tax paid by those still fortunate enough to have taxable income.

On September 23, 1931, the legislators responded to the governor's request with the passage of the Wicks Act. This act "to relieve the people of the state from the hardships and suffering caused by unemployment," gave the governor most of what he had asked for, including, to the chagrin of social workers who hoped for some specific recognition of the needs of the transient, a strict residency qualification for any and all such relief. The law read that all such aid outlined within its provisions be limited to those "who have been residents of the state for at least two years prior to the first day of November, nineteen hundred thirty-one, and to the dependents of such persons."[18] The rationale behind this qualification was quite sound. Even in the best of times, legislation threatening old cherished values and/or raising taxes had to be handled delicately. Thus, all reference to the Wicks Act was cushioned in statements about the emergency the state faced and the necessity for all of its citizens to pull together to share the common burden. Such appeals were effective and their logic persuaded persons to part with some of their traditional concepts about charity and with some of the cash in their pockets. To have attempted to extend the logic of the common good to outsiders would have threatened the concept itself; therefore, the residency clause was necessary. By the same token, a strict residency requirement was needed to keep outsiders from flocking to the state for its relief benefits.

All of this is understandable, but none of it helped to alleviate the plight of the individual transient. The Wicks Act, for all the praise it was to receive nationwide, provided nothing for those individuals who had been and still were being attracted to the glamour of the big cities of New York and to its industrial centers and farming communities in search of jobs. The treatment accorded to them would depend upon the interpretation of existing laws. It is interesting to note that one of the rules subsequently laid down by TERA was that there should be no discrimination on grounds of "political creed, religion, race, color, or non-citizenship." Thus, in practical experience, a United States citizen without residency could be turned down while a noncitizen with residency would receive aid.[19]

In New York State the existing apparatus for the care and disposition of needy transients was the much acclaimed 1929 Public Welfare Law. Within the basic provisions of this law, it was believed, there was sufficient attention given to transients to preclude the need for any additional mention under the Wicks Act. A law, however, is only as effective as its administration. Therefore, it is necessary to examine how the law was interpreted and administered by the appropriate state agency, the State Board of Social Welfare, Division of State Aid. Only then can we construct a true picture of how the state dealt with the ever-increasing flow of transients.

The State Board of Social Welfare was responsible for the overall implementation of the entire state welfare program as specified in the Public Welfare Law. During the early years of the depression, the office of Commissioner of the State Board of Social Welfare was held by Charles H. Johnson. In October 1932, upon Johnson's resignation, David Adie, Executive Secretary of the Buffalo Council of Social Agencies, assumed the office. He remained in that position for the duration of the economic crisis. Adie was a man whose name was well respected among contemporaries and is still recognized by historians as that of a champion of social welfare. Within the board, responsibility for various segments of society was delegated among specific divisions. Responsibility for state, nonresident, alien and Indian poor was assigned to the Division of State Aid. *State poor*, as defined by law and interpreted by the board, were persons "in need of public relief who have no legal settlement in any town or city of the state and who have not resided in any public welfare district of the State for sixty days prior to the application for relief." The state assumed full financial responsiblity for such persons. The term *nonresident poor*, on the other hand, referred to persons without legal settlement in the state but "who have resided in a public welfare district of the State for at least sixty days prior to application for relief." Such people were the responsibility of the county.[20] The state's only involvement was to provide for the transportation of such persons out of the state. The Division of State Aid was headed during the entire decade by Harry Hirsch, a sympathetic and outspoken friend of the transient and advocate of uniform settlement laws and federal aid.

Each year, as required by law, the board and each of its divisions presented the legislature with a report of the past year's application of the law. Table 2 has been compiled from the reports of the Division of State Aid to provide an overview of its operations between the time that the Public Welfare Law went into effect on January 1, 1930 and the entrance of the federal government into the realm of transient relief in November 1933.[21] (See Table 2, page 57). A review of this table demonstrates that the number of persons referred to the state government increased proportionately to the deepening of the depression. This fact was stressed year after year in the textual accompaniment to the reports. As early as 1930 Hirsch noted a 22.2 percent increase in the number of cases submitted over the previous year; by 1931 the two year increase mounted to 36.6 percent.[22] Rising even more rapidly were the number of cases pending at the end of the year. Such cases more than doubled in the four year period.

The interest of the officials was diverted in 1932 from the overall picture to the rising classification of state poor. This was particularly noteworthy because the law required that such persons be

TABLE 2. Summary of the Number of Cases of State, Non-Resident, or Alien Poor Under Investigation During the Fiscal Year (1930–34) and the Disposition of the Same

Report for the Year Ending . . .	Cases Pending at the Beginning of the Year	New Cases Submitted for Investigation	TOTAL	Discharged from Consideration After Investigation**	Removed to Other States & Countries	Cases Pending at the End of the Year
6/30/1930	406	6,116	6,522	4,039	1,768	715
6/30/1931	715	6,786	7,501	4,490	2,138	875
6/30/1932	873	6,737	7,610	**	2,456	1,456
6/30/1933	1,456	9,692	11,148	**	3,501	1,500
6/30/1934*	1,500	10,013	11,513	**	3,174	1,870

*By this date the federal transient program had been in operation for seven months therefore figures must be considered with this in mind.

**No specific figures were given in this category for the years 1932–34; it is reasonable to assume however that the difference between the yearly total and those removed and cases pending will produce a close approximation.

(Table compiled from the Annual Reports of the State Board of Social Welfare, for the years 1930–1936).

cared for at state expense without any distinction between them and any other needy resident poor. The rise which was thus singled out for attention is obvious in Table 3.[23] (See Table 3, page 59). The total number of state poor referred to the state for care and/or disposal more than doubled in the years 1930 to 1934. An increased case load of 1,086 in 1930, as compared to 2,486 in 1934, represents a 129 percent increase over the five-year period. Even more startling was the increase in the number of persons who remained under care at the end of the year. By 1933 this number had quadrupled from 98 to 440. It was only after a federal transient program finally alleviated some of this burden that the number dropped slightly to 349.

Both sets of figures, cases investigated and cases carried over, show a definite increase in the state's acceptance of its responsibility to care for the state poor. However, the proportion of those who remained under care at the end of the year, despite the rapid inflation of the figure, is still small compared to the number investigated annually. For example, in 1930 less than one-tenth of the 1,086 individuals referred to the state remained under its care at the end of the year. In 1933 only 440 of the 2,278 individuals investigated were given care beyond the fiscal year. Even this small number may be misleading in that it may be more reflective of the number of persons only just taken in at the end of the year and not yet disposed of. For example, an individual referred to the state on June 29th of any year would be recorded in the column, "Total Under Care at the End of the Year," even if his removal were effected within a matter of days. Therefore, it is safe to conclude that aid to the state poor, just as with the nonresident poor, was not a long term process. Thus it is important to continue an investigation into these statistics to understand just how such transients were disposed of and to determine if such disposal was within the terms of the law and whether it was for the best interest of the individual.

Of those cases disposed of, the largest number were recorded as "Discharged as Able to Care for Selves." Unfortunately, there is no information to explain how such ability was determined; therefore, we cannot meaningfully assess the state's very liberal use of this device to dismiss the large majority of cases submitted. The fraction of persons who absconded or died needs little comment. Those who fled may have been freeloaders testing the generosity of New York State or persons fearful of being removed. For those who died, New York may just have been their last stop after years of troubles, or

TABLE 3. Summary of the Number of Cases of State Poor Under Investigation During the Fiscal Year (1930–34) and the Disposition of the Same

Report for the Year Ending . . .	Number Under Care at Beginning of Year	Number of Persons Received During Year	Total Individuals Cared For	Number Discharged as Able to Care for Selves	Transferred	Absconded	Died	Removed to Other States	Total Under Care at the End of Year
6/30/30	76	1,010	1,086	736	2	*	33	217	98
6/30/31	154	955	1,109	664	*	2	32	259	152
6/30/32	*	*	1,527	850	*	14	33	352	278
6/30/33	*	*	2,278	1,256	*	27	44	511	440
6/30/34	*	*	2,486	1,520	*	9	32	576	349

*Figures not available.
(Table compiled from the *Annual Reports of the State Board of Social Welfare*, 1930–34).

they simply may have taken too long in coming to the attention of the state. The second most used means of disposal was to remove the individual out of the state altogether. Nonresidents were transported out of New York as quickly as they were reported. Their removals proceeded apace with the deepening of the depression: 1,357 in 1929–30; 1,658 in 1930–31; 1,715 in 1931–32; and 2,557 in 1932–33. The pace only began to slow down after a federal program became operative in 1933; then 2,257 were transported by the state.[24] This procedure was well within the law. Nonresidents were the responsibility of the county welfare district. The state only was to become involved when it was previously decided that removal was necessary. The state poor were supposedly a different matter. Removal in their case was only to be a final expedient taken under very specific circumstances; yet, a perusal of Table 2 shows that removals in this area also increased proportionately. According to these figures, the number of removals of state poor increased 165 percent over a four year period. The very year after the Public Welfare Law was passed shows a 19 percent increase in removals. When these removal figures are compared to the number of persons retained by the state at the end of the year, it can be seen that in each year those removed exceeded those taken under care. While the officials were noting the phenomenal increase of 128 percent in the number cared for, the increased percentage of persons removed far exceeded it with a figure of 165 percent. Only discharge was a more readily used recourse for the state.

The officials of the Board of Social Welfare and the Division of State Aid felt that their interpretation of section 73 of the Public Welfare Law, which allowed for the removal of persons to their place of legal settlement when it was judged to be in the best interests of the state and the individuals, and the subsequent removal of over one-fifth of all cases referred to them, was consistent with the letter of the law. Each year when they presented the ever-escalating removal figures to the legislature, they repeated their rationale. Removals, they explained, were only made when settlement had been definitely established outside of the state and authorization had been received from the appropriate out-of-state welfare officials, or when responsible relatives were found to provide for each individual. Commenting upon the record number of removed state and nonresident poor in 1931, Assistant Commissioner Hirsch explained:

> All those removed were persons who because of age, disease or other disability gave promise of becoming public charges for an indefinite period or even permanently.

In this explanation he put the interest of the state, that is, the elimination of potentially lifelong charges, before those of the individual. The law, on the other hand, specified that the interests of state and individual should be complementary. He went on to elaborate that the state's policy was also beneficial to the individual:

> Many of these persons are suffering from social and economic conditions, language difficulties and the separation from friends and kindred; it is a real service, when conditions permit to return them to their friends and native environment. [25]

This description may have applied to some of the persons referred to the state; however, it is inconsistent with the profile supplied by sociologists, statisticians, and social workers, of a young, virile, eager migrant seeking employment and betterment in a new environment. It was with the same argument each year that hundreds of persons were sent off to forty-four different states, Puerto Rico, the Virgin Islands, Honolulu, and thirty-nine different countries.

Another consideration necessitating the large number of removals, and a very understandable one, was financial. This was, after all, the depth of a severe depression, and a state can feel the economic pinch as keenly as an individual. Thus, state expenditures were watched as carefully as a family guards its budget in hard times. Those directly responsible for reporting budgetary matters had to remember that, despite the innovative Wicks Act, both the legislators and the governor were fiscal conservatives, and they would expect a fair accounting. Certain items were automatically paid. The support of the disabled poor, for example, was as acceptable to the State Board of Social Welfare as the paying of the milkman was by the individual. But this business of paying welfare to the able-bodied was a new idea, and appropriations in this area were granted only because of emergency conditions. Thus, during the years 1929–34, state officials watched with dismay as these figures skyrocketed.

In the annual report of 1934, Hirsch tabulated the expenditures within his division for the past five year period to illustrate such increases.[26] Table 4 (p. 63) is taken from his report. What was particularly disturbing about these figures was not the first set of numbers, the cost of removal. What was upsetting was the cost of maintenance. Caring for the state poor, despite the vigorous removal programs, was costing the department more each year than it cost to remove all state, nonresident, and alien poor combined. In other words, the handful of individuals who remained under care at the end of each year cost the state far more than the thousands who were processed and removed. By 1933–34 the state was paying close to $100,000 to maintain the state poor, almost as much as was expended in its total Indian program. With these figures in mind, the board justified its removal program as a fiscally necessary approach to a growing problem. Each year the commissioner pointed to the considerable savings that were made by removing the poor rather than maintaining them. In the year ending June 30, 1930, it was estimated that that year's removals had saved the state $17,860 per week. If maintained within the state for the entire year, those persons who were removed would have cost an estimated $919,360. These estimates rose each year as did the logic for removal: 1931, $1,111,760; 1932, $1,277,120; 1933, $1,820,620; 1934, $1,650,048.[27] The savings are significant when one considers the amount of money being expended at the time by the TERA to care for its own. The original twenty million dollars appropriated was used within a matter of months, and a steady stream of new appropriations was needed to keep the agency operative.

The legislators must not have found any inconsistencies between the law and its application, for they voiced no objections to the yearly reports. In fact, they went so far as to strengthen the very section of the law that gave validity to the removal procedure. On April 26, 1933, an act to amend section 73 of the Public Welfare Law was approved by Governor Herbert H. Lehman. The amendment repeated the previous wording of section 73, giving the board authority to remove indigent nonresident persons when it was in the

TABLE 4. Financial Statement for the Cost of Removals of State, Non-Resident, and Alien Poor and the Cost of Maintenance of State and Indian Poor for the Fiscal Year (1930–34) Inclusive

	1929–30	1930–31	1931–32	1932–33	1933–34*
Removals					
State Poor	$ 3,528.63	$ 2,728.74	$ 2,852.11	$ 9,166.09	$ 4,376.51
Non-Resident	23,673.07	29,471.19	32,197.80	41,136.73	40,974.24
Alien Poor	2,704.37	2,723.80	6,865.54	9,697.18	10,233.96
TOTALS	$29,906.07	$34,923.73	$41,915.45	$60,000.00	$55,584.71
Maintenance					
State Poor	$26,495.45	$ 46,994.72	$ 52,829.09	$ 71,301.33	$ 86,425.09
Indian Poor	47,504.55	72,705.28	94,806.81	112,495.93	92,915.08
TOTALS	$74,000.00	$119,700.00	$147,635.00	$183,797.26	$179,376.17

*1933–34 figures reflect seven months of federal aid under FERA transient program.
(Statistics gathered from the *Annual Reports of the State Board of Social Welfare*, 1930–34).

best interest of the state and the individual. There then followed a new clause:

> After notification of the proposed removal, if such person shall refuse to be so removed, the commissioner of the public welfare district wherein such person is being cared for may apply to the county judge of his country for the issuance of an order to the sheriff of the county, or to some other person or persons, for the removal of the person to the state or county, or district therein legally responsible for or willing to support him, and cause his removal thereto. [28]

The Department of Social Welfare now had the power to forcibly remove persons who refused to leave the state. It was a power they were to make full use of. Such authority had already been given to remove resident poor from one welfare district to another. Now it was applied to the out-of-state removal of nonresidents.

The purpose of the amendment was purely an economic one. When the bill was sent to the governor for his signature, it was accompanied by statements from Assemblyman Wilson Messer who introduced it, and from the commissioner of social welfare. Both urged Lehman to sign the bill as a financial necessity. Messer estimated that one million dollars could be saved annually if the bill were enacted as law. Adie confirmed that the bill would mean a "considerable savings," and he passed on the endorsement of the New York State Association of County Public Welfare Officials and Town Welfare Officers which had voted approval for the bill at its latest convention. [29] When Lehman signed the bill into law, it became apparent that the financial woes outlined in the board's annual reports had been well heeded; whereas, the suffering of the individuals recorded therein went unnoticed.

The fact that such a law was considered necessary undermines the very argument that the board had been using to justify the already high number of removals. Each year it was reiterated in the report that removal was beneficial to the people. There was a strong "it-is-for-their-own-good" flavor about these reports. Now, in endorsing the bill, the board had acknowledged that there were persons who did not agree that saving money for the state was necessarily in *their* best interest—persons who could only be removed by force. In Adie's memorandum to Lehman, he pointed out that there were many persons under public care who were only there because the board did not have the authority to forcibly remove them. This was of special concern, he explained, because, if these people remained in the state for one year, they would probably lose their old settlement and gain one here thereby making them the permanent responsibility of the state.[30] These comments meant that the board was ready and willing to augment the already high proportion of removals by removing people by force. In other words, the disproportionate number of persons removed was *low* compared to what it could have been if and when the board's authority had been expanded.

The brief clause added to section 73 by the amendment is symptomatic of the basic flaw in the administration of the Public Welfare Law in regard to transients. The law had been designed to assume the state's responsibility for needy persons, despite their settlement or lack of it. For this reason, it was cheered by contemporaries as a modern welfare law that took the state out of the poor law past. Transients referred to the state as state poor were to be treated with the same respect and concern as that afforded destitute residents. Care was the primary consideration — removal was secondary. The administration of the law between the years 1929 and 1930 reversed these priorities. The law specified care, but the system emphasized removal. This change was made obvious in the annual reports by the overriding concern with the money to be saved by removing the state poor. Preoccupation with that priority blinded the administrators to what was supposed to be their primary function — the *care* of the state poor. Tied to the restricting concepts of settlement and removal, they were unable to administer the modern law in a modern way. The inclusion of a few sentences in section 73 by the amendment of 1933 completed the transition. The approval of the legislature and the signature of the governor signaled their compliance in keeping New York State in its poor law past.

Thus far we have been considering the state's policies and practices for removing persons as if the state were the final recourse or an omnipotent benefactor to whom one made appeals and then humbly accepted its decision. The issue of removal, however, is larger than the state. A quick perusal of the Constitution of the United States makes it apparent that persons subjected to removal had grounds to at least appeal their removals as violations of their constitutional rights. According to article IV, section 2, clause 1:

"The Citizens of each state shall be entitled to all Privileges and Immunities of Citizens in the several states."[31] If this indeed be the case, then citizens summarily removed from one state to another because of poverty, by force if necessary, had sufficient grounds to protest such treatment. The Fourteenth Amendment, with its stipulation that "no state shall make or enforce any law which shall abridge the privileges or immunities of citizens of the United States; nor shall any State deprive any persons of life, liberty, or property, without due process of law; nor deny to any person within its jurisdiction the equal protection of the laws,"[32] provides additional justification for a legal appeal. If all else should fail, the laws of removal could be challenged under the catch-all interstate commerce clause. Was not the forcible removal of citizens an interference with the federal government's sole right to regulate interstate commerce? Despite all of these avenues of legal appeal, a careful review of the judicial records of the state show no reported cases of legal protest by a removed person over his removal. Out of the total of 1,913 state poor and 9,544 nonresident poor removed between 1929 and 1934, no one apparently chose to challenge the law or their treatment by the State Board of Social Welfare.

A number of possible explanations come to mind. Perhaps the department reports were correct and removal did provide a service. This may have been so in cases involving individuals whose flight had been ill-conceived in the first place and who welcomed the free transportation home. Nonetheless, given the composite profile of the typical transient, it is highly unlikely that persons who migrated out of a depressed area purposely to avoid welfare and to find employment elsewhere would be thankful to be returned to the debilitating environment from which they had fled. Another possibility is that proud persons, making such a journey to avoid the shame of poverty and the stigma of public relief, would be reluctant to make a public gesture such as a court case which would bring unwanted attention to themselves and their plight. The simplest explanations, however, are often the best. It is very probable that the parties so removed were either unaware of their constitutional rights or of the procedures necessary to secure them. Even if they were knowledgeable about the legal system, their very poverty may have precluded any attempt to demand these rights through the judicial system. We must not lose sight of the fact that these persons were alone and often penniless in unfamiliar surroundings. Given such a situation, it is easy to see how they could have been, and were, swept up in the bureaucracy of the system.

Whatever the real reasons, the courts were not used at this time by the victims. It was not until 1940 that a person removed from New York State was to make full use of this recourse, taking his case all the way to the United States Supreme Court. Instead of providing a vehicle for persons to challenge removal, the courts continued to be crowded with representatives of various public welfare districts vying with each other over issues of settlement, each trying to rid itself of an unwanted burden. Thus Onondaga County took the Town of Milo to court in 1930 in an attempt to recover funds expended for the children of Harry and Freda Jones over a contested question of settlement, while the towns of Manlius and Pompey resorted to the courts to settle a technicality involving the settlement of the financial responsibility for one Jesse Turvey, his wife, and their four children.[33] Over and over again, the courts were urged to resolve settlement technicalities in cases such as these.

On the state level, it must be concluded that the application of the Public Welfare Law did not live up to the expectations of those who heralded it as a momentous leap into the future — at least not for the transient. All blame, however, need not be focused on the misdirection of the administration. There were other reasons for the apparent circumvention of the spirit of the law. One problem was that the Division of State Aid lacked a sufficient number of field workers and was, therefore, unable to receive and analyze adequate information about the transient. Under these circumstances, the preoccupation with the disposal of individual cases referred to them is understandable. In addition, on the local level, communities were passing transients on so quickly that there was little opportunity for local welfare departments to properly register the great bulk of potential state poor. Considering that the acquisition of sixty days' residency converted state poor into nonresident poor, that is, a local responsiblity, the urgency with which communities resorted to passing-on is also understandable. Thus, according to a survey conducted by a specially appointed Governor's Commission on Unemployment Relief for Transients, only four cities out of twenty-six were referring state poor cases to the State Board of Social Welfare via their county commissioners; one city did so only when medical care or hospitalization was required. Families fared somewhat better. One-half of the cities referred all such cases to the state. Similarly, only eight counties out of thirty-five registered transients for the purpose of determining settlement, and in only ten had the towns referred all transients to the county commissioner. Based on these figures, the commission reported: "It may be presumed that the cases registered with the Division of State Aid presented an extremely incomplete picture of the actual problem of transient jobless men cared for in some fashion or other by towns and counties."[34]

For these reasons the state system of transient relief, with all of its inadequacies, was only reaching a small percentage of the transient population. Thus far we have been talking about annual numbers never exceeding twelve thousand for state, nonresident, and alien poor alike. In addition, those figures represented only reported cases. The cases actually dealt with were much fewer. When compared to the admittedly incomplete statistics on New York State compiled by the NCCTH during its nationwide census of the transient and homeless population, this becomes glaringly apparent. The 1933 census recorded 32,143 transient and homeless in New York State.[35] The census counted transients in municipal lodging houses, charitable institutions, shanty towns, parks, roadside camps, and boxcars. They did not, however, reach everyone. Many small towns and cities were not recorded, and persons "on the road" were also missed. With this in mind, a comparison of the figures makes it apparent that those persons who had even the most remote chance of receiving aid from the state were those who happened to come to the attention of local officials and who were then accepted by the social welfare department. Those not so assigned, the greater majority, were left to be cared for at the point of their discovery, in the cities, towns, and villages of the state.

⧙ 4 ⧘

Immediate Impact
of the Depression:
Local Reaction, 1929–33

THE local level treatment received by transients in New York varied across the state depending upon the size, financial wherewithal, and attitudes of each community. While private and public agencies struggled to extend their already hard-pressed resources to the newcomers, more often than not, they were only able to offer limited, life-sustaining, and very temporary assistance. Even this minimal aid was often available only in the larger cities of the state. Smaller cities and towns adjusted their assistance to their own resources. When pressed to their limits, communities usually reserved their tax dollars and charity for the resident needy, and transients, as in the days of the poor law past, were generally passed-on.

In the state's largest cities the municipal lodging houses* were heavily used in a valiant effort to meet the staggering increases in the number of homeless, needy individuals, resident and nonresident alike. In upstate New York, the annual reports of the Erie County Department of Charities and Corrections reflect the phenomenal pressure that was being put upon these facilities. The number of homeless men registered with the municipal lodging house in Buffalo rose from 65,493 in 1929 to 750,732 in 1933, a 1,046 percent increase. Correspondingly, the number of persons receiving lodging went from 24,633 to 461,646, and the number of meals provided from

---

*Familiarly referred to as muni-houses.

124,372 to 1,359,201.[1] These figures reflect increases of 1,774 percent and 992 percent respectively over a mere three-year period. The volume necessitated the opening of annexes in the Broadway Auditorium in October 1930, at Terrace and West Eagle Streets in January of the same year, and at 620 Washington Street in December of 1931. On November 5, 1932, a new, permanent Erie County Municipal Lodging House was opened on the corner of Carroll and Wells Streets.[2] Still the facilities were inadequate. This space problem, coupled with the emergency nature of the shelter, most often limited the care that could be afforded to the homeless to one day's food and lodging. By 1933 even this temporary, insufficient care was costing the county $125,709.25 per year.[3]

In New York City the problems of Buffalo were multiplied. During the depression, many people automatically gravitated to the city with hopes of employment or in search of excitement during their forced vacations. Here they mingled with the resident unemployed and homeless, complicating an already critical situation. Consequently, the number of persons registering with the city's municipal lodging facilities rose from 158,677 in 1929 to a phenomenal 2,230,086 in 1934, or from a daily average of 434 persons needing shelter and food to 6,110. As in Buffalo, the facilities in New York City had to be expanded just to attempt to meet such an increase. The existing municipal lodging house in Manhattan had been built in 1908 to provide shelter for up to 1,087 men, women, and children. By 1934 this obviously inadequate shelter was supplemented by the opening of two annexes.[4]

The Department of Public Welfare of New York City was very proud of the facilities in their municipal lodging houses. Each year, in its annual report, the department provided a fully illustrated presentation of the system at work. Attesting to the volume they handled were pictures of men waiting in lines the length of a city block, four abreast, for the food and lodging they provided. Inside the lodging house and its annexes the dining and sleeping facilities were displayed at their best. "Ready for that noon-day meal" captioned one picture of the huge sterile kitchen of the lodging house. It was quite impressive indeed to associate all those homeless, bedraggled, poor individuals in line with the meal they were about to receive from this kitchen. The dining room of Annex #1 was highlighted in another photographic series. The food served here, according to the report, was both wholesome and hearty. Breakfast consisted of a bowl of rolled oats, coffee, and bread. At the noon meal and at supper each man received a large bowl of beef or mutton stew with potatoes, tomatoes, onions, carrots, and turnips, and a cup of hot coffee with milk and sugar. According to the report, the men were never rushed during their meals or refused seconds, even with a turnover rate of thirty-five hundred hungry men per hour.[5]

The lodging facilities were displayed with equal pride. Their mere size and capacity was one feature highlighted. With the main municipal house accommodating over one thousand, the South Ferry Terminal Annex another thousand, and Annex #1 capable of sleeping fifteen hundred men in the "largest bedroom in the world," this boast was well substantiated. Again the facilities were photographically displayed to reiterate their effectiveness. In the world's largest bedroom one could see fifteen hundred cots set up in a warehouse-type building, six across and hundreds deep, with three aisles between them for walking. The beds were all lined up side to side and head to head in an attempt to fit as many as possible in the shelter. Each bed was clean and made up with blankets, sheets, and feather pillows. Linen was changed daily. The building also boasted a first-class heating system and "perfect" sanitary facilities consisting of four toilet rooms, eight long wash basins, drinking faucets, and liquid soap containers. The addition in 1932 of a building to be used during the day for recreation and "sprucing-up" for job interviews, completed what the city and frequent visiting dignitaries considered a model institution.[6]

The facilities in New York City were open to anyone who was homeless and in need, providing that space was available. A person merely presented himself at the lodging house and was admitted. From there he was fed and provided with a bath and a cursory physical examination while his clothes were being sterilized. He was then offered a night's lodging. The next day the newcomer would be sent to the Central Registration Bureau for the Homeless. If the person was a resident of the city, he would be registered and returned to the house for a five-day period which could be renewed indefinitely. Nonresidents were limited to a stay of one night per month. The department, "mindful that the taxpayers of the city are paying for the relief," felt it would be unfair to allow that institution to care indefinitely for the nonresident; thus, only 26,871 nonresidents were reported to have received shelter in 1931.[7] In actuality many more nonresidents were served. Because investigation was minimal, one could claim to be a resident and circumvent the rules. Women and children were handled in a similar manner in separate shelters.

Both Buffalo and New York City expended large sums of money to maintain this form of shelter as a refuge for the resident and, to a lesser degree, the nonresident homeless. In due course, Rochester and Syracuse were also forced to open similar shelters to relieve the heavy load of homeless in their cities. Each municipality took pride in its humanitarian concern for these victims of the depression, feeling that they were indeed doing their best to meet the emergency.

From the outside looking in, the neat rows of beds and sparkling clean kitchens may have indeed appeared worthy of praise. However, the view of the occupant of that bed or dining room seat was quite different. This distinction was dramatically pointed out to the readers of *The New Republic* by the cutting pen of Matthew Josephson in an aritcle entitled, "The Other America." Using the jargon of the street and perspective of the recipient, Josephson described the experience of a night in the New York City lodging house in a manner sharply contrasted with the boasts of the city.

The entry procedure, described as so simple and efficient in the annual reports, took on a new dimension when the experience was perceived from the participant's point of view. The procedure began at that moment when the individual lost all hope for the future, swallowed his pride, and decided to approach the Central Registration Bureau. At that point he was required to give up his individuality and submit himself to mass processing. Name, age, "where slept last night" were all recorded by the welfare officer. Each applicant was asked if he was a New Yorker of two-years residence. If the answer was yes, he could expect at least two weeks shelter; if not, he would be allowed a single night and be ordered to move on. Josephson implied that a small white lie here kept a man from disappearing into the unknown of subways and Skid Row. From here the person proceeded on to enter the first of the many lines that constituted a way of life for the destitute. This particular line was for supper at the South Street Annex. The line for the 5:00 p.m. meal formed early in the afternoon and was well supervised by the police. When the dinner hour approached, the guards drove "the cheerless crowd along the gallery much in the way cattle are driven in." With the signal "all right!" a race began as the hungry men tried to secure seats at the first sitting. The wholesome hearty meal described by the reports turned out, upon close examination, to be a coarse vegetable stew "reddish brown or brown yellow in color." Sometimes there was beef in it—when the mayor or some other dignitary was expected to visit. The stew was served with three slices of stale bread and a tin cup of weak coffee. While the report was correct in saying that the men were never rushed, the sight of other relays of men standing by with arms folded waiting their turn cast a gloomy atmosphere over the place and prompted the men to hurry, and, while they were not denied seconds, the departing recipients were heard to grumble among themselves that they did not get enough to eat and that they felt weak and tired during the day.[8]

If the person was to receive lodging as well as a meal, he proceeded along to the next stop. For the newcomers this meant they must first turn their clothes over for fumigation and then, wearing only a brass check that served as a receipt for all of their worldly possessions, they were hurried along for a quick doctor's examination and a mass shower. After being so "deloused, washed, and ticketed," each was clad in a "rough fumigated nightshirt which hangs down to the knees and opens at the sides," and sent to bed. Because there was nothing else to do in the shelter in the evening, no smoking or reading being allowed, one went to bed between 6:00 and 6:30 p.m. Now the newcomer was able to share the experience of sleeping in the world's largest bedroom with approximately two thousand other men. When the public welfare officials looked at this facility, they saw efficiency and cleanliness; when the participant looked, he saw a spectacle "like nothing else under the sun, perhaps a scene from Dante." Now the rows upon rows of neat beds came to life in a very unpleasant way. Now the 1,724 persons lodged there all lay down to sleep together. "Truly a man need no longer feel himself alone or 'forgotten,'" Josephson explained.

> Here he is in the bosom of an immense family of his fellows who will be coughing and snoring at him all night; hundreds upon hundreds of them in their rumpled nightshirts, now sitting up in bed, or climbing out or getting in, or leaning down to talk to a neighbor in the lower bunk, or simply sitting still and staring at their feet. Here are Negroes and White, Jews and Gentiles of all kinds, their faces haggard and wild under the ghastly light that falls from big lamps overhead, which are turned low not long after seven.

All mingled together in a stench composed of disinfectants and human odors "less sweet than cows', less fragrant than horses'".

From this experience the lodger emerged early in the morning, after a breakfast of "watery oatmeal and black coffee," into a day without purpose. With nowhere to go, no job to attend to, the army of men who had just shared bread and bed scattered about the city.[9]

After describing the situation at the New York municipal house and its annexes, Josephson left the reader with the same invitation that the public welfare officials had. Come, see the houses in operation, he urged. But his purpose was different. "A few hours' tour of their quarters," he explained, "would convince anyone that our society, with regard to its seamy fringes, grown so much broader nowadays, is, in actual practice, scarcely less hypocritical and brutal than in the darkest hours of the eighteenth century."[10] Later in the decade the Governor's Commission on Unemployment Relief for Transients confirmed that the experience Josephson described was true of New York City and common across the state. "Shelter facilities," they concluded, "were almost invariably inadequate; and mass care was the accepted practice. Men were fed and housed in large numbers in one building without even the privacy of cattle kept in separate stalls."[11]

One of the basic problems with the municipal lodging house was that the attitudes by which it was run had not changed for generations, while the clientele had. As Josephson pointed out, the lodging house treatment still reflected the theory of the bum. The men confined there were given enough food and shelter to sustain their bodies while their spirits were left to die. This was done despite the repeated observations by outsiders and insiders alike that the profile of the inmates had changed dramatically since the onset of the depression. In Erie County the Department of Charities and Corrections confirmed that the majority of their lodgers were white, native born, unattached, between twenty and fifty years old. In New York City it was noted that there was a marked decrease in the use of alcohol among the lodgers in the municipal house, from approximately 80 percent to 33 1/3 percent, thus separating these men from the more familiar Bowery bums. The change was reflected in the words of one unnamed city official quoted by Josephson: "We are getting a very good class of people in here nowadays. Half of them are not bums at all."[12] The lodging houses were now sheltering out-of-work men, men who were ready and willing to work, if their spirits had not yet been broken by the combined total of many depression experiences including the mass care of the lodging house.

At best the lodging house system was a stopgap effort. Given the circumstances, the swelling number of unemployed, and the unprecedented influx of transients into the large cities, it is understandable that officials had neither the funds nor the creativity to see beyond their emergency functions. They were faced with a mass problem, and they handled it in a systematic, efficient, and cost-conscious manner. The problem with this logical approach was that the individual, along with his self-respect and very identity, was lost somewhere in the endless lines and sea of mass beds. Without being offered even the slightest pretense of individualized care, the lodgers were allowed to slip even further into the faceless masses from which return, even in an economically-revived climate, would be nearly impossible. Normally decent God-fearing people, temporarily unemployed and destitute, were forced into an environment of hopelessness and degradation, the impact of which was devastating to the individual.

Despite the claims of city officials, the municipal lodging houses, with all of their mass facilities, could not accommodate the ever-increasing numbers who wandered New York's largest cities in search of food and shelter. Applicants were turned away daily. In his story Josephson reminisced about a day in 1932 when more than three hundred unassigned men were turned away from the door of the registration bureau in New York City because of a lack of beds. Ordered to move on, they "scattered after the feeblest murmur of protest." Besides those turned away there were unknown numbers of other "freer and hardier spirits, loathing or dreading the public asylum" who chose to fend for themselves wherever they could find shelter in doorways, railway and subway stations, or in the many hoovervilles scattered about the outskirts of all large cities throughout the state.[13] For those turned away and for those refusing to submit, another recourse in times of need was private charity.

The services offered in the state's large cities by private agencies ran the gamut from the indiscriminate distribution of bread or soup to the block-long lines of hungry men that have become by now symbols of the depression, to the maintenance of small, specialized shelters that provided individualized, rehabilitative care to society's outcasts. In the vast in-between were efforts to feed and shelter as many of the needy as possible with as much dignity as could be retained given the circumstances. All of this was financed within the confines of very limited, already overly strained budgets.

In some cities the private charities combined their resources and talents in cooperative, well-planned and administered programs for the transient. The private agencies of Rochester, for example, won for that city the distinction of appearing as one of sixteen model cities in *Community Planning for Homeless Men and Boys*, a self-help manual for communities across the country prepared by Robert S. Wilson for the Family Welfare Association of America. Rochester's transient and homeless program centered around the Bureau of Homeless Men, later known as the Men's Welfare Bureau. The bureau, which opened on December 1, 1930, was a joint effort of the Family Welfare Society, the Catholic Charities, and the Jewish Welfare Council. Its purpose was to serve as a central registration point where all applicants for aid would receive a thorough investigation as to their identity and need, after which they would be referred to the proper cooperating food stations and lodging houses. As its sponsors pointed out, an efficiently run system could be a matter of civic pride, as well as a way of redeeming needy persons before they fell totally into a state of mendicancy from which they could never be totally restored as functioning members of society. The severity of the winter of 1930–31 forced the bureau to open its own lodging facility in the basement of the city Armory where they cared for seventy to one hundred men daily. According to the author, the care they provided was generally superior to that of the lodging houses.[14]

Similar interagency cooperation was evident east of Rochester in the city of Syracuse. Community concern over the rapidly increasing population of homeless and transient persons found loitering in the parks, panhandling on city streets, and begging from housewives at their backdoors prompted the Syracuse Community Chest and Council to organize a Committee on Homeless and Transient in November 1931. The move was initiated because of the recognition that the approximately twenty-four hundred such persons in the city each day did not represent "hardened vagrants" but were, instead, people, often quite young, who had been displaced by the economic crisis. Common humanity, Chest members explained, dictated that they be helped. To that was added the equally acute realization that, if the problem was not corrected, it would soon get out of hand, and, according to the Chest, it would become "a serious threat to the well being of our community." The committee, which was composed of representatives of both public and private agencies that were familiar with the problem, in turn, established a Central Application Bureau to register the homeless and forward them to the appropriate agencies, that is, the YMCA, the YWCA, the Salvation Army, Travelers Aid, the Rescue Mission, veterans' barracks, and others, for the necessary aid. They also implemented a system whereby certificates were distributed to the general population to be used in lieu of cash handouts when an individual was approached by a panhandler. Each certificate entitled the bearer to an interview at the Central Application Bureau, a meal, and a bed for the night. The bureau was temporarily closed due to depleted Chest funds; however, money from the public welfare department restored its services. Thus, we have a unique example of public and private agencies pooling their resources and talents in an effort to care for the homeless and transient.[15]

In addition to these cooperative programs, private agencies continued their individual efforts to supply aid to the nonresident in need. In many large cities the YMCA and YWCA offered an inexpensive alternate to the cheap hotels of Skid Row. The Y also served as a referral point to which both public and private agencies sent needy people for a night's lodging. Young transients in Syracuse were weeded out of the general population and sent to the YMCA where a special effort was made to find them jobs and generally to help them "shake a life of vagrancy." The YWCA performed the same service for women and girls. Various Jewish agencies provided similar services as they extended their traditional welcome for the Jewish immigrant to their fellow transients.[16]

In New York City, much good was done in reclaiming the youthful transient by the New York Children's Aid Society. Originally founded in 1853 by Charles Loring Brace to deal with the problem of the city's vagrant street children, the society expanded its care during the depression to transient youth from across the nation. The society maintained the 250-bed Brace Memorial Newsboy's Lodging House, to which the police referred the youthful vagrant, and two industrial farms where the boys were taught useful occupations. Here they learned farming, auto-mechanics, painting, carpentry, horticulture, and other trades, while representatives of the society scoured the city to find them employment. The society also offered the boys the option of placement in upstate farm homes. In return for their help around the farm, the boys received room, board, and an allowance. About four hundred boys were so placed.

In all of the options offered its clients the principal goal was to provide something worthwhile to occupy the boys' minds and thereby to "redeem" them. Three thousand boys, from forty-two states, were so occupied in 1932 alone. This case load represented a 77 percent increase over the previous year, forcing the society to incur a deficit of over $200,000, and, according to the president of the society, threatening a curtailment of services.[17]

Travelers Aid also offered tireless service to transients of all ages. Since its inception, Travelers Aid's chief function had been to provide aid for persons in transit. The very first society was organized in New York City in 1905 in response to the alarming number of unescorted young ladies who were reportedly being abducted from train stations by "white slavers." Travelers Aid posted agents in its depots to meet and give advice and directions to such women. From that time on Travelers Aid has been recognized nationwide as the welcome friend of all unsuspecting and vulnerable travelers. On the very eve of the stock market crash their services were reaching over one million people annually.[18]

Despite increasing financial burdens that forced the closing of literally hundreds of its local branches, Travelers Aid continued throughout the depression to intercept needy travelers, to advise them, to provide food, clothing, and transportation, and, if necessary, to provide medical care. When shelter was also necessary, as was increasingly the case, Travelers Aid referred clients to other private agencies, such as the YMCA, YWCA, and the Salvation Army, with which they had made prior agreements. In 1932 alone over eighty-nine thousand persons received such services in Buffalo, New York City, Rochester, Syracuse, Albany, Attica, Schenectady, and Niagara Falls.[19]

Travelers Aid's service to the transient did not end with the care extended to the individual. On the contrary, the association took on a nationwide campaign to better the overall treatment of the transient. A constant flow of publications, countless mimeograph sheets, interdepartmental bulletins, journal articles, press releases, and books were all directed toward educating the country to the needs of this roving citizenry. Association papers such as: "Standards of the Care of Transient and Homeless," "Men Off the Road," "Casework with Moving People," and "Children Under Sixteen Travelling Alone," all emphasizing that the transient was an individual who must be treated with corresponding dignity, found their way into the homes of America and into the halls of Congress. Through their constant research and involvement, Travelers Aid became so expert in the transient question that the federal government turned to the organization repeatedly for aid and advice. When the emphasis of the government was on promoting self-help, it chose to print and distribute copies of the association's pamphlet, *A Community Plan for Service to Transients*, and, when the U.S. Senate began to consider a more lucrative involvement in the transient problem, they called upon the association to send members to testify as experts before the appropriate hearings. The publicity generated by such activities apparently produced some positive results in New York State. The Albany society reported in September 1932 that increased publicity had helped them to finally change the attitude of the Council of Social Agencies toward the transient, especially the young ones. In Rochester, the local organization reported at the same time that Travelers Aid's publicity had moved the Citizen's Council to at least conduct a survey of the problem. [20]

Another organization that strained its financial resources and personnel almost beyond endurance to meet the needs of the destitute transient was the Salvation Army. The Army had, of course, a traditional identification with the needy homeless. Army corps with their uniformed personnel and marching bands were regular features of the New York Bowery and similar Skid Row districts across the country. Salvation Army shelters, familiarly referred to in hobo jargon as "Sally," and food depots and soup kitchens were fixed institutions long before the depression. The traditional role of the Salvation Army, however, was primarily one of individual salvation. They fed and maintained the body in order to save the soul. Increasingly during the depression years, however, the Army was forced by the sheer press of numbers and need to deemphasize soul saving for the more immediate needs of the body. [21]

The Army's weekly paper, *War Cry*, generally an inspirational review of happenings in the Salvation Army, began noting signs of increasing need in the spring of 1930. An April 12th article, "Bowery Breadlines Longest Since 1914," described the chaos that resulted as needy men pressed in on a beleaguered Army worker dispensing ten cent meal tickets. Not only was the total desperation noted but so too was the changing composition of their numbers. Standing in line alongside Bowery bums were "carpenters, roofers, firemen, engineers, toolmakers, railroad workers, waiters, cooks, pantry men, cigar makers, metal polishers, bricklayers, pipe fitters, garage men, chauffeurs, common laborers, men with trades, and men of the white collar class." Responding to the obvious need of their clients, old and new, the Army expanded its service to New York's homeless in September, making regular rounds to local restaurants collecting unsold food to serve in a make-shift dining room in the basement of their Bowery hotel. By October an executive decision was made to close ranks to meet the crisis. The Army then went into the business of soliciting donations to fund a series of emergency projects. Their purpose: "To minister to those who have been wounded in the struggle for existence."[22]

The first need of their clients was for food. To meet this need, the Army opened fourteen free food stations across the city. Within a year, it found itself serving forty-eight hundred meals daily to the unemployed, homeless, and transient. Lodging was the next priority. When it became apparent that the six hundred beds of the men's hotel could not meet the need, the Army began opening new facilities.[23]

Definitely one of the most innovative of the new shelters was the S. S. Broadway. Christened appropriately enough on December 18, 1930 with a bottle of hot coffee, the 3,600 ton, 320 foot, reconditioned river steamer provided a "floating hotel" for destitute mariners who found themselves stranded in the port city of New York suffering from the combined effects of a lack of settlement and unemployment. At peak, the Broadway provided food and temporary shelter for approximately eight hundred mariners in a setting purposely designed to replicate their normal environment as closely as possible. The ship was captained by a seaman, and the men were required to stand four-hour watches and perform routine maintenance on the ship. A mariner's employment bureau, fresh clothes, and car fare were available to help the men find new jobs. Over sixteen hundred jobs were secured during the first year of operation alone.[24]

The steady increase of "landed" clientele also prompted the opening of a new men's lodging house in 1932 on the corner of Corlears and Cherry Streets. The Gold Dust Lodge, a reconverted, six-story flour mill, so named after the label of the company that donated the building, was able to accommodate two thousand men in its four floors of dormitories and serve them two meals a day from "menus suitable for any table" in the dining room. In its beds and at its tables

slept and ate men from every state in the union, of ages ranging
from twenty to seventy, and of "every trade and vocation going down
the alphabet from A-Z." In return for room and board, the men were
expected to pay a token fee. If they were unable, they were not pressed. All were required, however, to perform some work each day,
either in the Army's salvage operations or in the maintenance of the
lodge. Both the fee and the work were intended more as a method
to help the men maintain their self-respect than to raise funds.[25]

The Salvation Army took special pride in this building and its
operation. In November 1933 the *War Cry* offered its readers an on-
site tour of the facilities in an article by Jean Johnson. Under the title, "Pure Gold at Gold Dust Lodge," Johnson described an environment with "spic and span corridors, clean beds, spotless walls and
snow-white floors," an environment where the morale of the men
was treated with as much importance as their physical well-being.
"No opportunity is given for mental attitudes to get run down," she
explained, "for plentiful recreation is provided." Baseball games,
chess and checkers tournaments, entertainment by the men and by
outside guests, band concerts, and lectures were offered to fill the
men's idle time. The lodge also operated an educational program offering classes in English, arithmetic, bookkeeping, salesmanship,
and navigation taught by teachers from the New York State Department of Education. Spiritual guidance was available, but, according
to Johnson, the men were not forced to attend religious services.[26]

Ms. Johnson was obviously impressed. But we may suspect
that her enthusiasm was prompted more by her loyalty to the Salvation Army than an objective appraisal of the facilities. Yet what
evidence there exists from the perspective of the lodgers shows, in
this case at least, a remarkable consistency between the views from
inside and out. According to Matthew Josephson, for example,
residents of the Gold Dust Lodge were looked on with envy by their
counterparts over at the city muni-house. Gold Dust, he found, had
a city-wide reputation among the transient and homeless for providing "tolerable cuisine" and a good deal more comfort and privacy
than the public shelters. According to a long-term resident of the
lodge, a Harvard-educated but presently unemployed construction
engineer, referred to only as Mr. Eldridge, this reputation extended
beyond the city. Word had it on the transient grapevine that Gold
Dust had the best food and general care in the country. Eldridge
agreed. In his opinion, the lodge was very well managed, the men

were reasonably content, and he was pleased with the way they were treated. His gratitude for the assistance provided him was so great that he refused to accept the small stipend offered for the classes he taught his fellow lodgers. His appreciation was seconded by others who had been able to use the lodge as a first step to independence. "My stay at Gold Dust Lodge," wrote one former resident, "was the first contact I have had with Salvation Army and I am deeply impressed with the way in which such a large, mixed group of men was handled."[27]

The Gold Dust Lodge, like all mass facilities, still suffered the effects of congregate care. The dormitories were filled with hundreds of double-decker beds, row after row, and the dining room fed en masse. Yet the difference was that the Army personnel made every effort to provide a clean and healthy environment and to treat the men with dignity. This was what was remembered; this is what was appreciated by the men who returned to visit old friends and to express their gratitude.

Another Salvation Army facility that was opened to meet an immediate recognized need was the Harlem Lodging House for black men. This old, converted telephone company building on 124th Street was equipped to accommodate just over one hundred men. As it was the only such facility available exclusively for blacks, it usually ran at full capacity.[28]

While present-day sensibilities may recoil at the obvious segregation, nowhere in the Salvation Army literature is there any questioning of the need to provide separate facilities. Furthermore, it seems that the black occupants were more than pleased to have their own lodging house. That, at least, was the opinion of Mr. Clark, a resident of the Harlem lodge. The men, he explained, did not feel comfortable at the municipal lodging house, and preferred to be at "home" in their own community. Furthermore, they found the Salvation Army house to be cleaner (a responsiblility that they shared), the food better, and washing and laundering facilities superior. The house was so popular, in fact, that a rotational system had to be devised to allow all to share the privilege. The men were allowed to stay for three-week periods after which they were returned to the city's Central Registraton Bureau for referral to other agencies for the next three weeks. After that they could return for another three-week shift. Those men assigned to the municipal lodging house, Clark explained, often refused to go, choosing instead to ride the subways or stay in speakeasies until the time came for them to return to the Harlem lodge.[29]

Salvation Army units across the state carried on the battle to the extent that their means would allow. In Syracuse the Army was considered one of the most important elements in the city's transient and homeless program. The agency collected clothing and other salvagable articles donated for the homeless and employed transients to transport and repair such articles, giving them food and shelter in return for their efforts. In Buffalo, Lt. Colonel Thomas E. Hughes reported in 1930 that the Joint Charities, recognizing the Army's natural jurisdiction in the field, doubled their budget to "handle the needy transient and homeless man." In 1931, 27,566 of the 90,764 afforded relief in Western New York by the Salvation Army were transients. In Albany, a building donated to the Army by the J. B. Lyon Company became the Lyon Lodge, a model institution that received the praises of the mayor, the state commissioner of public welfare, and even the first lady, Eleanor Roosevelt, who took a personal tour of the facility. Unfortunately for the transient, the lodge was designed primarily for the local homeless. While friendless transients were not turned away, they could stay only on a temporary basis.[30]

Of special concern to many social workers was the plight of unattached transient women. Often overlooked in the emergency efforts to feed and shelter the overwhelming numbers of their male counterparts, few facilities were designed specifically to meet their needs. A couple of the very rare exceptions, however, were in operation in New York City. Travelers Aid operated a facility that served as a temporary home for eighteen to twenty transient women and children for a limited length of time. The Guest House, as its very name and capacity implies, offered a great contrast to the shelter provided to transients in public lodgings. Thus it was considered a model establishment. The house was staffed by a hostess, a cook, and a maid. Each was specifically instructed to provide a "wholesome, homelike atmosphere" for their guests and was hired for her ability to do so. Two case workers and a recreation worker completed the staff. A doctor and psychologist were available if needed; however, the visitors were not subjected to routine examinations unless there was a present and pressing need. Unlike the mass shelters, the Guest House provided separate bedrooms and an intimate dining room for the privacy of the visitors. The house also provided a large living room with a radio and piano to provide entertainment and a social environment in what would otherwise be a long interval between the routine of meals and bed. Here women were able to mingle, share their experiences, and establish a modicum of security and relaxation. For the similar needs of the children, a playground was available. What made the Guest House unique was that each visitor was respected as an individual. In this more relaxed environment case workers were able to take a longer look at each client and give her needs the kind of assessment that the quick contact of a mass shelter precluded.[31]

The Salvation Army also took a special interest in the unattached woman who found herself alone and friendless in New York City. As early as 1931 a free food station for women, the Marjorie Post Hutton Depot, so named after its benefactress, was established so that women could avoid the "harrowing experience of having to eat the bread of charity in public" and the humiliation of standing in line with the general Salvation Army clientele, that is, men.[32] The generous donation of two virtually rent-free buildings by the New York Telephone Company in January 1931 allowed the Army to expand its services to women by establishing the Woman's Canteen and Rest Room on East Twenty-ninth Street near Fifth Avenue. The purpose of the canteen was to offer an "appetizing meal" and a temporary rest for job-seeking women who "tramp the streets foodless" each day. It offered "a place in which to sit down at intervals during the day's search, play the piano, or listen to the radio and have tea and a little refreshment served by the Salvation Army women." The environment was intentionally attractive and specifically noninstitutional. Pictures show an attractively decorated lounge with upholstered furniture, rugs, curtains, and plants that resembles a comfortable hotel lobby. A similarly inviting dining room, arranged in tables of four with upholstered chairs, added to the environment. Women were asked to pay ten cents a meal, if possible, but none were turned away or embarrassed if they were unable to pay. The yearly financial statements of the canteen attest to the latter fact. During its first year of operation, 11,761 meals were served at the cost of $3,290.17. Receipts from the same period totaled only $1,011.40. The following year's report told a similar story.[33]

The Army also operated a Women's Hotel at 297 Tenth Avenue, which predated the depression, and an Emergency Home for Women and Children at 414 and 422 West Twenty-second Street which opened in March 1930 in response to the crisis. Again, the philosophy behind both operations was to provide protection, encouragement, and much needed security. Again, the surroundings were homey rather than institutional care was individualized rather than congregate. The Emergency Home, actually two refitted residential homes, was specifically "furnished with a view to avoid any formal appearance of an institution." Photographs of the facilities attest to the success of that goal. Women shared comfortable bedrooms, not wards, four to a room. They were served their three daily meals in a pleasant refreshing dining room, also arranged to accommodate parties of four. Again, the women were asked to pay what they could, but "if they have no money they are just as welcome." The home also offered an employment bureau and a confidential counselor to serve the women on an individual basis.[34]

In addition to their work in the field, personnel from many of the same private agencies contributed their time and expertise as members of the National Committee on Care of Transient and Homeless. The NCCTH was an autonomous group of concerned individuals recruited from the ranks of the social work profession, the academic community, and the lay citizenry to formulate and carry out an organized and coordinated campaign to resolve the problems of America's transient and homeless population. As such it was the only national group whose sole function was to serve this forgotten segment of society.

Consistent with its objectives and training, the committee collected its data: they thoroughly researched the current literature, conducted their own field investigations and hearings, and performed the first relatively accurate counting of the transient and homeless. With the evidence in hand, the committee put the transient issue before the public whenever opportunity allowed. Individually and collectively members spoke to conferences, penned articles, gave interviews and testified before Congress, in each instance describing the plight of the transient with facts and figures and presenting their recommendations for transient relief. The NCCTH took pleasure in associating the comprehensive ground work they had done with the passage in 1933 of a federal program for transient relief. Without their efforts, they believed, the government would have had neither the incentive to pursue transient relief nor the information necessary to formulate effective legislation. During the federal program, the NCCTH would continue to contribute information and to serve as a watchdog guarding that the program not stray from its original intent. After the demise of the program, the committee redoubled its efforts in a campaign for a resumption of federal responsibility.[35]

Over the course of its tenure, from its inception in 1932 to its absorption by Travelers Aid in 1939, the NCCTH maintained an impressive roster of members. Included were Dr. Ellen C. Potter, a tireless advocate of the transient who served as committee chairperson; Professor Nels Anderson of Columbia University whose sociological study of the hobo had gained him a national reputation as expert in the field (It was Anderson who coordinated the committee's January census and reported its findings to Congress.); Bertha McCall, executive director of the National Association for Travelers Aid (NATAS) (One of the transients' most faithful friends, McCall was always available to speak on their behalf. She was, in fact, the only witness to give testimony before both the 1933 and 1940 Congressional hearings on transiency.); Professor A. Wayne McMillen, University of Chicago, who had conducted the 1932 U.S. Children's Bureau investigation of boy transiency and authored the subsequent report; and Gertrude Springer, who as a reported for *The Survey* kept the issue of transiency fresh in the minds of her readers with a series of sensitive yet incisive articles on the issue. Other names from the rolls are also readily identifiable as friends of the transient by virtue of the study done, articles and book written, and testimony given on their behalf. Prominent were: George W. Rabinoff, Council of Jewish Federations; Margaret Rich, Family Welfare Association of America; Lt. Col. John J. Allan, Salvation Army; David H. Holbrook, National Social Work Council; Russell H. Kurtz, Russell Sage Foundation; Edith E. Lowry, Council of Women for Home Missions; Genevieve Lowry, National Board, YWCA; and MacEnnis Moore, Travelers Aid. Personnel from the Association of Community Chests and Councils, Child Welfare League of America, American Red Cross, YMCA, National Urban League, New York School of Social Work, New York City Welfare Council, and American Public Welfare Association also served.[36]

While the focus of the NCCTH was decidedly national, the New York influence was strong. Headquartered in New York City, many of the members in regular attendance were associated with New York agencies or organizations that shared the city as their headquarters. The witnesses who appeared before their hearings, especially transients, were at least for the time being living in New

York. In addition, the executive secretary, Philip Ryan, had earned his experience doing field work in New York State. He would continue his association with the state later when he was commissioned to do a comprehensive study of relief to nonresidents in New York by the Department of Social Welfare. Similarly, Homer Borst came to the committee after serving as chief administrator of the federal program in New York. All of these state contributions add a pronounced New York flavor to the national committee.

For all of the best intentions and genuine efforts of private agencies such as those described herein, and the many other smaller religious missions and charitable organizations that operated quietly without undue attention or publicity, the needs of the the increasing number of dispossessed, growing proportionately to the deepening economic crisis, were simply beyond their means. Even a facility as large as Gold Dust Lodge could not satisfy all applicants, residents or not. Very few could afford the transient the security of permanent residence. Furthermore, the economic strain threatened even that which was currently available. The Salvation Army's Harlem Lodge, for example, was forced for financial reasons to close its doors for five months in 1932.[37]

Perhaps even more discouraging to the social workers involved was the difficulty of applying individualized care and case work technique for the benefit of their clients. Such care on a wide scale was precluded by the sheer volume of people in need. Where individualized care was offered, the number of people able to avail themselves of the services were minimal. The Travelers Aid Guest House, for example, considered a model of constructive, rehabilitative care, could only accommodate approximately twelve hundred persons annually. Furthermore, it was the only such Travelers Aid facility available in the entire state. Likewise, the Salvation Army Emergency Lodge could accommodate only ninety women at a time. To render similar service to the tens of thousands of transients in the state was beyond the resources of Travelers Aid, the Salvation Army, or any other private or public relief systems then functioning.

In most small cities, towns, and villages across the state even the limited aid discussed thus far was not available to the transient. This was confirmed early on in the depression by the results of a survey conducted in December 1930 by the New York State Department of Social Welfare and the State Charities Aid Association. The objective of the study of forty-five cities within the state was to determine what type of aid was being given to those transients not referred to the state as state poor. Respondents from fifteen cities explained that the police were solely responsible for their care; another fourteen explained that the police were primarily responsible, but that the Salvation Army or other missions supplied meals and/or a small proportion of the lodging costs; two cities claimed that the agency administering such care was unknown; and three admitted that no care at all was given. Out of the total of forty-five cities, only five reported that the county department of public welfare participated in the care of transients, and only four reported having any organized system of care. Therefore, in most cities, in 1930, the chief mode of care was supplied by the police.[38] What this most often meant was that the transient, if not jailed for vagrancy, was allowed the dubious pleasure of bedding down in the basement of the local jail, often on the bare floor or on a wooden plank, and the next day he became the problem of the adjacent town.

The inadequacy of the care available locally to transients was reaffirmed three years later when the U.S. Senate Committee on Manufactures conducted a nationwide survey of mayors to determine how transients were faring locally. Thirty-two mayors from New York responded to the question: "How are you meeting the problem of the transient unemployed in need of relief?" Four localities, Canton, Potsdam, Hamburg, and Fulton, indicated that they gave transients one night's meal and lodging and then sent them on their way. Another four, Greenport, Baldwinsville, Tonawanda, and Cohoes, reported that they provided temporary emergency relief and then sent them back to where they came from or where they had legal residence. Four other localities, Monticello and Wellsville, as well as cities as large as Batavia and Dunkirk, relied on private charities, including the Red Cross, Catholic Charities, and the Salvation Army, to provide such relief. Even more localities still resorted to their police to provide temporary shelter and, sometimes, one or two meals. Gowanda, a city of only three thousand people, reported that their police station had sheltered eight hundred individuals in 1932 alone. Massena, Granville, Olean, and Irvington also reported this type of improvised care. Granville did make note, however, that veterans were an exception. They were referred to the American Legion. Fredonia, Amsterdam, Kingston, Johnstown, and Lackawanna, all middle-to-small cities, combined the services of public and private agencies to provide temporary one-night care. Only East Syracuse reported the exclusive use of town and county welfare relief, and only one respondent, the mayor of Amsterdam, made any reference to referral to the county commissioner of public welfare. Three localities admitted outright that they were not meeting the problem at all. Frankfort and Lynbrook stated simply that no relief was given, while the mayor of Seneca Falls explained that his town had no means available for handling transients.[39]

It is apparent from both sets of responses in the foregoing studies that little had changed in the years between them, or, for that matter, for the centuries intervening between the passage of the first settlement law and the twentieth century. Communities still operated on the premise that outsiders were not their responsibility. Thus, in all the responses cited, there was a common attitude that the transient presented a temporary emergency situation which should be dealt with as quickly as possible. What this meant was that, while common humanity often moved communities to supply food and shelter temporarily, the transient was to be on his way the next day. Nowhere is there any indication of an attempt to provide a wide-scale, long-term, individualized solution. Casework rehabilitation and reclamation were obviously considered to be beyond the responsibility of the community. What most communities were in essence doing was resorting back to the centuries-old practice of passing-on.

Many explanations were offered as to why communities reacted so laggardly to the transient. Health hazards, moral dangers, job competition, local and state ordinances all played a part. The common denominator in all of these possible explanations, however, came from deep in the past. The rejection of the depression-spawned migrant, just as that of the hobo and the tramp before him, lay in a traditional sense of community exclusiveness and a centuries-old fear of strangers.

The latent feelings of community exclusiveness, existing even in times of prosperity, were brought to the fore during the depression. In the earliest days of the prolonged economic crisis, when the first dislocated persons began to appear on doorsteps and street corners, sympathetic housewives would extend them a bit to eat and the passersby might drop them a few coins. But, when the trickle became a torrent, attitudes stiffened. As the economic crisis deepened, as factories closed and jobs became more scarce, as private charities strained under the ever-increasing burden of the un-employed, and public welfare was pressed to its limits, the atti-tude of most communities became more and more exclusive as car-ing for their own became their prime concern. In New York State this transition from trickle to torrent was rapid. Port Jervis reported seven thousand lodgers a year at the police headquarters in the first three years of the depression; Hornell reported that ten thousand "floaters" a year passed through.[40] In an industrial state these num-bers not only meant an increased charitable burden, but they also meant cheap labor, thereby contributing to the fears of those persons tenaciously holding on to their jobs, as well as those paying the taxes that were supporting the unemployed. Under such circumstances, when a community's very survival was being threatened, there was neither the time nor the money to take on the extra burden of out-siders. Private charities, using the rationale that the resident unem-ployed were already more than they could handle, often reverted to a charity-begins-at-home stance. Public agencies, confined by either local ordinances or community opinion, also failed to reach these people. Looking back on this period, the Governor's Commission concluded that, even when the avenues for relief were available, local welfare officials were often reluctant to take on the responsi-bility of the transient because "local opinion was generally opposed to providing care for 'people not on their own,' and socially minded commissioners were subject to criticism by taxpayers for 'giving care to outsiders.'"[41]

To these conditions communities responded with increasingly restrictive measures. Vagrancy laws were stiffened and arrests were accelerated. Headlines such as "37 Homeless Men Seized in Sub-ways" and "23 Jobless Sent to Jail" typified the plight of many a tran-sient in New York City. In the first case the judge took pity on these homeless unemployed and suspended their sentences. In the second case, the twenty-three jobless, admittedly neatly dressed and seeking work, were fingerprinted and sent to the "Tombs" for thirty days like common criminals. In most communities vagrancy ordinances were not intended to provide thirty days' room and keep for the transient; rather, they were used either as a temporary expedient to get them off the streets or else to threaten them out of town altogether. In ad-dition to a vigorous use of old laws, new exclusive ones were also added. For example, when the state passed an act enabling New York City to raise $10 million to provide work relief for the unemployed, the law specified that any persons hired under the program must be legal residents of the city in addition to having voted for the two preceding years.[42]

Adding to the accelerated sense of community exclusiveness was the continuation of age-old attitudes and fears about strangers. Speaking from her experiences in the New York City Travelers Aid Society and her knowledge of the nationwide situation, Bertha Mc-Call explained this fear:

> Way back in our subconscious we dislike the strangers who come in and we think they do not merit any special assistance and this feeling has stayed in the minds of a great many people. Newspaper clippings come though, 'Jobless descending on the town,' 'Boy bums,' 'Vagrants in hordes,' 'Gypsy families,' . . . . This reacts in the attitude of those responsible for allocating funds for services to people in need.[43]

The latent dislike of strangers reported by McCall was exacerbated in this economic crisis by the real dangers that were raised by the mass migration of the destitute.

The health hazard that migrants presented was one such practical concern. Forced to live in impromptu shelters set up by mosquito-infested river banks or in the close quarters of shanty towns near junk yards and garbage dumps, sustained by substandard diets, without proper sanitation or health precautions, the body of the transient was susceptable to many ailments including, to the chagrin of the towns through which they passed, communicable diseases such as malaria and the much-feared tuberculosis. A representative of the National Tuberculosis Association expressed this concern before the National Conference of Social Work as early as 1929. The migrant, explained Jessanine Whitney, provided the association with one of its biggest problems in its effort to control the disease. That organization had estimated ten thousand as the minimum number of tubercular migrants in the southwest alone. When the exposure to their families was taken into consideration, the number soared to thirty thousand. In addition to the danger presented by those contracting diseases while traveling, there were also those who traveled because of their health searching for better climates or medical facilities. The latter reason attracted many to New York State even before the depression, thereby necessitating specific exclusion clauses in the Public Welfare Law to prevent hordes of sickly persons from gaining settlement while hospitalized in the state.[44]

Besides threatening the physical health of the community, the transient was also feared by many as a moral danger. This was especially true for people who could not separate the uprooted of this economic crisis from the tramps and hobos of the past. In the most active of parental minds the onslaught of ragged and tattered folk into their communities could conjure up stories of child-stealing gypsies growing out of their own childhood fears. More realistically, others looked at the transient as an unwanted teacher of their impressionable children. The very presence of such people, they feared, offered their children the lesson that work and responsibility were not the only alternatives available to them. Furthermore, the sight of an apparently unending trail of destitute, homeless Americans undermined the very confidence that President Hoover had been trying so desperately to bolster.

Finally, the existence of a horde of hungry, cold, and sometimes despondent individuals *seemed* to increase crime. The very nature of their poverty, especially in communities that offered them little if any sustenance, turned many normally law-abiding persons into harassing street corner panhandlers and petty thieves, while their despondency threatened more personal crime to women and children, who feared to walk the streets in their presence. As such individuals congregated on the edges of towns, they could be likened to roving bands of criminals from days gone by and feared as such. These feelings were encouraged by studies done in the opening months of the depression. *The New York Times* carried an article in February 1930 that confirmed for many people an instinctual belief that transients were naturally inferior people. Under the caption, "Finds Mental Ills Factor in Vagrancy," was reported the findings of a year-long study of homeless Jewish men and boys in New York City conducted by the Jewish Committee on the Homeless. The report showed that out of 640 cases investigated by the committee, 33 percent had "obvious physical ailments." From this figure the report concluded that "a large number of the homeless men are either mentally unbalanced or of defective intelligence."[45] Similarly, a study done at the University of Buffalo by sociologists Niles Carpenter and William M. Haenszel equated criminality with migration in the Buffalo area. Comparing the place of birth of 100 males convicted of felony in Buffalo during 1929 to a control group composed of 220 male students in Hutchinson Central High School, the sociologists found that there was a "marked and statistically significant difference between the two groups in the categories 'Born in Buffalo' and 'Born in the United States outside of New York State.' The felons are under-represented in the first group, and over-represented in the second." From this they conjectured two possible explanations: either criminals by the nature of their profession were mobile, or else the strain of migration caused personality breakdowns that led to criminality. If the latter be the case, then the communities need well be aware of the danger within their midst of persons experiencing such a breakdown.[46]

The messages projected by both these sources were frightening ones, especially to the communities that watched this type of person pass by their windows and through their streets each day. The problem with both studies, however, is that the groups they were studying represented the pre-depression migrant. Carpenter and Haenszel studied felons who were convicted in 1929, either before the stock market crash or in the early months of the depression before mass migration set in. The same was true in the first case. The year-long study they reported on in February 1930 had begun before the effects of the economic crisis were reflected in mass migration. Therefore, the findings of both were projecting the characteristics of one group of persons who became migrants because of a completely different situation.

Social workers tried to dispel the image of the dangerous transient with articles describing his personal plight. Titles such as "Mustering Out the Migrants" and "America on the March" were common in professional journals. A larger audience was reached with the same message when journals such as *The New Republic* and *The Ladies' Home Journal* took up the issue under headings such as "Forgotten and Scrapped" and "Vagabond Children."[47] It would be another five years, however, before John Webb was to present statistics to counter effectively the image that such reports conjured up. In the meantime, what of the transient who was being so maligned and guarded against? What effect did transiency and rejection have upon him? What was it like to be rudely awakened one day to find that the stable and secure world upon which you had depended was no more? What was it like to swallow one's pride, to appeal to the town, city, or state for assistance? What, that is, did transiency look like from the transient's perspective?

5

Immediate Impact
of the Depression:
From the Transient's Perspective,
1929-33

For those transients who failed to qualify for state assistance or who had used up the hospitality of the local community, the final recourse was to rely on their own wits and "shift for themselves." In so doing the lone male transient became to many minds indistinguishable from the hobo, the tramp, or the bum. There were, of course, very definite distinctions between the estimated half a million transient men and those they were being so indiscriminately lumped together with. To begin with, the terms being used were not synonymous — each represented a distinct life style and attitude. As explained a few years later in the constitution of the Hobos of America: "A hobo will work, a tramp won't and a bum couldn't if he wanted to. . . . A hobo believes the world owes him an opportunity, while the tramp thinks the world owes him a living and the bum just exists." More specifically, the hobo was a migratory worker who chose to pay his own way by his labor; the tramp, while also leading a migratory life, chose not to complicate it with work. The bum was generally stationary but homeless and decrepit and usually alcoholic.[1]

The association between tramps and bums and the transient can be easily dismissed. Unlike either, the transient was very willing to work. In most cases, he was on the road for precisely that reason. He did not presume upon society to provide him with a free ride while he idled his life away like the tramp; and becoming a bum, a spent and sedentary Skid Row derelict, was one of the hazards of his adopted life style that he dreaded most. The association between hobo and transient is closer but still not accurate. Hobos, like transients, actively searched for jobs. In better times hobos had constituted a valuable mobile itinerant or casual labor force that fit well our expanding economy. Temporary jobs cutting timber, laying rail, or harvesting crops gave them the means to pursue the independence and detachment they freely chose. The transient, on the other hand, longed for the security and social acceptance of a permanent position in an established community. Travel was the means to that end. In the words of Nels Anderson, depression migrants "migrant because they must, and most of them will stop if they can."[2] While the transient did not share the professional hobo's commitment to wander, he did learn the art of getting by from his well-experienced contemporary; and he did, at least temporarily, share his life style. Hence the frequent confusion between them. One easily identifiable indication of the hobo's influence on the transient was the transient's ready adoption of his means of travel.

Whether ordered to move on by police, lured by job prospects somewhere down the road in another town or state, or struck by wanderlust, the transient did travel. Some walked the distance with a stoic endurance and determination. Others who were able to maintain a good "front," that is, a good suit of clothes and a neat appearance, were able to hitch rides from passing motorists. When the appearance deteriorated and the feet swelled, most turned to the railroads as the fastest and most reliable means of transportation.

Not being conventional passengers, the transient had to first learn from the experienced 'bo just how to use the rails. If the yards were not well guarded, one could simply choose a destination, board an appropriate outbound freight, and, if he could avoid detection until departure, he would be on his way. Most often, however, railroad crews and detectives kept the yards clear. This complicated the situation as the hopeful rider now had to wait down the tracks to "nail," that is, jump or hop onto, the now moving train. This took the skill and precision that only experience could bring: "I judge my distance. I start running along this track. I hold my hands up to the sides of these cars. They brush my fingers as they fly by. I feel this step hit my fingers, and dive." Knowing what is coming next, the veteran rider tightens his grip. "I slam against the side of the car. I think my arms will be jerked out of their sockets. My ribs feel like they are smashed, they ache so much. I hang on. I made it."[3] The inexperienced rider may miscalculate and be sent flying into the cinder railroad bed, or worse yet, if he was not a "smart stiff" and had caught hold of the back step instead of the front, a fall could send him between the cars and under the wheels.

Once he was safely aboard, the rider selected his berth. If he had caught a passenger train, he could ride the "blind," that is, the space between the locked door of the baggage car and the locomotive. This was, however, a precarious perch, and the rider had to take care not to doze, lose his balance, and slip beneath the wheels. The cold was another disadvantage. Freezing to death was a distinct possibility. And then "there was always the risk of being pelted with coal lumps or hot ash by a hostile fireman."[4] Freight trains offered more choice. One could go "top deck" and ride atop the car and bask in the sun. However, the sunbather would also have to contend with wind, soot, and various obstructions along the railroad's right of way that could send him over the side. A better choice may be in the boxcar, cattle car, or gondola. Often, however, the rider would find himself sharing the boxcar with a load of freight, the cattle car with assorted livestock, and the gondolas with a load of coal or steel, any or all of which would shift dangerously as the train speeded up, stopped short, or turned a bend.

By far the boxcar provided the preferable berth, but it was not necessarily a comfortable one. Under the heat of the mid-day sun, boxcars became ovens; in the cold of winter or cool of the evening, they became iceboxes. To warm themselves, riders snuggled between newspapers or built small fires from cargo, tar paper flooring, or wooden scraps carved from the interior beams of the car—anything that would fuel the fire to warm numbed feet and thaw frozen fingers. While the rider suffered, he did not suffer alone. He had companionship—sometimes too much of it. One young transient testifying before a Washington panel described his experience riding a boxcar with eighty-six other men. "These box cars," he testified, "are in pretty bad condition." Without toilets, "it was awful." The car his was coupled to held nearly twice as many occupants.[5] Finally, one never knew until it was too late which one of his traveling companions might show a knife or "gat" (gun) and mug the rest.

Riding the rails may have provided cheap transportation, but it definitely had its risks. This was confirmed in cold statistics each year by the Interstate Commerce Commission. In its 1932 report, for example, the ICC counted 1,886 trespassers killed on railroad property. Another 2,791 were injured. Included as trespassers were any unauthorized persons found on railroad property. The numbers, therefore, could include persons walking the tracks or passengers in stalled automobiles straddling railroad crossings, as well as transients and hobos riding the rails. Increasingly, however, the accidents recorded fell under the headings: "Coming in contact with structures," as in being hit and swept off the top of a boxcar; "Getting on and off cars or locomotives," as in miscalculating one's move when nailing a moving train; "Struck or run over, not at public crossing," as in falling beneath the wheels from any one of the rider's improvised berths; and a miscellaneous category that included "falling from locomotives or cars," "being pinched between cars or locomotives," injuries caused by "load shifting," and others.[6] All of these accidents, in other words, were common to the transient and his companions. Additional physical danger was faced when the brakemen or railroad detective confronted the trespasser. Many a rider sported some scar from his encounter with either as they did their job of clearing off the trains.

As the transient traveled alongside the professional hobo, he became less distinguishable from him, seemingly confirming the public suspicion that they were one and the same. When the transient stopped to rest along the way, the only shelter that was often available to him was that which the hobo had long utilized—"jungles," rescue missions, municipal lodging houses, "flop houses," and the like. As the transient adapted this aspect of the hobo's life style, the identification between them was furthered.

When the climate was good or the season right, the transient accepted the welcome of the hobo jungle. Simply put, in the words of one young man who had by age eighteen frequented several, "a jungle is where a group will get together and build a fire and sort of share out all of the provisions they have."[7] More specifically, a jungle was a temporary camp set up by a few men on a site convenient to food, water, and fuel for a fire. Choice locations were usually close enough to a city or town to offer access to jobs or supplies, but far enough away so as not to excite the community or raise the suspicions of the local police. Garbage dumps, river banks, railroad crossings and irrigation ditches were all ideal locations. As the invitation of the jungle's camp fires drew new wanders to it, the small group could swell into a sizeable community. As a community its members shared their resources. Vegetables and chickens gathered from sympathetic farmers, or stolen from the not so generous; bits and pieces of meat begged from butchers and grocers in the nearby town; leftovers and scraps solicited from restaurants, were all contributed to the communal pot of "mulligan stew," an imprecise recipe that called for whatever was handy. If pickings were good, the stew could be appetizing and nutritious. If supplies were limited, the stew suffered. The jungle offered more than just food to share. It also offered companionship and camaraderie, job and travel information, and tips on the hospitality or lack of it in communities en route. The novice was taught the tricks of the trade by the professional 'bo or the experienced transient, and each had the opportunity to tell his story or listen to others do the same.

Should this image become too cozy or romantic, one need only to imagine a jungle as the winds begin to blow or the rain to fall, as the hard ground turns cold and then wet, as makeshift tents and shelters constructed of cardboard and bits and pieces of scrap melt away. As the pleasant outdoor camp erodes, the men therein turn from the overage boy scouts to the desperate stiffs that they were — ragged men in ragged clothes, with "sunken cheeks," "hollow, dark-rimmed eyes," and sagging shoulders — desperate and forlorn men who "are here because we have no other place to go." "For three years, I have laid in the cold and the dark like this," explained one old man, "Is this goin' to last forever? Ain't things never goin' to be different? How long is a guy suppose to put up with this?" Even this limited community, this makeshift existence, only existed by courtesy of the local police. At any time, night or day, in fair weather or foul, the residents of the jungles knew that they could be, and often were, rustled out and instructed to move on by blackjack-toting "bulls."[8]

When the weather was good, most men seemed to prefer the independence of the jungle. A significant decrease in the numbers of applications for public and private shelter during the summer months reflects this preference. But as summer turned into fall, and winter threatened, the jungles began to break up, their residents deciding, one by one, whether to turn southward or to head for the shelter of the city. Those who originally chose the former often rejoined their friends in a short time after experiencing the decided inhospitality of the Sunbelt states. Together they headed for the city's main "stem," or Skid Row.

If one had been able to raise a stake during the summer months, or could beg four-bits, he could choose a room in a Skid Row flop house — a "cheap hotel or relief station where the homeless sleep poorly and the bedbugs live well."[9] Of course, at that price, one would probably have to share the room with a score or more of others. Louse, soiled bedding, and snoring, drunk roommates also came with the price. For food the neighborhood offered a variety of cheap restaurants. A cup of coffee and a roll had here for a nickel could go a long way to stave off chronic hunger pains. Most cities also had enough bread lines and soup kitchens to provide for the winter influx. In the winter of 1931, much to the chagrin of social workers who deplored the disorder and waste of indiscriminate giving, New York City alone could boast of eighty-two going bread lines that served more than eighty-two thousand meals a day. "If he is smart enough to time himself properly and spry enough to cover the ground," Gertrude Springer reported, "a homeless man may without doubling on his tracks, get a good hot handout at any hour of the day or night."[10] Of course, one had first to swallow one's pride, if any were left, before submitting to charity in plain open view.

If the four-bits for a flop was hard to come by, or if one's stake was already spent on other Skid Row diversions, brothels, speakeasies, or gambling houses, most large cities had their rescue missions to turn to. Rescue missions operated in much the same way and for the same purpose as foreign missions. As foreign missionaries ventured into the depths of an uncivilized, heathen world to rescue its inhabitants for the Lord, so too did their equally dedicated, domestic counterparts venture into the very den of iniquity, Skid Row, to minister to the souls of the derelicts therein. Their clients learned quickly. For the price of a sermon, the hobo taught the transient, one could usually receive a meal and bed down for at least the night. A conversion, real or affected, could possibly extend the stay.

While the missions provided a real service for the men who lined up at their doors, ate at their tables, and slept therein, a corresponding graditude is conspicuously missing. Most first-hand accounts are, in fact, decidedly hostile, with the authors referring to the mission as a last resort, often less desirable than remaining shelterless. Among their complaints were monotonous diets of meatless stew or beans and weak dishwater coffee (sometimes laced with saltpeter); overcrowded and makeshift accommodations sometimes on floors or in pews; the indiscriminate mixing of young and old, drunk and sober, clean and unclean in common rooms; and, in some missions, the application of a work test to prove worthiness, or, as the client suspected, to provide free labor. Topping the list of complaints and evoking the most resentment and bitterness, however, was force-fed religion. With soul saving their priority, many missions ministered first to the soul by demanding attendance at religious services before providing the food and lodgings that had attracted the men to their doors in the first place. Transients especially looked at mandatory attendance as an exploitation of their present vulnerability and indignantly rejected it when they could or stoically endured it in bitter silence when the cold winds outside reminded them they had no other choice.

These generalizations were, in fact, unfair to those missions that made a concerted effort to provide constructive programs and decent accommodations and to those directors who recognized the need to temper their religious zeal in light of a changing clientele.[11] Furthermore, the quality of care, or lack of it, was more often due to limited budgets that could only be stretched so far, than to a purposeful effort to demean the client. Nevertheless, the mission continued to offer food and shelter and those who received the same continued to complain.

Some transients were fortunate enough to find themselves a more stable, but nevertheless temporary home by joining together with the local homeless in any one of the many makeshift shanty towns that sprang up profusely, dotting the landscape in or around the towns and cities of the nation in the opening years of the depression. More commonly referred to as hoovervilles in dubious recognition of the man to whom the residents credited their present condition, such encampments could be found wherever shelter was available, under bridges or railroad els; where running water was plentiful, by rivers or hydrants; and supplies for constructing their homes were handy, at the town or city dump.

New York City was host to a number of such communities. At the foot of Henry and Clinton Streets in Brooklyn, for example, stood Hoover City. This odd assortment of makeshift shacks or "cottages," built on an abandoned dumping ground, was home to some six hundred or so dispossessed persons, and birth place to at least one child in the winter of 1933.[12]

An insider's view of the City is provided for us by two residents, Mr. Blair, an unemployed, middle-aged machinist, and Mr. Lyon, a fifty-six-year-old seaman who, like many others in his trade, found himself abandoned and without residency rights in one of the many ports serviced by the now-depressed shipping industry. One of the most striking aspects of the stories they told was the ingenuity shown by the residents. Mr. Blair, for example, originally constructed his home out of the body of a discarded truck and his bed out of two old sailors' bunks. He later added an extra room by joining a second truck body to the first. For cooking and warmth, he constructed a stove out of old pipes, iron bars, and ash cans. Mr. Lyon's place, a two-room cottage furnished with some overstuffed furniture that he salvaged from the garbage heap and repaired, and floored with some old discarded linoleum, was appropriately enough referred to by his neighbors as "The Palace." Top soil carted from a vacant lot provided the bed for a vegetable garden he cultivated outside his door. Others similarly improvised their own homes and implements and a community grew.[13]

The organization of the City was informal. Prospective residents simply came in, looked around, picked out an unoccupied spot and settled down. Neighbors were friendly and visted back and forth. Supplies to construct or improve one's home were readily available from the dump, water was available from the hydrant on Columbia Street, and food was had from various stores or friends who sympathized with the residents. The police visited frequently but did not trouble them. While the winters did get admittedly cold, and conditions were basic, few people moved out once they established themselves. When they did, they were able to sell their homes to newcomers for as much as fifty dollars.[14]

Both men expressed their preference for this life over that which was offered to them in the various municipal shelters. Mr. Blair valued highly the "sense of personal freedom" the City allowed him, while Mr. Lyon explained that he liked living there because it gave him his independence. He appreciated knowing that he could go to look for work in the morning, which both he and Blair did regularly, and know that he had some place to come back to when he was tired. Generally speaking, both felt there was an atmosphere of contentment in Hoover City. Even the "Reds" who had tried to organize the people were not able to break their spirit.[15] Blair and Lyon and their neighbors, apparently, had found themselves as good a place as any to wait out the depression with a stoic acceptance.

For those others, those without a Hoover City, or even a flop or a mission house to tuck into, the city's parks, doorways, bridges, railroad stations, subways, window wells, abandoned buildings, and the like offered a final refuge. Any place where a dry spot was found could be home for the night. Again the ingenuity is remarkable. One man, for example, after being given a solemn promise by the Salvation Army worker with whom he was speaking not to reveal his secret, admitted that he and one or two others slept regularly in an unused sewer pipe in a certain part of Manhattan. "It was a trifle cold sometimes," he explained. "That is why I am carrying these newspapers. They help to keep out the cold a bit."[16] Another man had climbed two-thirds of the way atop the Hudson bridge seeking a nook to call his own one cold December night before police rescued him and jailed him as a vagrant. The arrest was not so bad. At least he had a less precarious place to sleep that night. Many a hungry and homeless individual may well have envied him his new luxury, for people were known to break the law purposely to achieve the relative warmth and security of a jail cell. Only a few days before the above described man attempted to perch himself above the Hudson, *The New York Times* carried the human interest story of a penniless and jobless young man who reportedly walked up to a police officer on the beat and asked to be arrested on vagrancy charges. If not, he explained, he would have to break a window to guarantee his arrest. The judge in this case took exception in light of the boy's story, dropped the charges, and even found him a job.[17] To this story there was a happy ending, but many others were playing out the same plot to a less satisfactory conclusion.

To these deplorable living conditions must be added the less tangible but equally destructive psychological effects of the stigma and rejection that the transient bore. For the most part, the individual transient had been born and bred in middle or working class America as heir to the American Dream. Only yesterday he had his home, his family, and his friends who shared his values and expectations. They were all part of a community. Now, for reasons most often beyond his control, his dreams were shattered, his ambitions thwarted. He found himself detached and rejected by the very America that he had so short a time before felt an integral part of.

Mistakenly labeled tramp, bum, or hobo, respectable communities shunned him. Restaurant owners, gas station attendants, and merchants did not want him begging food and supplies in front of their customers; relief officials did not want to assume financial responsibility for him; law enforcement officers did not want him hanging around contributing to a potential police problem. So merchants turned him away, relief officials gave him a night or two of care and passed him on, and the police ordered him out of town. Even those communities where the transient was recognized for what he was still felt impelled to guard their limited resources by moving him on.

We have already looked at the whys and wherefores of the community's reaction to the transient. What we need to do now is to consider the impact of that rejection on the individual: consider the effect of seeing fear and suspicion in the eyes of those you approach with outstretched hand; feel the scorn in the voice of the police who run you out of town; appreciate the sting of injustice of being called a bum or accused of being worthless, the public humiliation of standing in a bread line, the indignity of being arrested and fingerprinted like a common criminal, the horror of the jail cell. How long, the transient's friends asked with growing apprehension, could a man's character resist the combined effects of his enforced life style and the rejection it solicited? When does the will break? When indeed would the distinction between transient and hobo cease? When would the transient become a tramp?[18]

To answer their questions, it is necessary to listen to the voice of the individual transient. Yet, generally speaking, transients peopled that part of the inarticulate past that so frustrated historians. Very few left their personal experiences behind for us to analyze, interpret, or sympathize with. Evidence is fragmentary, a word here and there. Occasionally, however, an exception occurs, and an individual does speak up through the ranks giving voice to his more silent fellows. In such a manner, the feared effects of repeated frustration were poignantly recorded by one Tom Kromer, transient, in an autobiography appropriately entitled *Waiting for Nothing*.

At the time he was writing, Kromer was still a young man in his twenties. He had, by American standards, a good start in life — three years of college and two years' experience teaching. Yet the story opens with the author at the point of total desperation. He is ready to mug, rob, submit to perversion, and deny his God and country. What has driven him to this point? Too many nights sleeping in four-bit flop houses, cheap boarding houses, and hotels, scores of beds to a room:

> I walk into this room. It is a big room. It is filled with these beds. They do not look so hot to me. They are only cots. They look lousy. I bet they are lousy, but a stiff has got to sleep, lousy or not. . . .I can hear the stiffs as they sleep. I pick me out a flop at the other end of the room. There is no mattress. Only two dirty blankets. They are smelly. Plenty of stiffs have slept under these blankets.

Eating too many nondescript meals at too many missions and shelters:

> They shove this stew before us. It is awful. It smells bad. The room is full of the stench of this rotten stew. What am I going to do? What can I do? I am a hungry man. Food is food to a hungry man, whether it is rotten or not. I've got to eat.

Listening to too many mission sermons:

> These stiffs are in this joint because they have no place to get in out of the cold, and this bastard asks them to stand up and tell what God has done for them. I can tell him what God has done for them. He hasn't done a damn thing for them. I don't though. It is warm in here. It is cold outside.

Suffering the humiliation and pain of waiting in a soup line for hours as passersby scoff disparagingly:

> I wait, and Christ, but the hour goes slow. I stand in the soupline. Back of me and before me stretch men. Hundreds of men. . . .For two hours I have stood here. . . .The wind whistles round the corners and cuts me like a knife. . . .Across the street people line the curb. They are watching us. We are a good show to them. A soupline two blocks long is something to watch.

Succumbing to a homosexual seduction because the "seductress" had a warm room and food for him:

> I am so ashamed of all of this. What can I do? What I am doing is all I can do. A stiff has got to live . . . . [The affair is aptly con-

sumated with the words], You can always depend on a stiff having
to pay for what he gets.

Consistent through all of these experiences are pathetic reminders
that being a transient, a stiff, was not his choice. He is not pleased
with the life he has been forced into, the humiliation he must endure, but "what else can a stiff do?"[19]
 He is bitter and resentful that the rich feast while he starves,
that their women are bedecked in jewels and furs while he freezes.
He is frustrated over a justice system that brands him a criminal for
seeking shelter in an abandoned building, and then sentences him to
hard labor in a mass trial in a kangaroo court where he cannot even
voice his own defense. He is ready to lash back at the police who
roust him and his fellows out of their jungles and beat them indiscriminately, but he knows that their blackjacks and firearms give
them the advantage. And he is tired of religious hypocrites who
could not see that the men they were forcing through the charade of
conversion and salvation had long ago given up the God who had,
they believed, deserted them. Throughout the piece there is a
building resentment and rising class consciousness, yet there is also
the realization that a bowl of stew or a warm bed will quickly take
the revolutionary zeal out of his fellows. While he lies awake con-
templating his fate, they acquiesce in a stoic resignation. So, "what
can a stiff do?" In final resignation, in the middle of the night, from a
mission bed, amidst the snores and stench of hundreds of others like
him, at age twenty-three he concedes:

> What is a man to do? I know well enough what he can do. All he
> can do is to try to keep his belly full of enough slop so that he won't
> rattle when he breathes. All he can do is to try to find himself a
> lousy flop at night. Day after day, week after week, year after year,
> always the same — three hots and a flop.[20]

A similar story was told to the readers of *The Forum* by another transient, Frank Bunce, in February 1932. In an article entitled, "I've
Got to Take a Chance," Bunce described the gradual degenerative
process that took him, a twenty-five-year-old, law-abiding young
man, a typical all-American type who had played semi-professional
baseball and football, from the security and stability of employment
to the point where he could say, after two years of wandering, "I lost
any loyalties to my country, to God, to mankind, that having lived

like an animal, I am taking on the ethics of an animal, that I have become, in short, a public menace."[21]

Mr. Bunce's story began in 1931 when the young mechanical draftsman, despite the continuing reassurances of his supervisor that he would "take care" of him, found himself unemployed. After a fruitless search for a new job, unwilling to be a burden to friends and relatives, and wanting to maintain some semblance of pride, he left his home town and began his two-year odyssey. Sometimes he worked briefly as an itinerate farmer, but, for the most part, his experiences were in flops, boxcars, soup lines, missions, and, finally, on the streets begging. Describing the process, he explained:

> It is the first couple of weeks at tramping that hurt a man most. Added to the uneasiness of any animal in a strange environment is the human feeling of depravity from his beggar's status. One talks badly, goes hungry for unnecessarily long periods of time, walks needlessly after nightfall, goes blocks out of his way to avoid policemen.

Bringing himself to beg was one of the first hurdles he had difficulty in overcoming: "I recall that, when I finally brought myself to hit my first door for breakfast, I told the people a clumsy compound of lies about a job waiting for me in Tennessee, a post office remittance that hadn't reached me yet, and a wildly improbably tale of my past life." With time, however, he grew much better in his technique and soon pride no longer intruded upon his scam. To finally stop looking for a job took him much longer. To stop traveling to every place and any place, no matter how far, where rumor said employment was to be had, only came with time. It took him a full year to become a "wise stiff," that is, "one who has sensibly resigned himself to the futility of looking for more than the merest means of subsistence." Nevertheless, skilled though he became, he did not learn to like the humiliation of living the hobo's life. He still wanted a job, home, and family. At this point, however, he had decided that he must make a change, by which he meant the final resort to a life of crime. Others he knew had done it. Some wound up in the penitentiary, but, after all, he explained, "get me cold enough and hungry enough and bored and sick with futility, and I'll probably decide to take a chance." He must, he felt, do something to at least show that he was still alive.[22]

In the course of this true confession the author reflected on a number of attitudes and opinions that separated these men from the communities through which they passed. To those who charged that the fault of poverty was that of the individual and not of society, he retorted that a man cannot be independent in modern society. His present life, for example, had not been determined by himself; it was instead the product of

> the ill-judged votes of men I had nothing to do with electing, the bad judgment of the superintendent of the factory where I work or the president of the bank I use, the wild betting men I never saw on the floor of a stock exchange I have never entered.

As to society's advice that he return home, he replied with indignity: "But we're not on the road by choice; it's hard compulsion. We're foraging animals in thin pastures and we have to cover an incredible lot of territory to keep alive." Furthermore, he asked, "What, I wonder, would they have me do? Blithely chisel quarters from old schoolmates? Circulate at the back doors of people who knew your mother, and yourself when you were in rompers? Or just crawl into a hole and starve?"[23]

Here was a man who conjured up a picture of all the values America prided herself on. He was robust, educated, had plenty of drive and initiative, was repulsed by the idea of turning to others for charity; yet he was being driven to the life of a criminal. He was one of those independent-minded Americans which Hoover was "saving" by refusing them a federal handout. This man, however, was not thankful that the President had saved his self-initiative; instead, he was crying out in desperation that the hopelessness of his situation was forcibly turning him against his God and his country, and, he warned, if the one, five, or seven million others who shared his experience "have undergone a metamorphosis, spiritual and emotional, like mine, then our threat to society is immediate and immense."[24]

Sympathetic and knowledgeable contemporaries, social workers and the like, anticipated with growing apprehension the hostility and class consciousness voiced by Kromer and the threat posed by Bunce. With hindsight we know that the transient was remarkably resilient. He did not succumb to revolutionary propaganda or realize the fears of the community. Kromer finally acquiesced along with his fellow mission house roommates, and Bunce apparently spent his anger by putting it into writing. The transient remained basically law-abiding, except when need necessitated the pilfering of food or supplies, and he was there to answer the nation's call to arms when war broke out. The end result, however, should not be used to diminish the anger and frustration expressed by these two men or the thousands of others with whom they traveled. Rather, a realization of the physical, emotional, and psychological stress under which they lived, some for the duration of the depression decade, should increase our appreciation of their endurance.

As Americans started getting used to the Kromers and Bunces in their midst, they were forced to face a new depression phenomena. Among the transients there were women. Fellow transients were the first to notice:

> Women on the road these days? Sure. Not so many as men, but—well, nine girls traveling together hopped off the same car I was in when we hit the freight yard last night.

> Women on the road? Sure. Saw a funny thing yesterday—woman with seven little kids. She was hitch-hiking from Alabama to Boston where she used to live. Husband went off job hunting and she don't know where he is.

> Women on the road? Sure. Yesterday saw three of them in a rattedy-bang old car asking a service station fellow if they couldn't clean up his place in exchange for gas and oil.[25]

Sociologist Thomas Minehan saw them and he told America:

> There are girls on the road today—thousands of them. . . . They live in box cars, in jungles on the edge of towns or near lakes and streams, in the basements of old deserted warehouses near railroad yards, in caves along a river bank. They eat whatever they can beg or steal, or what the men or boys beg or steal for them. . . .Outcasts of society, they live a semi-criminal gypsy life, hunting food, clothing, and shelter, being hunted by railroad detectives, police, and degenerate men.[26]

Estimates of their numbers ranged from the 14,482 recorded in the January census (2,783 of which were under twenty-one years of age) to a highly inflated figure of 250,000. A 1933 Women's Bureau survey counted almost ten thousand homeless women in eight hundred cities nationwide, more than nineteen hundred of which were found in hobo camps. The numbers cited, however, do not adequately reflect the full extent of the problem. Many women avoided the very agencies that were participating in the surveys and thus were not counted. The standard social work policy of the day, to return stranded women to their homes, deterred many women from entering agency offices. Women who had fled unpleasant family situations did not want to go back to them, and young girls from relief families would not be persuaded to contribute to their family's problems by returning. "Knowledgeable" friends warned one girl to stay away from the charity organizations when she traveled with her baby for fear they would take the child from her. For others it was simply a matter of pride. Even the Women's Bureau's inclusion of hobo jungles would not have accounted for those women to be found sharing rooms with friends or living in cheap lodgings. Taking these factors into consideration, Anderson estimated that there were approximately forty-five thousand transient women and girls in the United States in 1933.[27]

The number of women counted in the surveys and the adjusted estimates of Anderson were still relatively low compared to the corresponding male population. Yet the presence of any unattached homeless women wandering the country was cause for alarm. Before the depression this problem was almost nonexistent. In an earlier 1923 sociological study of the hobo, Anderson made specific reference to the exclusively male character of that culture. Tradition had protected the place of the woman in the family. No matter how desperate circumstances became, it was expected that some relative would shelter or care for her. Some lady hobos, hardened, rough, social outcasts from the radical fringes—IWW organizers, anarchists, revolutionaries, prostitutes, and drug addicts—as well as women simply stricken by wanderlust or fleeing from bad family situations, were to be seen on the road in pre-depression America, but their numbers were few, and they still were the noticeable exception, even within their own circles. Hitchhiking college girls were also a fairly familiar sight in the twenties as the fad ran its course.[28] The women counted in the 1933 surveys, however, were not out on a lark; they did not traverse the radical fringes. They were desperate, homeless, unemployed women, products of the economic crisis, and, ironically, of the very independence they had so recently won.

Since the turn of the century, women had been entering the job market and gaining an independence outside of and often far away from the home. An active demand for their labor, especially in the clerical field, left very few stranded without family or friends. Those who were in need were referred to a number of private agencies which provided specialized care. The job security of the newly independent working woman, however, often did not survive the depression. Pay cuts and then unemployment left many women in desperate circumstances. Increasingly, hitchhiking and hoboing women wore signs of past prosperity—business dress, now rumpled and torn; soft hands becoming calloused and stained; pretenses of gentility fading fast in boxcars and roadside camps. All were quiet reminders that these women were neither hobos nor bums.

In most instances these women had, as had their male counterparts, taken to the road looking for work. Bertha McCall gave the story of one nineteen-year-old woman as typical of the cases that her agency was seeing with alarming frequency. The young woman had hitchhiked from a small Pennsylvania town to New York City in search of a job. But there was no job, and the police sent the exhausted, hungry girl to Travelers Aid. The agency contacted the family, but, as in too many similar cases, the family did not have the financial resources to send for her.[29] Speaking from fifteen year personal experience hoboing, back and forth across the country, Bertha Thompson, alias Box-Car Bertha, told a similar story in her autobiography, *Sister of the Road* (as told to Dr. Ben Reitman). "The most frequent reason they leave," she explained of her traveling companions, "is economic." "They usually come from broken or poverty-stricken homes. They usually want to escape from reality, to get away from misery and unpleasant surroundings."[30]

Once they had made the decision to "hit the road," or it had been made for them, transient women found themselves sharing many of the same problems that men did—the daily search for food and shelter, the quest for the ever-elusive job or stake, the dangers of travel. In some instances, however, these problems proved to be magnified for the woman. Part of this had to do with the fact that neither society nor she knew how to deal with her present situation. Unlike the homeless man, the woman had no hobo lore or tradition in which to slip with relative comfort. She was an anomaly to the culture from which she sprang as well as that into which she was being forced. She had, as yet, no "hobohemia" or jungle society to

which she could readily turn with a perverted sort of social acceptance as was the case for the man who adapted the hobo life style. As
one contemporary explained, "Women have not had time to build up
their own communal homeless life."[31]

Women also appeared to be more resistant to seeking public
relief or private charity and would make every attempt to make it on
their own, sometimes to the bitter end. This resistance was used by
at least one contemporary observer to explain the conspicuous
absence of women in bread lines. A woman's experience with relief
had by tradition been as a member of a family in the privacy of one's
home or out of view in the almshouse. The display of standing in an
open line, exposing oneself to the public view, was alien to them.
The bread line was humiliating, and women simply had "no philosophy for its graceful acceptance." They would half starve themselves
rather than submit. Consequently, "any one who has marveled
because there are no women in bread lines should realize that it is
not because there are no hungry women. It is because they believe
that any public parade of poverty is degrading."[32]

A similar story was told by Agnes V. O'Shea of the New York
City Central Registration Bureau for Women regarding the plight of
the homeless, unemployed women with whom she worked. After losing their jobs, or resigning in protest of pay cuts, the women usually
moved from one relative or friend to another until "their benefactor's
resources gave out." In some cases "as many as half a dozen girls
crowded into one room apartments, sleeping in relays, and pooling
their clothes to assemble one outfit presentable enough to pass
muster with a prospective employer." When this recourse was not
available or ran out, women would ward off applying to relief agencies for as long as possible. Many entered the domestic work field
where they were often exploited as to pay and living conditions and
were physically and often mentally broken. Even when totally
destitute, the women would first go without food and ride the subway for shelter before they would apply for relief. In some cases they
would finally enter the registration bureau in such a state of mental
and physical exhaustion that they would be removed directly to a
hospital.[33]

Yet, while women may find the adustment more difficult,
"there is no reason to assume," the contemporary observer cau-
tioned, that "the homeless women cannot bring themselves to make
adjustments to life on the road, in the boxcars, flop houses, in

Shantyvilles — in general, to the life of a bum or hobo."[34] While making this adjustment to a previously all-male domain, however, the woman transient faced additional problems peculiar to her sex, from the inconvenience of her dress to the dangers of the predatory male.

Single women traveling alone were especially vulnerable to sexual assault or exploitation. Male motorists expecting sexual favors in return for a lift, railroad crews demanding sexual payment for a ride on a boxcar, and rapists lurking on the lonely highways or in dark train yards were but a few of the perils they faced. For protection many women traveled in pairs or took on lovers. Box-Car Bertha, for example, started out her traveling career at age seventeen with her sister at her side. Later she substituted a series of casual lovers for much the same purpose — companionship and protection. In his research on the juvenile transient issue, Minehan found the same to be true of young girls. A tender scene from a hobo camp of a young girl and her two sixteen-year-old male companions sleeping, each with a protective arm around her, effectively made his point. Single women, in pairs or alone, were also attracted to hobo camps for the safety of their numbers. Younger girls similarly traveled in "tribes" with scores of other youthful companions that offered camaraderie, much as a sorority would under more normal circumstances, and protection.[35]

On the other hand, contemporaries also reported that transient women often relied on their sex purposefully as a means of survival. Both Box-Car Bertha and Minehan referred to sexual barter quite casually in their accounts of women and girl transients. A typical example from Box-Car's experience was that of young, attractive Virginia, who traveled regularly with one or more hobos and traded sex for protection. "They had hustled food for her and in return she had given them what sex expression they wanted."[36] Sex was similarly open and free among the juveniles Minehan studied. The girls were readily available for the satisfaction of boys and men alike. "They go from jungle to jungle and from box car to box car without discrimination. . . .They enter a box car or jungle — and without much ado the line forms to the right."[37] In a more recent article about the sexuality of women hobos, historian J. R. Roberts referred to these sexual arrangments as part of the "giving-in" rule. "By 'giving in' to the male hobos, to drivers offering rides, to railroad workers and detectives," she explained, "a women could receive the benefits of male power: money, privileges, protection, food, shelter, or free transporation."[38] In other words, what may on the surface appear to have been casual promiscuity, was, in reality, part of the fine game of sexual politics.

Clothing was another particular concern for women transients. Clothes were hard to come by and harder still to maintain. This was not unique to women. However, hopping boxcars, hitchhiking, and walking endless miles on foot was not possible in the long skirts and high heels fashionable in the thirties. For comfort and to preserve the skirts and hose packed neatly away in "bindles," many women chose to adopt men's clothing while on the road and then return to their own for job interviews, visits home, and other special occasions. Minehan's book is peopled with young girls wearing overalls, army breeches, and caps. In many cases even the author could not tell a sleeping girl from a boy until noting more closely the gentle curve of her figure under the coarse fabric or the soft features under the cap.

For most women, men's clothing was simply a practical alternative to ruining their own. It provided comfort and convenience. For others, it served as a helpful disguise. A young girl, literally tripped over by Minehan in a crowded lodging house, had escaped the cold night outside by passing as a boy in the men-only dormitory. Passing was, in fact, a method of survival. "Disguised as a man," Roberts explains, "a woman hobo would have more chance of escaping the 'giving in' rule and possible rape. Plus she might find more equal treatment as a comrade of the road." Passing, however, could also put a woman's sexuality in doubt and imply lesbianism which, again according to both contemporary and historical accounts, was not an unusual preference in this culture.[39]

There are very few surviving first-hand accounts of life on the road from the woman's perspective that can be used at this point for illustration.* There is the autobiography of Bertha Thompson which chronicles some fifteen years of hopping freights; living in jungles, missions, and flops; and criss-crossing the country in one seemingly endless escapade filled with free love and adventure. But Box-Car

---

*Work on the history of the woman hobo which includes those women defined here as transients is being done by Nan Cinnater. A sampling of her findings and a synthesis of the available literature can be found in the paper "Women Hobos of the Great Depression: Survival in Hard Times" presented at the Sixth Berkshire Conference on the History of Women, June 1, 1984. Also included in the paper is some of the only material available on black women transients.[40]

Bertha was admittedly a lady hobo long before the depression swelled the ranks of her sisters of the road. What compelled her to the life, furthermore, was not economic necessity but an overwhelming wanderlust that was born out of childhood play among the boxcars adjacent to her mother's diner, hence the moniker "Box-Car Bertha." There too she was weaned on that particular brand of American radicalism preached by the "red card" carrying hobos that frequented the establishment which accounts for the proletarian tone of her story, as well as her later associations with assorted radicals and their causes. Consequently, the autobiography tells us more about traditional hobo cultures and radical America than about the woman transient and her experience.

Despite these disclaimers, however, the autobiography is valuable as a confirmation of what we have already learned about hobo life, from the camaraderie of the jungle to the dangers of riding the rails. It is also interesting to know that Bertha and a handful of other women were able to penetrate that life with remarkable ease, thereby contradicting the opinion held by a host of other participant observers and students of hobo history that this was an exclusively male domain before the depression forced open its membership. Through the words of this one woman, we are also able to personalize the struggle with conscience and pride that preceded one's first experience panhandling, as well as the ease with which one could slip after that into shoplifting, various other forms of petty larceny, and prostitution. Bertha is also able to corroborate Robert's giving-in rule with specific incidents from her experience. Finally, she adds her own feminine brand of class consciousness to complement that of Kromer, especially in her criticism of the hypocricy of a society that would brand a woman hitchhiking by the roadside or hopping a train as a deviant while rich women stricken by the same wanderlust as the hobo were called globe trotters.

While Bertha may have been a hobo of the old order, she was sensitive to the fact that that life was passing. The depression had brought changes in the homeless population that would inevitably have an effect on the hobo's existence. Bertha was there to observe and record those changes. One of the first things she noted was the increasing number of women to be counted among the ranks of the transient and homeless. After a temporary hiatus from her hoboing life, Bertha had returned to find, to her surprise, "that a great army of women had taken to the road, young women mostly, gay, gallant, sure that their sex would win them a way about." She also noted that there was a distinct difference between the women she was seeing on this lap around the country and Truck House Mary, Lizzie the Queen of the Hoboes, and Yvonne the Tzigane of her earlier tours. Unlike their predecessors, these women were on the road primarily for economic reasons. Personal problems and/or the wanderlust that had stirred Bertha might still be there, but they were now secondary. "Their stories are very much the same—no work, a whole family on relief, no prospects of marriage," and, she added, maybe out of her own personal sense of nostalgia, "the need for a lark, the need for freedom of sex and living, and the great urge to know what other women were doing."[41]

Another first-hand account, one that falls more precisely into our definition of depression transient and provides personal insight into the conditions of the road from the women's perspective, is that of one Mrs. Metzger (a name she adopted to shield her true identity). Her story was told in 1933 to a sociologist gathering research on the subject of transiency. At the time of her interview Mrs. Metzger was thirty-seven years old, unemployed, well-traveled, and homeless. After a long history of steady employment in a semi-skilled trade, interrupted only briefly by an unsuccessful marriage, she had found herself without a job and alone. After two and a half years of job hunting, with her savings depleted, and realizing that she could live more cheaply on the road than in her present boarding house, she decided to satisfy a long suppressed desire to travel and see the country, and she hit the road. A failed relationship and other personal reasons also prompted her on her way. She then began a journey riding the rails, hitchhiking, and, when all else failed, walking the highways, from D. C. to Florida, from Mississippi to California, and back again, and then on to Little Rock, Memphis, and Nashville. In the course of her travels she had been thrown off trains by railroad detectives; been locked in one boxcar, and ridden with up to fifty men in others; begged at back doors for food, clothing, and a place to wash up; hitched rides from passing motorists and friendly truck drivers; walked mile after mile when the hitching was not good or trains inaccessible; slept in numerous jungles, under bridges, and outdoors under the stars with a series of male companions; and generally "got by."[42]

Sexually, she experienced the giving-in rule several times and was assaulted on other occasions. She was raped by a railroad watchman who "said he would hit me in the head if I didn't give in." "I fought him," she explained, "but he took me by the neck and threw me down on the floor of the car." In another instance her accoster turned the burden of guilt onto her, telling her "if you don't give in, you have no business on the road. He said it was his car [the boxcar] and he would put me off." Despite these attacks, she did not fear the men with whom she traveled; instead, she counted on them for protection. In more than one instance, including the latter, the intercession of another man saved her from the assault. "Some men are always near me and protect me—like some countries have a protectorate." On those occasions when she was assaulted, she had been traveling alone.[43]

While she obviously did not appreciate these violations, she did seem to take them in stride and with a certain amount of philosophic resignation. "Men on the road," she explained, "never have a woman and when there is a woman they always come around every time." "It ain't the looks of me," she conceded. "It's just because I'm a woman." She was more than willing, if her interest were peaked, to accommodate them. The simple admission, "yes, he made love to me," regarding truck drivers, motorists, and traveling companions, punctuates her story with a casual regularity that reinforces the similar attitudes reported by both Box-Car and Minehan.[44]

Seeking some indication of the effect of these experiences, the interviewer asked her how she felt about her present life, to which she responded that, aside from the attacks, "I am real happy on the road." By her own standards, she took pride in the fact that "she has never begged for money, never stood in bread lines, and never taken money for sex." In other matters she accepted that "you have to put up on the road with certain things and you got to give in when forced." Adopting this perspective, she found the experience rewarding. She now had independence; she knew that she could make it on her own, and was proud of that fact; and, she now had a "career" to fall back upon. While she was presently traveling back home to live with her sister, she knew "I can always go again . . . anywhere I like to go." Her options were limitless.[45]

This attitude, her willingness to compromise all but a few values, represents one of those very effects that the transient's friends feared most about the experience. This woman was adjusting quite nicely. She felt this was an accomplishment. Social workers, sociologists, and friends, however, saw it as a sign of degeneration. In this case the interviewer concluded that "the chances are very favorable . . . that she will continue in a semi-transient state and that she might later become a chronic transient," and, he was probably right.[46]

Women hobos were a hard pill for Americans to swallow. Harder still was the fact that many of their number were little more than children, some as young as thirteen. Yet both boy and girl "tramps" were becoming a distressing reality.* The January census counted 16,538 homeless boys under the age of twenty-one and 2,783 girls. These figures, however, as was the case with women, included only those individuals who had sought assistance at one of the participating social agencies, and youthful transients, fearful of being returned home, avoided these very same agencies. Taking this into account, Anderson revised his estimate to 135,000 homeless boys, 50 percent or more he believed were transient. The number of young girls was not specified in his estimate of 45,000 unattached females. Another student of the problem, however, calculated that approximately one in twenty of the young transients were girls.[47]

While others were just beginning to be aware of the problem of the child transient, Minehan was in the field collecting his information first hand. Leaving his University of Minnesota classroom, he donned the attire of the tramp and spent two years living with and studying Texas, Happy Jo, Bo Peep, Lady Lou, and hundreds of other boys and girls he met on the road. He rode with them, ate with them, walked with them, and even went to jail with them. He shared their camps, their food, and the dangers of their lives. As they traveled in boxcars, lingered over campfires, or waited out their sentences, he asked questions as one friend asks another—Why are you on the road? What was it like back home? Did you ahave a job? Did you go to school? Got any family left? And he listened to them talk about sex, religion, politics, their hopes, their dreams, their fears, and their frustrations. What he learned and what he lived was put into print for others to share in the classic *Boy and Girl Tramps of*

---

*The term tramp was freely used by contemporaries when they referred to the youthful transient. This was probably done more for shock value than any other reason since the majority of young transients did not meet the negative criteria ascribed to the tramp. Like their adult counterparts, they generally looked for work as they traveled and, from all accounts, did not conceive of their present status as permanent.

America. Within these pages were answered some of the most pressing questions of the day.

Why were these boys and girls on the road? Minehan asked his young friends. "There's seven of us kids at home," explained seventeen-year-old Joe, "and I'm the oldest." "Last fall they cut down on our relief. We had to go to bed because our house was so cold." Joe tried to get jobs to help out, but the jobs were not there. "Then, before the old man could start giving any more hints, I scrams." Pete faced similar pressures at home. "Work! Work! 'Why don't you get work?' That's all I hear from the old man for a year. Cripes! What does he expect a kid to do?" What this kid did was to leave. Jennie's family was also feeling the effects of the depression, yet she sympathized with her father.

> Dad tried to keep a home for the four of us kids. Cripes! He was as good as any man could be, considering. But what could he do? I was willing to work but nobody hired me and the rest of the kids were too young. So a home took the three kids, my married sister in Allentown took my father, and I just sort of scrammed.

Out of the 466 boys and girls he asked, 387 told him that hard times drove them away from home. Not wanting to add to the financial burdens being carried by their families, many of these youngsters felt that leaving was the greatest contribution they could make. For the rest, a combination of tense relations between parent and child, troubles with a boyfriend or girlfriend, and adolescent curiosity drove them to their present situation. Why did they leave home the "touch" asked the boy beggar: "Hard Times, lady, hard times . . . ," and, Minehan added, "the difficulties and desires of adolescence and the lure of the open road."[48]

Where exactly were they traveling? Sixteen-year-old Bob answers: "Fellow, I've traveled to every drag in this country big enough to have a flop house. . . . You can't name a main I haven't hit or a road I didn't ride." The children that Minehan knew were well traveled. At first they chose their destination out of curiosity to see "the appearance of the Rockies, the coast of California, the color of the deep South blacks." But the traveling did not stop after the curiosity was satisfied. Instead, a regular pattern or routine developed — to the cities in the winter, to the country in summer; North in search of industrial jobs, West to follow the harvests, South for warmth. Always moving.[49]

But why don't they stop? Why don't they settle down? Minehan's answer: They can't. "No matter how tired he or she was, how willing to work, how weary and disgusted with the road and its aimless wandering, he had to take to it." The combined effectiveness of relief authorities who gave a meal and an invitation to move on, and police who roused them when they attempted to rest, forced the child to keep on the road.[50]

Once it had been accepted that they were out there, and it was understood why, the next question was, how did they survive? How did they find food, clothing, shelter? Boys and girls, Minehan answered, got by in much the same way as men and women. They could usually rely on most communities to provide at least one free meal and a flop before instructing them to move on. After that, they were on their own. For food the boys could make the rounds of the mission houses, soup kitchens, and Sallies for their single bowl of meatless stew or beans, more commonly referred to by the diners as "swill" — "food fed to transients and hogs." For girls it was somewhat harder. The few agencies to which they could apply invariably wanted to return them home. Not agreeing with that solution to their problems, the girls avoided the agencies and the food and shelter they provided. A girl could sell her body to meet her needs, but chances are "she will find nobody in the market with desire and a dime."[51]

Begging was their next recourse. With the right story, physical deformity, real or affected, or a good racket, a child could usually secure sufficient food or funds to get by. Housewives who found them on their back steps, farmers approached in their fields, shopkeepers, grocers, restauranteurs, and passerby were all fairly easy touches for a young beggar. When panhandling was poor, and begging was difficult or unproductive, they stole. Pies out of a bakery truck, fruit from a grocer's stand, a chicken from a farmyard, clothes off a clothesline, all supplemented the young tramps' meager resources when local generosity failed. In their eyes this was not criminal. It was just part of their day-to-day existence.[52]

In summertime supplies gathered from these various sources were contributed to the communal store back at the jungle. Sometimes the young tramps gathered with older transients and hobos in their camps; more often they set up their own where tribes or packs of youth settled down until the season changed or the police routed them. Each jungle had its own hierarchy of leadership and loyalties, and, where boys and girls traveled together, a traditional division of labor with boys providing the food and protection and girls keeping camp and preparing the food. When the weather was good, these camps offered freedom, companionship, and a relatively nutritious diet from a communal pot of mulligan stew prepared from the fresh seasonal foods begged or stolen from farmers and grocers. Changing weather sent them back to the overcrowded lodging and mission homes as they sought shelter from the elements.[53]

Not all of the children living this life survived unscathed. Minehan's story is filled with children with bent and crippled bodies. There was Peg-leg Al who got his name from the wooden leg he fashioned to replace the one he lost between railroad cars in Texas, and there was Blinky who wore a watery socket where an eye had been before he caught a live cinder from the freight he was riding. Bo Peep, who was not yet fifteen, displayed a cheek scar from a blow by a railroad watchman. Hopping fast moving trains, perching precariously on boxcar tops, seeking shelter in rat-infested, leaky, old buildings, sleeping communally with disease-infested derelicts, maintaining an erratic diet, and the many other occupational hazards of hoboing, all took their toll on their young growing bodies. Many paid an even higher price. "More than once, . . . in more than one American city, a young tramp went to be outside to sleep the sleep that knows no waking"[54]

In addition to the physical dangers, contemporaries also worried about the child's bent and crippled spirit. What, they asked, would be the effect of such a life on an impressionable youth? For an answer to this question we can go directly to a boy transient. Eighteen-year-old Elliot Chapman speaks to us through the testimony he gave to a Washington panel five decades ago.* With credentials earned by hard experience, Chapman offers his expert testimony: to get by the boys usually begin by begging at restaurants and back doors.

> The main thing you have to do is keep yourself looking neat. Then you can get by except gradually you get dirty. Your clothes go and finally you can not do that any more. You get back to the place of being an ordinary bum, and that is when you have to start panhandling.

---

*Chapman's wanderings began when the high school graduate found that there were no jobs for him in his home town of Detroit, so "I thought I would just start out and see what I could do for myself." He thus began four and a half months of hitch-hiking, riding blind baggage, eating bad food in Sallies, listening to long unap-

But learning to beg coins on city streets is not easy.

> Most of the fellows, young fellows that start out, will not pan-
> handle. They have pride and are sort of scared to go up to a per-
> son. But you soon lose that.

Pride takes second place to survival, and the boys grow daring.

> There is just a feeling when you are tired and hungry you do not
> care much what happens to you. If you spend a night or two in jail
> you will get something to eat and a place to sleep.

They become frustrated because the jobs they sought were not there.
The neat appearance kept to impress the employer deteriorates as
does the spirit.

> When they try for a job, they are told there is not any such thing.
> That is when they first keep looking neat. They have no recom-
> mendations, or do not live in the city. They get the idea it is im-
> possible, and then, after they have been out for awhile and their
> clothes are looking shabby, they can not get near a place.

It is at this point, when they are most vulnerable, that the "professional bum" intercedes to teach them how to get by.

> When you get in with the professional bums your trouble starts,
> because they can tell you so many ways of managing, some of
> which are quite clever. . . .These men would tell these boys how
> easy it was in certain places to bum it, just how they could panhan-
> dle money, and would tell different ways of getting it.

In answer to the question, what effect is the life having upon them,
for the boys that Chapman traveled with, they were becoming ac-
customed to the road, and slowly but surely, they were learning to
become bums. Chapman had by this time given up the road and
returned to the security of his grandmother's home. The others he
traveled with and of which he spoke, presumably, were still out there
somewhere in a mission or a jungle continuing their lessons.[56]

---

preciated sermons at rescue missions, sleeping on the floors of flop houses, and
working temporary jobs, as he went from Detroit to California and back again, his
goal of a real job never realized.[55]

Minehan found the same degenerative process operating a-
mong his young friends. Initially they rejected the values, or lack of
them, of the hobos and tramps with whom they traveled. "I don't
want to be a bum" was reiterated with conviction. But, Minehan
warned, "there comes a day when they are alone and hungry, and
their clothes are ragged and torn, bread lines have just denied them
food . . . and a man of God at a mission has kicked them into the
street. . . .An old vagrant shares his mulligan with them and they
listen." The tramp will teach them about a new life—one without
work and responsibility, one with its own language, its own loyalties, its own moral standards—and anti-social life. They will learn
to steal without guilt, to deny God and country, to accept the idle life
as the norm. This, Minehan predicted, was the legacy America
could expect from its child tramps.[57]

The very first relief program to be established by the FDR administration was specifically directed toward meeting the needs of
such boys. The Civilian Conservation Corp (CCC), passed a mere
eight days after being introduced in Congress, established a network
of camps in the nation's parks and forests where America's jobless
youth could find work in return for relief. The scheme did include
the transient—if he was at least eighteen years old, had a residence
and dependents, and could provide references. Unfortunately, most
of the young boys Minehan met could meet few if any of the eligibility requirements. Either they were too young, had lost ties with
home, or were orphaned. Furthermore, they had their suspicions
that the CCC camps were thinly disguised military camps from
which recruits would be drawn in time of need. Their patriotism, according to Minehan, would not stand that test. Some of his friends,
however, did go—for a while—but then deserted these "prisons,"
"army chain gangs," or in friendlier terms, "Roosevelt roosts." Perhaps the most significant effect the CCC had on boy transiency was
a preventive one. Of its eventual two and one-half million enrollees,
it probably saved many from reaching that point of desperation
when hitting the road seemed to be the only choice. The camps offered one more alternative. But for those boys already on the road
the effect, apparently, would be minimal.[58]

The intent herein has been to recreate transient life from the
participant's perspective, especially in those cases where the transient was forced to make it on his own. To do this, individual cases
have been used at times to illustrate generalizations made by contemporaries who befriended the transient, often traveled with them,

but were not transients themselves. These cases are meant as samples of transient life since it cannot be said with complete assurance or statistical verification that they are representative of the typical transient, if there ever was such a person. The corroborating evidence, however, from the perspective of law makers, social workers, and participant observers, does confirm all that is said herein. Additional proof was forthcoming as these same friends took the transient's case to Washington in January 1933.

The Salvation Army's Gold Dust Lodge, New York City

Photograph courtesy of The Salvation Army Archives and Research Center

Men preparing for bed at Gold Dust Lodge

Photograph courtesy of The Salvation Army Archives and Research Center

A Salvation Army soup line during the Depression
Photograph courtesy of The Salvation Army Archives and Research Center

Tables set for a meal at Gold Dust Lodge
Photograph courtesy of The Salvation Army Archives and Research Center

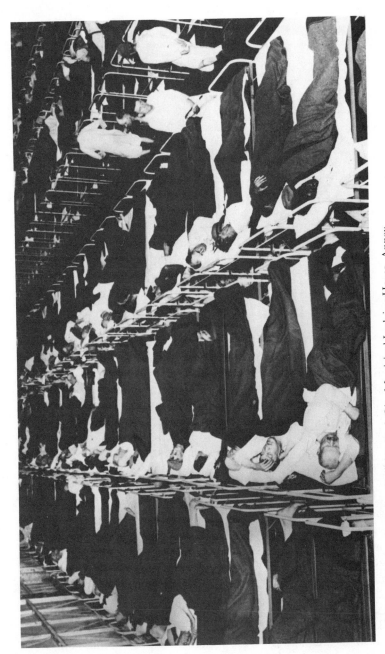

"The largest bedroom in the world." New York City Municipal Lodging House, Annex

The National Archives (No. 306NT174.969c)

۶ 6 ۶

The Federal Transient Program
In New York State I,
1933–35

THE estimates were in. The January 1933 census had shown the total number of the nation's homeless to be approximately 1.5 million, a vast majority of whom were transients. Both public and private agencies had by this time shown that they could not cope with this burden in addition to the ever-increasing needs of their own local unemployed. Three years of confusion and misery in trying to adapt antiquated poor laws to the severe modern crisis had once and for all proven the inadequacy of the old system. A federal program was needed, and this was precisely what social workers, public officials, businessmen, and university professors converged on Washington, D.C., that same January to tell Congress. They came with graphs, charts, statistics and personal stories to testify before the Senate Committee on Manufactures then conducting hearings on Senate Bill 5121 (S5121). The Cutting Bill, so named after its sponsor Senator Bronson Cutting of New Mexico, proposed to amend the Emergency Relief and Construction Act of 1932 to provide for the allocation of $15 million in federal funds to relieve distress among unemployed and needy transients.[1]

The sheer volume of the problem, increasing at a rate proportionate to the depletion of the meager resources available, was of major concern to the witnesses. In California, it was reported, transients were entering the state on the average of twelve hundred per day. As of December 1932, the total count was at one hundred thousand. Travelers Aid representative Dorothy Wyson explained that Los Angeles had more than ten thousand boys pass through the hands of the city's "vag squad" in a six month period in 1932. Four times the number of homeless women and girls had come to the attention of her agency in 1932 than during the preceding year. In Cleveland, Ohio, the president of the Cleveland Boys Boys Bureau reported that 240 youthful transients had sought help from that agency in just three months of 1932, while, at the same time, the local YMCA was feeding as many as five hundred others per month. Margaret Reeves of the New Mexico State Bureau of Child Welfare, reported that many small New Mexican communities were being inundated by westward-moving transients. As an example, she offered the story of one town of twenty-five hundred which gave help to a thousand transients in the month of December alone. While she praised this and other localities cited for their small town friendliness, she left no doubt that in such small communities, where the one-man police force often went home at 5:00 p.m., the people were understandably fearful of the hundreds who disembarked from freight trains in the dead of night.[2]

The witnesses agreed not only on the volume of the problem but also on the sad fact that the individual was being lost in the very statistics they were reciting. Recognizing the need for individualized treatment and care, they were forced to concede that in most instances the genuine problems of limited funds and/or state and local laws forced relief agencies to provide them with minimal subsistance, if even that. A nationwide survey of mayors conducted in conjunction with the hearings revealed that the usual treatment afforded to transients was to provide them with one meal and one night's lodging and then in the morning to simply pass them on to the next community. In some states and localities experimental programs placed transients in camps or tried to rehabilitate them vocationally, but, with extremely limited funding, only a fraction of the needy could be reached. For the rest, life consisted of municipal lodging houses, missions, boxcars, and jungles, with the ever present threat of arrest and imprisonment on vagrancy or mendicancy charges and, in some cases, detention on a chain gang.[3]

According to the witnesses, the rejection of the transient was as much the result of hostile community attitudes as it was due to the financial pinch. While touring the southwest, Professor A. W.

McMillen of the University of Chicago came face to face with some of this hostility. Outside of Tuscon, Arizona, for example, he found a highway sign which read: "Warning to Transients. Relief funds for local residents only. Transients, do not apply." "Do not ask for relief. You can be fed and slept at jail in return for 10 days' hard labor," was the message to be read in store windows in Deming, New Mexico. In a number of towns, he was informed, guards were posted at train crossings to escort out of town all of those who disembarked from the freight cars. Such attitudes were once again attributed to an instinctual and well-nurtured fear of strangers. J. Prentice Murphy of the Philadelphia Children's Bureau explained that the mere appearance of a stranger "of an unkempt condition" was enough to arouse suspicion and lead to quick and summary arrest. This deep-seated fear, he explained, resulted in the rejection of persons of honest needs and virtues. One such person dramatically impressed this point upon him. "Believe me, sir," said the tattered and torn hobo addressing him,

> three days in a box car, in zero weather, without water, sleep, or food, would make anybody look like a thug, but give me three days of heat, food, soap and water, a razor and a bed, and I will look just as I am—a graduate of the University of Chicago.[4]

Such immediate and fallacious identification of strangers and the subsequent treatment reserved for them were among the major concerns of the witnesses. How long, they asked, could any individual retain his/her health, morals, and overall character under these conditions? Agonizing over the immediate and long range effects of transiency, they could not but wonder if such persons could retain any sense of self-worth or love of nation, and, consequently, whether they could ever be salvaged after such an experience.

Of special concern was the young transient. Owen Lovejoy of the New York Children's Aid Society pointed out that the experience of being moved from place to place, unable to find employment, had a poor emotional, moral, and psychological effect on them. All of these influences, he explained, made the youth "feel that after all there is another way to live," and he predicted that "development of the professional tramp is more than likely to become one of the direct results of this system of wandering." Lovejoy was simply reiterating for Congress a nationwide concern over young transients that had prompted a U. S. Children's Bureau survey and report. Furthermore, this was an issue that had already been thoroughly explored by social workers. Articles such as "An Army of Boys on the Loose," "200,000 Vagabond Children," "Uncle Sam's Runaway Boys," and "Wandering Youth," filled both professional and popular journals in these early years.[5]

During his testimony, J. Prentice Murphy had explained that, "any fundamental program for the care of transients or migrants should be made an integral part of a larger and comprehensive relief program." "They can not," he emphasized, "be viewed separately."[6] Murphy was correct in his evaluation. Before the issue of transient relief or the fate of the Cutting Bill could be settled, the entire issue of federal relief had to be addressed once and for all. When the Cutting Bill did finally become law, it became so as part of a larger relief package. The development of that law, the Federal Emergency Relief Act, marked a break not only in the traditional treatment of the transient, but in the nature of social responsibility itself.

From the time that President Franklin Pierce had broken precedent by vetoing legislation to aid the insane, right down to Herbert Hoover's final presidential address, the position of the executive branch was that federal welfare benefits were the equivalent of a dole, a concept incompatible with prevailing American ideals and inconsistent with federal jurisdiction as defined in the Constitution. Yet the circumstances of the depression were steadily undermining the old concepts. Unemployment and its consequent miseries and hardships were soaring. According to the conservative estimates of the Department of Labor, 24 percent of the nation's work force was unemployed.[7] Private charitable agencies were incapable of keeping pace with the accelerating need resulting from the labor situation. In many cases annual allotments were being used up in a matter of months, and replenishing those supplies was becoming more and more difficult. According to the Association of Community Chests and Councils, fund raising in 1933 reached only 77 percent of the previous year.[8] Public relief, the twin partner of private charity in the poor law scheme, suffered from similar inadequacies. Increasing unemployment meant both an additional service load and a subsequent reduction in taxable income, that is, fewer tax funds available for relief. Caught in this vicious cycle, public resources quickly dried up. By 1933 many cities were on the verge of closing their public relief operations, a recourse that Philadelphia was forced to succumb to temporarily in June 1932.[9] At this point, the last line of defense permitted by the old system was rallied to the cause. The states, one by one, followed the example of Governor Franklin D. Roosevelt of New York and became involved in the business of relief. The rallying of state resources admittedly shored up some of the gaps in local relief; however, the states suffered from the same tax/relief cycle that the local governments did. Only the federal government, many believed, had sufficient and stable enough resources to break the self-defeating cycle. Public welfare officials, charitable organizations, and social workers were thus among the many who flooded the White House with petitions, requests, and outright pleas for federal cooperation. President Hoover, however, remained firm.

Since the executive branch showed no sign of weakening its traditional stand against federal relief, numerous attempts were made to break the deadlock between the poor law past and present reality in the halls of Congress. The most promising of the hundreds of relief bills presented to the Seventy-third Congress were introduced in December 1931 by two tireless advocates of federal relief, Senators Edward P. Costigan and Robert M. LaFollette, Jr. Both bills, S174 and S262, were referred to the Committee on Manufactures which held public hearings during December and January. On January 15, the bills were combined into a $375,000,000 relief proposal which, after much debate, was defeated. The Senate, apparently, was not ready to make such a dramatic and costly leap from the past into the future.*

While the states continued to petition the federal government for more adequate relief, the suffering continued. *The Nation*, vowing to "harp week by week until there is relief," kept up the constant pressure on Hoover. Directing personal responsibility for the needs to his door, the journal asked: "Is it to be Mass Murder, Mr. Hoover?"; "Shall Americans Starve?" and, "Must Americans perish miserably because of your fear that their characters may be sullied

---

*A more acceptable plan to loan the state relief money at 3 percent interest did, however, pass both houses of Congress and was signed into law in mid-year. The Emergency Relief and Construction Act authorized the Reconstruction Finance Corporation to make $300,000,000 available "to several States and Territories, to be used in furnished relief and work relief to needy and distressed people and in relieving hardship resulting from unemployment." The relief scheme, however, was fraught with difficulties from the very beginning. Ten weeks after the appropriation of the $300,000,000, Edith Abbott was able to report that only $25,000,000 of the funds had been thus far granted to the states. Due to the conservative leadership of the RFC, many states were granted only a fraction of what they needed and asked for, while others met with costly delays or outright refusals. [10]

by a dole?"[11] In a state of utter desperation, a delegation of mayors traveled to Washington, D.C. to literally beg the Senate Banking and Currency Committee to amend the RFC law to allow cities to borrow directly on the security of municipal bonds. Representing their counterparts in forty major cities, the mayors of Detroit, Boston, Milwaukee, and Chicago warned of impending municipal bankruptcy. "If the Federal Government won't help us," warned Mayor Frank Murphy of Detroit, "we don't know where we can turn." "We only ask what you have given to banks, railroads and insurance companies," pled Milwaukee's Mayor Daniel W. Hoan.[12]

Senators Costigan and LaFollette, undaunted by their senatorial rebuff a year earlier, again introduced separate bills for direct relief to the states. Again their two bills were combined and hearings by the Committee on Manufactures were resumed in January 1933. As proposed, bill S5125 of the Seventy-second Congress provided for "cooperation by the Federal Government with the several States in relieving hardships and suffering caused by unemployment, and for other purposes," and required the creation of a special fund of a half a billion dollars to be administered by a Federal Emergency Relief Board. The funds were to be allocated to the states as direct grants, with a special reserve fund to be set aside for transient relief.[13] Many of the same witnesses as the year before paraded before the Committee giving testimony that repeated their earlier statements and emphasized that conditions had worsened in the intervening year. They came from across the country, with their stories of suffering and distress. From New York, West Virginia, Maryland, Connecticut, Virginia, Ohio, Pennsylvania and Illinois came distinguished professionals and laymen. Harry Hopkins from New York; Dean Edith Abbott of the University of Chicago; William Green, President of the American Federation of Labor; and a host of representatives of a multitude of private and public organizations came to reemphasize to the sympathetic committee the extent of the problem and the failure of the RFC to alleviate it. Top RFC officals Atlee Pomerene and Charles A. Miller were also summoned. Their defensive statements, however, held little weight in light of the testimony of the foregoing witnesses.*

---

*The witnesses came to say that, despite optimistic statements from the White House, recovery was not just around the corner. Harry Hopkins, director of New York's Temporary Emergency Relief Administration, reported that one-tenth of the population of the state was at that moment on relief. This burden was costing

In unison, the overwhelming majority of the witnesses highly endorsed the proposed bill and warned against delay. Without federal funds, Hopkins warned, tens of thousands of persons would be without adequate relief in the upcoming months. "Whatever our theories of relative responsibilities of governmental units for relief of the unemployed," he explained, "it is perfectly clear that the unemployed will not get anything approaching adequate relief if the Federal Government does not bear a substantial share of the total amount." Others hinted of more foreboding consequences. Hunger marches, demonstrations, and a few riots had already occurred and in some cities, it was reported, and this growing bitterness and resentment was only a prelude to what would come should all hope of federal relief be squashed.[15]

As was expected, the Committee on Manufactures approved the bill and passed it onto the Senate where it was when Franklin Roosevelt took office on March 4, 1933. Two months later the newly elected Congress passed the Federal Emergency Relief Act, thereby assuming leadership in the battle for adequate relief. Explaining that the present economic depression, with its consequent deprivation and suffering, had made the cooperation of the federal government necessary, the legislators earmarked a $500 million fund to be administered by a newly created Federal Emergency Relief Administration (FERA). The administration was authorized to make outright grants to aid states on a matching fund basis of one-to-three to aid in furnishing relief to the needy "whether resident, transient, or homeless." Such relief was to be given in the form of "money, service, materials and/or commodities to provide the necessities of life to persons in need."[16] Ten days later FDR appointed the capable relief director of New York State, Harry Hopkins, to the role of administrator.

Few people, besides perhaps the outgoing Hoover, wept many tears about the passing of the old order. Rather, most looked on

---

$8,000,000 a month but was expected to top $10,000,000 in 1933, Illinois reported a rise in unemployment from 265,123 in 1930 to 1,400,000 in 1933. Chicago alone was serving a relief population ten times the size of its 1930 load, at an annual cost of $40,000,000. Corresponding to this increasing need was a regrettable but necessary reduction in the quality of care. In New York City, for example, only a few of the larger relief agencies were giving as much as $1.00 per day per person, approximately half of what was considered a level of subsistence. Unfortunately, lack of resources forced agencies nationwide to compromise their standards and strive for the minimal objective of "letting nobody starve."[14]

hopefully as the experiment in government responsibility evolved. Even many conservatives were willing, since the old way proved itself bankrupt, to give this "business of relief" a cautious try. Social workers, reformers, and municipal and state officials, on the other hand, were jubilant. Even before FDR put his signature to the bill, in eager anticipation, *The Nation* announced: "Direct Relief at Last." "After a two-year struggle, begun by Senator LaFollette in the spring of 1931," the journal explained, "the principle of direct federal unemployment relief has at last been accepted." The enthusiasm swelled until Gertrude Springer could report a few months later:

> There's a new spirit in Washington—a resolution to get on with things that will count. With a set-up of experienced men, a law giving it wide powers and half a billion dollars in its pockets, the Federal Relief Administration has set out on one of the greatest tasks of mass-relief ever undertaken—to get relief through to all those helpless millions who need it, to make it decent and to make it prompt.

Crediting the spirit of optimism to a "social minded President" and the "seasoned social worker" at the helm of the FERA, she explained, there was in Washington "a Green light, 'Go'!"[17]

The enthusiasm exhibited by Springer was shared by the social work profession at large. The mood of that year's National Conference of Social Work "was one of elation, triumph, bedazzlement." Looking back from the perspective of some fifty years in the profession, Jacob Fisher remembered vividly the hero's welcome that was given by the delegates to the newly appointed FERA administrator Harry Hopkins. Social workers, like most of the country, basked in the glory of the honeymoon period, giving almost unqualified support to the New Deal.[18] New Yorkers were especially elated. After all, the legislation that prompted the celebration, the FERA, was closely modeled after New York's TERA, the chief administrator of the federal program was their own fellow New Yorker and former chairman of TERA, Harry Hopkins, and it was their ex-governor who signed the bill into law. As historian Robert Bremer has shown, New York social workers had worked long and hard for this federal legislation and were now enjoying the fruits of their victory.[19]

The social work profession had made a very important about-face in a very brief period of time. When the depression began, social workers had met it with a traditional "we will take care of it" attitude based on the time-honored concept of local responsibility. The needs of the unemployed were very clearly a local responsibility preferably handled by the private agencies. By the time that FDR was inaugurated as president of the United States, however, these very same social workers were in the forefront of the battle for federal responsibility. This change was very ably explained and endorsed for the readers of *Survey Graphic* in July 1933 in an article by Gertrude Springer, "The New Deal and the Old Dole." Springer attributed the suffering experienced thus far in the depression to a "range of mistakes reaching back into history," the first of which was the old poor law. Likening the concept of outdoor poor relief to a "leaky old boat" which was "plainly unseaworthy for a great industrial people caught in an economic hurricane," she blamed a lackadaisical, irresponsible adaptation of the same for the "backward pattern of public relief" that existed on the eve of the depression. Carrying the metaphor one step further, she referred to the attempts to supplement the shrinking coffers of the private agencies with municipal and then state and/or RFC funds as a series of new mistakes intended to patch the old boat, but the efforts were in vain. As the passengers multiplied, the boat floundered, strewing its human wreckage upon the shores. Metaphors aside, what she was sayings, simply, was that the tradition of local responsiblity was obsolete. Furthermore, it was naive to expect that financial supplements to private charity from local, state, or federal governments would remedy the situation. The old dole did not work—what was needed was a new deal—thus her enthusiasm and that of her associates for the can do attitude in Washington.[20] In New York, Bremer tells us, two winters' "deepening chill" in 1930 and 1931, and the "icy winter's blast of 1932," were enough to make social workers realize the inadequacies of the old order and champion the coming of the new.[21]

Perhaps even more surprising than the federal government's assumption of responsibility for the nation's unemployed masses was the inclusion of the traditionally rejected stranger within this obligation. Incorporating the Cutting Bill into the final version of FERA, the legislators had specified the relief funds appropriated to the states be distributed among the needy "whether resident, transient or homeless." Furthermore, section 4C provided that the administrator: "May certify out of the funds made available by this subsection additional grants to States applying therefore to aid needy persons who have no legal settlement in any one State or community."[22] Pursuant to the legislative dictates, the newly appointed said administrator established a Division for Transient Activity within the FERA under the directorship of Mr. Morris Lewis, a former field representative for the NCCTH. To this division the individual states were to make application for transient relief funds.

Each state was requested to develop a workable special program for transient relief within its state emergency relief administration and to submit the plan to the FERA, which would release funds upon approval of the plans. The first such funds, earmarked specifically for transients, were granted to the state of Alabama in September 1933. By the following January, forty states and the District of Columbia were operating transient programs. Ultimately, the system was to include a nationwide network of treatment centers providing "care far superior to any ever before afforded to this group in the United States," at an estimated total price tag of $106,517,000 for four years of operation, or $5 million per month at peak.[23]

With the creation of the Federal Transient Division the transient had finally been recognized as a victim of the Great Depression and as deserving of aid as any of his unemployed fellows. With the appointment of Morris Lewis to head the division, he had also found a true friend. Known as a "social worker and practical idealist with a genuine concern for homeless people," Lewis promised to take the program beyond the realm of mere subsistence. "We must not stop at merely being good Samaritans," he wrote, "there must be a spiritual and cultural content in this program. There must be a realization that other qualities [beyond physical needs] consistent with human development are to be applied in connection with this work." Likening the modern wanderer to the heroic pioneers of old, he asserted that service given them should be considered their right rather than the benefactor's privilege. Consequently, he added that, "the recognition of public responsibility for people who are denied the chance to earn enough for the ordinary decencies of life presupposes their obligation, which must not stop with mere palliative measures."[24] The choice of Lewis as director was also a happy one for social workers. No mere Washington bureaucrat, he came to his new position from within the ranks. Not only had he previous experience as a field representative for the NCCTH, but he was, in fact, only "on loan" to the federal government from his present position with Travelers Aid. He, therefore, came to the national offices by compliment of the private sector and, more importantly, with the confidence of his fellow social workers. Social workers had been at the forefront in calling for a national program and now they had one of their own at the helm.[25] With such an advocate in Washington, the future at last looked bright for the transient.

Despite its reputation as one of the wealthiest states in the union, New York was in dire need of the new federal law. Human interest stories in *The New York Times*, such as "Party Tidbits Feed Homeless in Jail," were becoming all too frequent. The story of left over hors d'oeuvres and lady fingers being relished by the vagrants in the Mt. Kisco jail reflected the rising inability of localities to care for victims of the depression. At the same time, local private charities were increasing the urgency of their pleas for help. William Church Border, president of the Children's Aid Society, an organization which accepted responsibility for transient boys, exclaimed that, "The time has come when the Children's Aid Society can no longer bear the full burden for the care and training of these boys and I must therefore appeal to the public to help support this work."[26]

Work on New York's application had been progressing behind the scenes as Morris Lewis and officials of the New York TERA negotiated the terms of the state's proposal and appropriate funding allowances. On October 26, 1933, Frederick I. Daniels, executive director of the New York TERA, submitted the formal letter of application to Harry Hopkins to initiate a federally funded transient relief program in New York State. Eight days later, on November 3, 1933, Hopkins responded with the go-ahead: "Authority is hereby extended to the New York Temporary Relief Administration to effect a state program for the care of transients." An initial grant of seventy-five thousand dollars per month, to be adjusted according to need, was authorized.[27]

Included in Hopkins' letter of authorization were ten previously agreed upon conditions. A number of the points were purely administrative and designed to address anticipated problems before the fact. The state, for example, was required to adopt the federal definition of transient, that is, "persons in the state for less than twelve months," and to restrict program funds to their assistance only. They were also required to make a clear distinction between transient and migratory labor so as not to inadvertently allow employers to use the program to subsidize the artifically low wages of seasonal workers. The remaining conditions, to the obvious delight of experienced social workers, addressed standards and means of care as previously prescribed by workers in the field. Treatment and registration policy for transients, for example, must be uniform throughout the state. Adequate care, without any time limitations, was to be provided. Passing-on was not to be tolerated. The state was also required to employ "adequately trained case-work personnel" to provide professional services to transients. Work projects were to form an integral part of the transient program. All transients were to be provided with full physical examinations when registered, and full medical care (exclusive of hospitalization) was to be provided when necessary. Finally, reinforcing the reliance of the federal program on the expertise of the private sector, Hopkins wrote:

> It is expected that you avail yourself of the use of the personnel of private agencies wherever possible. Inasmuch as a great proportion of this work has been handled through private sources, it would seem that a continued responsibility might be assumed by them because of the burden now taken over with the application of federal funds. Many of these private agencies have qualified personnel, many of whom have developed techniques necessary to the proper service of your clients. The loan of such personnel should be encouraged where possible.

On November 27, 1933, TERA was ready to release the story to the press. "The practice of furnishing unemployed transients a cup of coffee and a boost out of town will continue no longer"—a federal program was being initiated.[28] Within seventeen days the Transient Division was established with Walter Kreusi, former TERA administrative assistant, as the first director. County and city welfare commissioners were authorized to begin providing relief to transients in anticipation of 100 percent reimbursement. Although but a brief experiment, the resulting program was to provide relief for tens of thousands of persons over approximately two years in a transient care network that spanned the state.

A number of administrative problems beset the program from the very beginning. One immediate problem was determining who exactly was eligible for federal transient relief. Section 4C of FERA had provided federal responsibility for all persons who had "no legal settlement in any one State or community." In subsequent rulings it was determined by the administration that, due to confused and varied state settlement laws, a blanket definition would be applicable to all states cooperating in the program. Henceforth, settlement was defined as "residence within the state for a period of one year or longer." Anyone without such a credential was to be cared for at federal expense.[29] Even this liberal definition, however, did not reach all persons in need. Owing to settlement law technicalities that in some cases prevented even persons who had resided longer than one year in a state from receiving aid, many persons still remained outside of the program.* To compensate, the administration chose to interpret FERA in such a way as to allow such persons to receive aid out of general FERA funds. As it now stood, persons classified under 4C as transients were cared for under special treatment funding, whereas, persons in a state more than one year, but without legal settlement, were to be treated as the bulk of the population out of general funds at the specified state-federal one-to-three ratio.

To further complicate the situation, federal laws had to be interpreted within the context of the still operative Public Welfare Act and Wicks Act. Under the former, the state assumed responsibility for the state poor, persons without legal settlement who had lived in any one specific public welfare district less than sixty days, while local communities were responsible for nonresident poor, those persons without settlement but who had resided more than sixty days in their district. The Wicks Act, furthermore, specified that persons were not eligible for state unemployment relief until accumulating two years' residency. Since the federal law was created to extend federal funds to help states support their own temporary emergency relief programs, persons without two years' residency were technically still without recourse to those funds. To resolve these problems an equally complicated system of definition and classification was devised. (See Tables 5 and 6, pages 137 and 138.) Even with such a well-

---

*Most states specified that the required years be accumulated without receiving any public assistance. Residency requirements ranged from six months to five years.[30]

TABLE 5. Eligibility for Transient Relief*

FEDERAL TRANSIENTS

1. Unattached single persons, who, *at the time of application*, have resided *less than a year continuously* in the state, with no legal settlement within the state.
2. Families that, *at the time of application*, have resided *less than a year continuously* in the state, with no legal settlement within the state.

STATE TRANSIENTS—UNATTACHED

A. Persons who, *at the time of application*, have resided *less than a year continuously* in the state but have a legal settlement in another welfare district within the state.
B. Persons who, *at the time of application*, have resided a *year or more continuously* in the state, but *not two years*, with no legal settlement in another welfare district of the state.
C. Persons who, *at the time of application*, have resided a *year or more continuously* in the state but *not two years* and who have a legal settlement in another welfare district of the state.
D. Persons who, *at time of application*, have resided *two years or more continuously* in the state but have no legal settlement in a public welfare district of the state.

STATE TRANSIENTS—FAMILIES

Families that, at the time of application, have resided *a year or more continuously* in the state, but *not two years* and which have no legal settlement in any welfare district of the state.

LOCAL HOMELESS

A local homeless person is any unattached individual not having a recognized place of abode who has legal settlement in the district in which he applies. The TERA participation in their relief is provided for in special instruction, bringing them under the home relief class.

*(New York State, Temporary Emergency Relief Administration, *Manual of Procedure*, April, 1935, Albany, Item 705).

defined system, it was difficult to translate rules into reality, and in many cases classification and disbursement of aid was erroneous.

A second equally complicated administrative problem that was worked out as the program became operative concerned who would actually administer relief. Ideally, all relief systems at the time tried to maintain at least the semblance of local responsibility by involving local officials in investigative procedures and the disbursement of funds. Therefore, as originally formulated, the New York plan provided that all transients be cared for by the public welfare official where said transient applied for relief, subject, of course, to 100 percent reimbursement. The need for cooperation and difficulties in providing a smooth flow of funds, however, necessitated a change in

TABLE 6. Residence with Source of Funds*

	Unattached	Families
Less than year continuously in State on application.		
No legal settlement within State	Federal Transient(1)	Federal Transient(1)
Legal settlement in another district	State Transient(2)	Home Relief Family(4)
Legal settlement in district	Local Homeless(4)	Home Relief Family(4)
Year or more continuously in State on application, but not two years.		
No legal settlement within State	State Transient(2)	State Transient(2)
Legal settlement in another district	State Transient(2)	Home Relief Family(4)
Legal settlement in district	Local Homeless(4)	Home Relief Family(4)
Two years and over continuously in State on application.		
No legal settlement within State	State Transient(2)	Home Relief Family(3)
Legal settlement in another district	State Transient(2)	Home Relief Family(3)
Legal settlement in district	Local Homeless(3)	Home Relief Family(3)

(1) Federal Transient Fund, 100% (disbursement).
(2) State Transient Fund, 100% (disbursement).
(3) Reimbursement Fund, 40%. Discretionary fund, extra percent or Federal Fund throughout, or either portion (reimbursement).
(4) Federal Fund, 75% (reimbursement).

*(New York State, TERA, *Manual of Procedure*, April, 1935, Albany, Item 705).

the basic plans. In May 1934 care of the unattached transient was generally taken out of the hands of local officials with emphasis changing to state operated and staffed centers and camps. With the exception of Buffalo, Rochester, and New York City, care for transient families was disbursed by the home relief division of the various county departments of public welfare, subject only to nominal supervision by the Transient Division but, nonetheless, fully reimbursed.[31]

The type of care to be given the transient was specifically outlined by TERA and set down in Bulletin #20, "Rules and Regulations on Care of Transients." Food was to be provided either in a designated shelter, at specified restaurants at previously agreed upon rates, or through food grants to the individual. Shelter could vary from congregate care in private or public lodging houses and/or camps, to individualized care in rooming houses, hotels, or private charitable institutions. However, the rules specified that any such shelter meet specific standards of quality regarding sanitation, cleanliness, and bathing and sleeping facilities. Clothing and shoes were to be purchased from predetermined merchants at stipulated rates. Personal services such as laundry and barbering were also to be provided. Medical care, including complete physicals and/or emergency care, was subject to reimbursement under the program. Hospitalization, however, was specifically excluded under federal and state regulations. Such expenses would remain the liability of the local public welfare district. In addition to such physical services, TERA specified that all local transient units have qualified social workers available to provide case work services to the transients. A subsequent bulletin from Washington required regular inspections of all buildings by local health and fire inspectors.[32]

To facilitate the program, the state was divided into eight transient districts. District offices were centrally located in Buffalo, Dansville, Rochester, Syracuse, South Schenectady, Elmsford, Binghamton and New York City. To fully understand and evaluate the impact of the federally funded, state-run transient program, it is necessary to look more closely at the care provided within these districts. Much of the footwork for such an evaluation was done contemporaneously, the year after the program was terminated, by the New York State Governor's Commission on Unemployment Relief. In an attempt to adequately handle the transient problem after the federal government had returned it to the states, Governor Herbert

H. Lehman ordered the Commission to conduct a thorough study of the entire question of transient relief, before, during, and after the federal program. Because the study was conducted to anticipate and adjust to an accelerated transient problem which the state must now face alone, the resulting report provides an invaluable look at the federal program in New York State, albeit with a necessarily critical eye.

Before beginning a discussion of these various types of facilities and the programs they offered, however, a word of explanation about a commonly shared feature is necessary. Throughout the contemporary literature on transiency in general, and the Federal Transient Program in particular, there is a repeated concern over rehabilitating the transient. From all that we now know about the profile of the typical transient, his generally upright character, employability, sound educational background, and initiative and tenacity, the high degree of concern over his rehabilitation seems inconsistent. Rehabilitation implies a state of uselessness or disability from which one must be delivered, but the typical transient was not useless or disabled. Yet the word is there. Social workers, FERA officials, camp directors, and the press all refer to the rehabilitative features of the transient program. This apparent contradiction can be clarified by looking more closely at just what contemporaries meant by the term. For this explanation we turn to an expert in the field, Robert Wilson, author of several Travelers Aid manuals on social work among the transients. Rehabilitation was, to Wilson, a broad term. It included providing personal services such as tailoring, laundering, and shoe repair; offering an opportunity for regular eating, sleeping, working and playing to restore the "energy and stamina which have deteriorated through transiency, unemployment, and irregular income"; and breaking down, in part, the protective shell of tough individualism and helping the individual to once again learn to fit into a group and acquire a sense of group responsibility; all of which were intended to help prepare the transient for a return to "regular community life." The bottom line of this treatment, the rehabilitation, was to increase the man's self-confidence, ingenuity, and self-respect. "The unemployed person," Wilson explained,

> has lost his sense of achievement and rewards of social approval. He has no pay check, which is the most concrete symbol of accomplishment, as well as the means of securing the standards of living

for himself and family which win social approval. . . .Underneath, he may share unconsciously the feeling of the community toward the transient and have a sense of failure or inadequacy.

The transient program was designed to help the man win back his sense of identity and approval by removing him from the debilitating environment that was sapping his vitality and by giving him the opportunity to participate in worthwhile projects "which in turn raise his own individual morale and offer him a legitimate basis for self-respect."[33] This is not to say that some of the men did not need more. As in any population, severe emotional and psychological problems that needed more treatment than a fresh set of clothes, a comfortable bed, and a temporary job could provide, existed. The ultimate goal of the rehabilitation process also often eluded the client. The program could not get him a job; it could not guarantee his reentry into society. But it could help to form a bridge to the mainstream that just awaited an upswing in the economy to be crossed. This, then, is what contemporaries meant by rehabilitation.

Within the eight transient districts, federally funded, state-administered aid to the unattached male transient was provided through four specific types of facilities: reference bureaus, transient centers, state run camps, and special rehabilitation centers. Each served specific purposes and provided different levels of care. (See Table 7, page 142.)

The reference bureau remained closest to local control and provided the least physical and/or rehabilitative care. Before the state consolidated its control over local transient operations, most of these twenty-odd reference bureaus were known as transient agencies. They were usually one-man local relief operations that provided overnight care and referral to state transient centers or camps. Even after these agencies were incorporated into the revamped state program and designated reference bureaus, their operations and functions remained basically unchanged.

By specified policy, care was to be remain limited. Food and shelter were to be provided overnight or on a strictly limited basis with the ultimate object being referral.[34] Thus none of the reference bureaus maintained their own shelters; instead, they relied on private agencies on a contract basis. The state paid a flat fee to boarding houses, missions, and restaurants to house and feed the transient. Such contract care referred him right back to the same shelters that had for years proved to be inadequately equipped and

TABLE 7. Types of Relief Granted to Unattached Transients*

	CAMP	TRANSIENT CENTER	REFERENCE BUREAU
FOOD	Continuous care three meals a day.	Continuous care three meals a day.	Overnight or limited
SHELTER	Extended dormitory care.	Isolation and general dormitory care, or rooming house or other contract agency.	Overnight or limited. Rooming house or other contract agency.
CLOTHING	As needed. Work clothing at discretion of director.	As needed. Work clothing at discretion of director.	Emergency only.
CASH ALLOWANCE	At discretion of supervisor. $1.00 per week up to $3.00 per week.	At discretion of director. Up to $1.00 per week.	None.
MEDICAL	Physical examination. Treatment. Appliances. Hospitalization.	Physical examination. Treatment. Appliances. Hospitalization.	Emergency given under TERA medical regulations.

*(Adapted from New York State, TERA, *Manual of Procedure*, April, 1935, Albany, Item 708).

overcrowded. Recreational and work programs were consequently nil, leaving the client with little to occupy his idle hours.

Inadvertently, the best intentions of the state program were circumvented at this level. Because of the limited field supervision on the local level, the state had little control over either the standards of care provided the transient or the time that elapsed between the registration of a transient and his referral to a better supervised treatment center or camp. This was especially apparent in a number of communities which had willingly accepted the establishment of transient bureaus because of the 100 percent reimbursement that came with them but failed to accept the corresponding responsibility to provide adequate care and competent programs. The result was that in many place bureaus often became drop-in centers for individuals who chose to remain footloose. Transients could easily spend a night in a poorly run bureau, check out the next day, and soon be on the way to another community for another free night. Critics of the program cited such cases as contributing to transiency by creating a system of way stations across the nation where the prospective transient knew he would not go hungry or cold. Referring to transient youth in particular, Thomas Minehan, for one, believed that easy access to this network of shelters tended to "aggravate the problem rather than allay it."[35] A similar complaint, but one motivated by a very different experience, was addressed directly to Franklin Roosevelt by a distraught father in Beaver Dam, New York, who believed he had lost his son to the road because of the convenience of the network of transient bureaus. "Such bureaus," Mr. W.* wrote the president, "have encouraged young men to seek a life which is a disgrace to the nation as well as the family and self." By offering the necessities of life free of charge, the bureaus lured boys who would never have dared take to the road otherwise. It allows them "to lose contact with home, favorable associates, defy laws. . . .They become restless, irresponsible, always seeking the road to ease, rather than effort." Carrying his criticism even further, and speaking "man-to-man," he went on to explain the physical

---

*A number of the following personal stories or histories were found in letters to President Roosevelt, Eleanor Roosevelt, and Harry Hopkins now housed in the National Archives. When these letters were written, they were written in confidence. Even after the passage of fifty years, the author does not wish to violate that confidentiality; therefore, initials will be substituted for full names in these instances only.

danger facing such boys. His own son, "a good boy," who left home a clean-cut, intelligent, eighteen-year-old boy, was now, according to his father's greatest fears, "a derelict, seeking empty thrills, a common prostitute, passed from one bum to another." His chief frustration seemed to be his inability to bring his boy home because the bureau would not return him against his will. While he made his appeal as personal as possible and literally pleaded with the president as one father to another, his letter was answered by an FERA officer thanking him for his interest in the federal program and providing him with the name of the director of the transient program where his son was staying.[36]

The second type of facility, the transient center, was much more effective in performing its assigned task: to offer the transient "a program of care for physical needs, such as food, housing, clothing, medical care and social service through consultation, work and recreations."[37] By June 1935 eleven transient centers were in operation statewide. It was the conclusion of the Governor's Commission that, given the conditions under which they were forced to operate and their hasty development, the treatment centers did offer well-rounded, adequate programs of care, especially those five centers that maintained their own shelters and/or dining rooms and, thus, retained direct control over "the quality of food and the livability of quarters." Meals, they found, "were quite different from the stew traditionally served homeless men and did represent a real effort to furnish some diversity as well as adequacy of diet," and the quarters were, in general, well maintained.[38]

They were also favorably impressed by the concerted effort that was made to provide employment for idle hours. Work programs, for example, were inaugurated in every facility where suitable projects could be found. In return of one dollar per week, transients of various skills maintained and renovated their environment, served each other as barbers, tailors, and cooks, and supplemented the clerical staffs of the centers by serving as typists and stenographers. In a few instances industrial projects were also carried out. In Buffalo a transient-operated printing shop did approximately one-half of the printing needed by the state transient operation, turning out ten thousand pages a week. In Elmsford Center and in Syracuse much of the office equipment and camp furniture used in the program was produced in transient-operated furniture shops. In Schenectady transients assembled metal cots for similar use. In addition, for public relations, as well as the need to keep busy, local community projects were undertaken by transients. Such projects were carefully chosen, however, to prevent competition with local workers.[39]

Work projects were initiated as much for their restorative value for the men so occupied as for the valuable man-hours they provided to supplement severely overworked staff and limited budgets. One such project in the Buffalo center illustrates this point well. Because of its location on Swan Street in the heart of downtown Buffalo, the center was not able to provide construction projects or outdoor work for the men. Therefore, a city office work project was initiated in June 1934 for the dual purpose of assisting the staff to service the increasing number of applicants at the center, and, "by means of needed work [as opposed to make-work], to improve the morale of the better trained and steadier transients from a higher socio-economic background." A select group of men was carefully chosen from the general transient population registered at the center. The selection was made on the basis of clerical and/or managerial skills and talents and aptitude. Those chosen to participate in the project were assigned to tasks as simple as messenger, "go-for," or clerk-typist, as well as more responsible "straw boss" positions as foremen, office managers, timekeepers, desk managers, and test administrators. Others were assigned to carpentry projects and general repair and cleaning about the center. Office project workers also assisted staff psychologist, Herman Schubert, collect and collate data on the transient population, and, in turn, found themselves, wittingly or not, the subject of his book on the Buffalo experience, *Twenty Thousand Transients.* When the project began, only three transient men were engaged. Their proficiency and the value of their work, however, led to a steady demand by the staff for more. By the end of 1934, 170 transients were assisting a staff of fifty.[40]

In return for their required twenty hours per week, and the overtime they voluntarily put in, the men received a dollar per day and were placed on special care. This meant a private room in a nearby rooming house or third-class hotel, a thirty-five to forty cent daily food allowance that could be used in a restaurant of their choice, and a "slightly higher class clothing." It is not surprising that Schubert was able to report that incoming applicants begged to be put on the project or that he was able to detect an improved morale in those so involved compared to the "downcast mien of the incomers."[41] For those chosen for the project and the beneficence of special care, the Buffalo center gave the opportunity to gain the self-respect that comes from having some change in your pocket and the freedom of movement that private lodgings and restaurant dining allows. It should be noted, however, that the preferential treatment received by this handful of elites could be a source of resentment among the unselect many. Among the letters of complaints filed away in FERA records, there are some bitter comments on the special treatment accorded these "pets."[42]

The project proved to be mutually beneficial, however, for both the staff and transients lucky enough to participate. After an initial period of adjustment, the staff grew to appreciate and "greatly depend" upon their transient helpers. Schubert noted that remarks like, "one really could not find better workers," became the "order of the day" among staff members. What was more important, staff came to see the men they worked so closely with as individuals rather than as part of an anonymous mass, an appreciation that transferred to the transient population in general, which in the long run aided in the treatment and care of all transients. Schubert experienced this conversion himself. He had originally come to his position on the staff not because of any particular interest or crusading desire to help this population in particular but because "it was a job" for the young Columbia University graduate. In short time, however, he developed a real affection for the men he worked with and even took them into his home. "He got to like these men," his wife remembers. "Many of them were very nice people." He and his wife even made one futile effort to arrange an introduction for Schubert's office manager and a co-worker of his wife's. Mary, unfortunately, did not share their sympathy with the lot and refused to date a "transient."[43]

As far as the men themselves were concerned, time occupied in useful, rewarding work was much better than long idle hours of brooding and worrying. When one man, for example, was asked why he showed up for work before he was scheduled, he answered simply, "I just couldn't stand doing nothing at the hotel any longer so I came over to see if there was anything I could do here." After just a few days on the project, Schubert reported, the men "were very cheery rather than morose, hopeful rather than despondent, and active rather than lethargic. They felt that they were doing something worthwhile and, many of them, that they were learning something."[44] It was not without good reason that Schubert included his report on the city work project under the heading, "Some Treatment Methods." Work definitely had its therapeutic value.

Schubert offered a number of stories to illustrate. One involved a young man of twenty who had come to the center after being turned out of his aunt's house. Hard times and a large family to care for had driven him from the only home he had known since he was fourteen. The six-footer came to the center weighing only 120 pounds, with unkempt clothing, and a "very withdrawn and shy" response to people. Yet, he appeared friendly and eager to work and was assigned to the janitorial service. When Schubert next saw him he almost failed to recognize him. "He was now scrubbed, his clothes presented a good appearance, and he greeted people with a cheery 'Hello!'." He was responding favorably to finally finding a place where he fit in and was useful—he was even beginning to gain weight. Another young man, still in his teens, "not quite as crushed and beaten as the general run, but nevertheless hungry, cold, bleary-eyed from travel and loss of sleep," showed up one cold April morning at the center. The boy showed quick intelligence, scored well when tested, and, besides that, he was just plain likeable. The staff took to him immediately and offered him a job assisting Dr. Schubert administer tests to applicants at the center. Before long he was conducting all of the testing himself, as well as composing and typing departmental letters. He was soon promoted to head the Work Office where he oversaw men much older and more experienced than himself. The young man's insatiable curiosity, eagerness to learn, and desire for increasing responsibility, prompted the staff to suggest that he enroll at the Collegiate Center in the city. Shortly thereafter Schubert was able to report that he was working his way through college "and having a very good time of it." The young man had made a lasting impression on the staff. Fifty years later, Bill Garno is one of the few transients that Schubert fondly remembers by name.[45]

Unfortunately, as Schubert pointed out regarding the Buffalo experience, only a select group, the "cream of the crop," could participate in such programs. At a time when the Buffalo Center was only processing approximately two thousand new registrations per month, only 170 men, at peak, were participating in the project. Of the 11,608 men being cared for daily in centers across the state, 3,005 or 25.9 percent had worked a total of 367,572 man-hours during the month. The low percentage was directly due to the limited number of projects available in New York City and Buffalo where 13.4 and 12.1 percent respectively were so employed. In the remaining nine centers the percentage of men working was better, ranging from 48.2 percent in Port Jervis to a high of 92.3 percent in Schenectady, but it was still impossible to provide work for all able-bodied clients.[46]

For those hours not occupied by work, the centers tried to provide a variety of recreational opportunities. While lack of facilities and open-air space made city recreation more limited than that available in the transient camps, most centers did provide fairly adequate lounging and recreational space. Each center differed in what was available. Most, however, could provide radios, checkers, cards, and similar diversions. Due to time demands on administration and staff, only one center had a continuous recreation program; however, any attempt to fill in the idle hours for the transient provided a pleasant contrast to the long and lonely days in the streets that had preceded the program.

Despite the best of intentions, the transient centers did not operate without their share of problems. In many cases the sheer magnitude of need and the numbers of people applying for admission made it virtually impossible to live up to the federal guidelines and expectations. Social services in the centers, for example, were severely lacking. In many cases an overworked staff, already pressed to provide for the physical needs of its clients, was simply unable to provide the anticipated social services. The persons designated as responsible for such services were already occupied in the time-consuming process of registering from one thousand to three thousand men a month. Case workers, similarly, were hampered by the multiplicity of forms and paper work which left little time for developing the free and informal rapport needed to help the individual.[47]

A lack of suitable facilities, and overcrowding also forced many centers to resort to contract care, that is, the providing of food and/or shelter in public lodging houses, missions, boarding houses, and restaurants on a contract basis. Approximately 75 percent of the total number of persons served in the state program were cared for by contract. At first the plan to use contract care was considered advisable because it would save the state a great deal of money in capital expenses buying, leasing, and/or renovating buildings for use in the program. The result, however, was a confusing administrative scheme whereby the state agency supplied the funding and supervision while the contract agency furnished food and lodging. This led to a problem of duality of control over the clients "with neither agency having complete responsibility for guidance of individuals or for the use of physical care as part of the treatment plan." Furthermore, agencies "set in their ways" were known to attempt to exert excessive control over the behavior of the individuals placed under their care, often trying to make them conform to shelter policies such as requiring a specified number of hours of work. Such control was highly resented by the transients, especially when it involved religion, an area they correctly believed had no part in a federal program.[48]

Even those contract shelters that tried to maintain standards could provide but a bleak existence for the inhabitants. In Buffalo, for example, those men not on special care or farmed out to supplemental shelters were housed in the Erie County Municipal Lodging House where, according to Schubert's observations, conditions were "from all angles at the bare subsistence level." Men were served two meals a day from a repetitive menu. They had very few personal services available to them, such as barbering, shoe repair and tailoring — little services that help lift the spirit while improving the appearance — and scarcely any facilities for activities, sports or hobbies to busy themselves. The result was a dull, monotonous existence from which most escaped after an average stay of only two days.[49] Contract shelters, furthermore, did not usually segregate federal transients from the general clientele, which meant that men duly registered with the program would find themselves once again sleeping side by side with Skid Row derelicts, habitual bums, drug addicts, and drunks, the very element that the program intended to segregate them from. From the People's Rescue Mission in Rochester came the complaint of one such federal transient on contract care. The drunks, he complained, are from three to five every day and night, and his sleep was being constantly interrupted by police coming in to remove them.[50]

Even in those centers that maintained their own shelters and dining rooms all the old problems that accompanied congregate care persisted. "Struggle as they did . . . with decent equipment, recreational facilities, and whitewash," explained Hopkins, "the hardworking transient directors could not make out of these converted warehouses, offices, stores, garages, school houses, or cheap hotels anything but thinly disguised flophouses."[51] Longtime advocate of individualized treatment for transients, Robert Wilson, elaborated on this dilemma before the 1935 annual Conference of Social Work in Montreal. "Most of the present so-called 'emergency' shelters," he explained, "are hopeless both because of size and impossibility of ever making them livable." He heartily suggested the abandonment of approximately nine-tenths of such shelters, including many of the present municipal lodging houses. For all the reasons cited earlier, he found the warehouse type of shelter to be a "social anarchism in modern day social work."[52] A number of residents at the centers agreed. From the Syracuse Transient Center, for example, came complaints from a World War veteran of "food worse than in a German prison camp," and being forced to sleep in a common dormitory with men infected with venereal disease and tuberculosis.[53]

Few supporters of the program could or would in the final analysis claim that the transient center provided a final solution to the transient problem. There are some good examples of men who did stop long enough to be reabsorbed into society, but, proportionately, there just were not that many Bill Garnos. This was understood and expected at the centers. They operated under very few false illusions. "Most of the measures now possible are at best palliative," Schubert had admitted. "They keep the men off the road only a short time. They stay for a week or even a month, and many of them just continue wandering." For men who were used to being self-supporting, men who wanted to reenter society, who wanted to establish normal relationships, one dollar a day on a temporary project simply was not enough. So they came, stayed a few days, a week, a month, and moved on.[54]

This is not to say, however, that the program was a failure. The centers provided valuable service to all those who sought them out. They gave the transient a place where he knew he could stop, rest, and recover from the "buffeting of the road." For the first time he knew that there was a place he could seek shelter from a wintry blast or the soaking of a summer storm, food for an empty gnawing stomach, and a warm bed, and know that he would not be turned away because of a lack of residency, passed on to the next town, or "shipped back willy-nilly to the same conditions that sent [him] on the road in the first place."[55] For some the shelter provided the first security they had known in years. "I had a hard time since 1931," explained one such man, "but when the government opened up these things, . . . things were different. A man could get three squares again and a roof over their head."[56] How long they stayed may be an indication of how basic the roof was, but at least it was there.

The personnel at the centers also did their best, considering the numbers, needs, and limitations, to provide treatment for their clientele. The core of that treatment was usually very simple: occupy idle hours with constructive, worthwhile projects, and, more basic yet, treat the client as an individual worthy of respect. Schubert repeated this formula throughout his 1935 book, and he still repeats it fifty years later. Looking back on the experience, he explains: "My idea was, if you are giving them something to steady them, to support them, and then the man catches hold, then that's rehabilitation. If you let him go and further beat him down . . . then you are pushing him into more trouble." As to critics who claimed that the centers failed to individualize care, Schubert asks, "How much are you going to say that being treated as a worthwhile person, and given at least a part-time job, and not being told you can stay here for one night, but tomorrow you are on your own, get the hell out of here, how much of that is positive individualized attention and how much isn't?" What the center offered the individual was a welcome that he had not heard in a long time: "We will take you in and consider you a worthwhile citizen." Ultimately, the goal of the centers was, according to Schubert, to "establish a condition where men could grow, at least not negatively deteriorate." They could do little more. For in the final analysis, as Schubert recognized back in 1935, "the one thing the men are looking for and the one thing that would hold them is a job paying fair wages. This the treatment centers cannot offer. Until there are jobs enough to go around, this milling around the country will continue." And it did.[57]

Despite all of the drawbacks, the care afforded by the transient centers was decidedly better than that provided the local homeless. In New York City, for example, the Unattached and Transient Division paid a contractual rate of fifty-five cents a day per client, while the City Department of Welfare paid only forty cents to the local homeless. In addition, those agencies providing service to transients at fifty-five cents were required to conform to Federal Transient Division standards, that is, three meals a day, clothing, and specific facility requirements. The difference, it was noted among a variety of observers, prompted local men to "forget" their residency and to apply for relief as transients. This point was graphically illustrated by a little story supplied to the *World Telegram* by the deputy commissioner on the New York

City Department of Public Welfare. The story related the story of four brothers, all victims of the depression:

> FIRST BROTHER, a New Yorker, but by a twist of luck not classified as homeless, gets $6 a week from home relief, not working.
>
> SECOND BROTHER, also a New Yorker, gets $6 a week for working five eight-hour days at Camp Greycourt.
>
> THIRD BROTHER, a New Yorker, lands in the Municipal Lodging House. He gets free shelter and three meals a day, but if he wants cash for cigarettes and clothes must panhandle. He can't spend the day in the lodging house, and wanders the streets daytimes in the cold without an overcoat.
>
> FOURTH BROTHER, He is a middle westerner, and has never lived in New York. Hearing rumors the unemployed are treated better here, he boards an eastbound freight. Arriving, he registers, and the first day of his visit, gets warm underwear, an overcoat, a pair of shoes, and in the newly acquired outfit, encounters his astonished, raggedly clothed brother.

Such unequal treatment provided fuel for critics of the program, but it also illustrates the laudable attempt being made to alleviate some of the transient's woes.[58]

7

The Federal Transient Program in New York State II, 1933-35

For as long as the issue of transient care had been contemplated one suggestion kept repeating itself: consolidate unattached transient men in work camps where physical and emotional rehabilitation could be realized through hard work and a clean and healthy environment. General William Booth, founder of the Salvation Army, had made such a proposal in 1904, and Edmund Kelly raised it again in 1908 as a means to "eliminate the tramps."[1] By 1933 many social workers had come to agree that this would be the best way to provide relief and rehabilitation for transient men. Not only would the transient benefit from the healthy atmosphere of the rural camp sites and the elixir of hard work and companionship, but the change of environment, it was hoped, would encourage the restoration of self-respect. Fortunately for the supporters of the proposal, Hopkins agreed. An integral part of the Federal Transient Program from the beginning was to encourage states to explore the possibility of transient camps—the cost of which would be totally reimbursed by the program. On April 28, 1934, Hopkins gave added encouragement to the plan in FERA Bulletin T-42. The further development of a camp program for transients was referred to as the most satisfactory method of meeting the problem of the unattached male transient population. With this added stimulus, the 95 federal camps then in operation in March 1934 nearly doubled to 189 by July 1934. All but five of the states cooperating in the Federal Transient Program operated at least one camp: California topped the list with twenty-eight.[2] The establishment of transient camps provided the third type of transient care facility.

In New York State a network of camps was established shortly after the federal government gave the green light for the state's transient program. In February of 1934 a gang of twelve men broke through the winter snow at Bear Mountain Park to begin construction of what was to become the first federally funded transient camp in the state, Camp Roosevelt. Within five months, a working camp complete with army-type barracks, running water, and a sewage system stood where only an old shack had been before.[3] This process was repeated six times more as pioneering bands of men trooped into the parks, forests, and reserves of New York State and pooled their skills to build homes out of the rough and primitive environs. Within the first six months of 1934, Camp Greenhaven (Dutchess County), Elks Park (Port Jervis), Camp Saratoga (Saratoga Springs), St. Johnsville (St. Johnsville), Stony Brook (Dansville) and Camp Frontier (North Collins) were complete and operating. Eight more camps were set up along the southern tier in July 1935 to serve as emergency work units in assisting in clean-up operations resulting from disasterous floods that had inundated the region.

In anticipation of community objections and to allay suspicion, each project was preceded by a careful information campaign directed at nearby communities. The initial announcement of each project was accompanied by guarantees that the men were "safe," that they were only seeking a chance to work, and that the work they would be doing would be to the benefit of the community. In Saratoga Springs, for example, it was carefully explained that the camp population would be composed of men whose wanderings were the result of a persistent search for employment, not chronic bums or tramps; that the men who were registered in the program by the state were in fact, "characteristically American and in many instances of surprisingly good antecedents"; and that all had already received physicals and Wasserman tests and were, therefore, not a threat to community health. The men were there, it was further explained, to landscape park property and to build picnic sites, paths, and even a golf course. None of these projects, it was stressed, would create any competition with local labor since these were jobs that would not normally be undertaken by the community. In case one still had his doubts, it was added that the men would "occupy their spare time in the camps" and that "strict discipline" would be maintained at all times. Furthermore, the camps would be purchasing their food and supplies locally.[4] In light of the depressed economy, this could be the clincher.

Publicity campaigns, however, were not enough to totally dispel the fears and suspicions of communities which still felt that the state was dumping bums and tramps in their backyards. Only the men themselves could convince the community through their hard work and good conduct that they were deserving of the recommendations offered on their behalf by the State Transient Division. In many communities and with many individuals they were able to do just that. In short time the men at Camp Frontier had won over the community and were even competing at baseball with local teams in the vicinity.[5] In other places, however, the relationship was never an easy one, and numerous contemporary accounts comment on community hostility as one factor in the eventual liquidation of the whole project.

In return for their new homes, the men were expected to contribute their labor both in the operation of the camp and in the outside projects promised the community. In the very beginning most of the men's time was taken up in building the camps from the ground up or renovating existing buildings for camp use. After the initial construction projects were completed, the men were expected to contribute to the maintenance of the camp and the duties required in feeding and sheltering the camp population. At Camp Frontier, for example, mechanics, blacksmiths, carpenters, plumbers, and various other skilled and unskilled tradesmen and laborers worked in their respective shops, repairing and maintaining camp tools and equipment, as well as building and landscaping the grounds. Cleaning dormitories and kitchens and guarding the grounds were among the jobs of others. A number of the camp's population were engaged in jobs directly serving their fellow men. Cooks, waiters, cobblers, barbers, tailors and laundrymen alike kept up the health and appearance of the men. Other self-maintenance projects included the raising of vegetables and poultry to supplement the camp's food supplies. A noticeable weight gain among the residents attested to their effectiveness.[6] "In the final analysis," the Governor's Commission reported, "the camps were operated to keep every transient interested in some camp function that would tend to make him believe that he was earning his keep."[7]

In addition to helping run the camp, the men were also expected to work from thirty to thirty-six hours per week on various outside projects. In many cases transient labor was used to improve state parks and develop recreational facilities. Again, the projects were carefully selected so as not to compete with local labor and fan the flames of community suspicion. The men at Camp Saratoga, for example, contributed valuable man-hours to the development of a park system to compliment the multi-million dollar facilities of the Saratoga Spa. The men constructed water and pipe lines, filled in stump holes, and cleared bush and wood to construct foot trails for hikers.[8] Transients also contributed their services to nearby state institutions. Camp Frontier provided services for Gowanda State Hospital while Camp Greenhaven served Hudson State Farm. In all, it was estimated that approximately 90 percent of the men in camp were working, as opposed to about 25 percent in the city centers. Of the time spent in work, the largest percentage went to the daily maintenance chores of office work, farm work, wood supply, and personal services. The rest of the time, approximatley 50 percent, was divided between community work, property improvements and the production of consumer goods.[9] A later study by TERA estimated that during the transient camp project, New York State had benefited to the extent of approximately seven million man-hours, most of which contributed to the beauty or utility of public properties.[10] The work provided by the transients did more than just beautify the vicinity and leave a lasting legacy in the state's parks and recreational sites. When local communities saw the positive value of the work being performed and observed the men at work, much good was done to break down local resistance and to dispel the negative image of good-for-nothing loafers living off of Uncle Sam. From one camp came the good news that initially hostile public opinion that had typecast the camp population as "professional Knights of the Open Road" now "realizes that this is far from true and that by far the majority of the enrollment are men who have been responsible, self-sustaining, and worthwhile citizens." This change in attitude was attributed to the satisfactory conduct of the men and the positive contribution they had made to the surrounding park areas. The men in Schenectady also won themselves some very positive goodwill when they took on a special project repairing broken toys for the children of the poor at Christmas. "With no other pay than the satisfaction of giving some underprivileged child the chance to have enjoyment that would otherwise be denied him," the local press reported, the men donated selfless hours, after a full day's work, to complete the project in time for Santa's appointed rounds.[11] Also indicative of a changing attitude and appreciation of their neighbors was the protest heard when the liquidation of the camp project was announced. Many of the same communities that had complained the loudest about the establishment of the camps now became their chief supporters. In St. Johnsville, for example, the town board adopted a resolution requesting that Hopkins keep the camp open until such time as all projects therein were completed.[12]

More important than public opinion, perhaps, was the opinion that the transient held of himself. Egos and self-esteem, badly beaten by months and even years of unemployment, were bolstered by the sense of accomplishment that comes from a job well done. "Work is the real medicine of the camp," Gertrude Springer reported to her readers after personally touring several camps in New York State. But, she made it very clear, "busy-work is no good. Leaf-raking does not fool these men." When they work they want to know that something constructive is being accomplished, and with that they will receive the "medicine," the self-satisfaction that comes from their labor. "Given useful, constructive work, calling for personal ingenuity, with definite measures of progress and a modicum of outside appreciation," she explained, "they will toil tireless and enthusiastically." As an example she shared the comments of one worker among a gang she found, long after quitting time, who were trying to complete a rock-lined, sand pathway through the woods to a lake. Sweating under his heavy labor, he explained, "Want to finish it before Sunday when a lot of folks go through here. . . .Nobody could get to the lake before. Bet a lot of 'em never knew it was here."[13] This man was working for a purpose, and he knew his efforts would be appreciated. This was something that few city shelters could offer the men, but it was something, as Schubert recognized, that was vitally needed to keep them from wandering and to restore their sense of self-worth.

In return for their labor the men received room and board. The army-type barracks they constructed were often quite primitive, but they were warm and dry, unlike the previous sleeping arrangements many had known, and one's neighbor was usually clean and sober. Food was generally plentiful; the quality, however, depended greatly on the experience and talent of the man chosen to play chef. On the day of her surprise visit to Camp Roosevelt, Springer dined with the men on a meal of roast beef and potatoes, string beans, cole slaw, canned pineapple, bread, butter, coffee and milk, "with seconds for anyone who said the word."[14] This was not necessarily the case at all camps at all times. There were a sufficient number of complaints about food addressed to Albany and Washington to warrant suspicion that not everyone shared meals such as described by Springer.[15] The men also received a small cash allowance of one to three dollars per week to buy personal items, to pay for barbering, laundering, and tailoring services, to go into town for a movie or a drink, or to save up to purchase a front. Very emphatic efforts were made by camp directors to make it clear to the men that this allowance represented relief not pay. The distinction was an important one because as pay these few dollars were in no way equal to the amount of work performed. The camp directors Springer talked with referred to the weekly allowance as the weak link in the program. "How can you retrain men in work habits," explained one director, "without the psychology of the pay envelope, without recognizing the principle of honest pay for honest work."[16]

It was recognized early in the program that the free time of the transient far exceeded the amount of work available to fill it. To prevent this time from becoming wasted in idle lounging, a great deal of consideration was given to recreation. In this aspect of the program the camps had a decided advantage over the city centers. The location of the camp, often in a park or similar rural setting, provided the necessary space for organized athletics: baseball, football, soccer, and so forth. In addition, the camps were often built with recreational and lounging facilities in mind. Unlike the make-do recreation rooms and/or lobbies of the city shelters, rooms were specifically built and decorated to create true "living rooms." In three or four camps recreation rooms large enough to be used as gymnasiums were available. In some communities local YMCA's also opened their doors to campers. Many camps had radios, pianos, checker boards, cards, boxing gloves, horseshoes, ping-pong, tennis courts, croquet, darts, shuffle board, bingo, and billiards, to help occupy the idle hours in a constructive manner.

Despite the best organized efforts, some men preferred their solitary hobbies. A man at Camp Greenhaven, for example, took to spending his spare time adorning the tops of stone walls with bits of stone and cement reminiscent of the Mayan ruins he had seen during his travels in Central America. Another at Camp Roosevelt worked endless hours with bits of scraps and odds and ends constructing the likeness of one of the ships he had sailed on in better times.[17] Others preferred lounging and reading in quiet or swapping tales about their adventures on the road.

Another outlet for one's creative impulses could be found working on or contributing to the camp newspaper. Each camp published a paper, usually a few mimeographed pages, that reported on events around camp and local gossip, shared some jokes and stories, most of which related to the experiences of the road, and displayed the art work, prose and poetry of those men who were so inclined. In most cases the camp director served as editor while the men supplied the content and saw to its collation, printing, and distribution. The tone of the papers, their humor, the men's good-natured ribbing of each other and their new homes says a lot about the camaraderie and sense of shared experience and common goals of each camp.

Finally, some camps experimented with educational programs ranging from on-site lectures and college credit course at neighboring institutions to occupational training and modified apprenticeships. Such endeavors were designed not only to fill the idle hours but to help prepare the men for reentry into the job market. In the New York camps purely academic programs were usually not as successful as vocational courses that clearly exhibited their practical usefulness. The men showed real enthusiasm in those courses that could be translated into jobs outside. In one New York camp, for example, a course in radio "resulted in strangely contrived receivers all over the place," while another in motor mechanics led to the construction of a jerry-rigged "weird looking vehicle" made from bits and pieces of abandoned wrecks about camp which "by some miracle actually ran."[18]

While the camps were most often out of sight, being located in isolated regions, well outside of town, they were not out of mind. Many people, out of curiosity over the experiment, because of a vested interest in the project, or due to concern over the proximity of a camp to their community, were concerned about the behavior of the men in camp. Some of their most frequent questions were answered for Gertrude Springer by the director of Camp Greenhaven. When asked about discipline, he responded simply. "They know what is expected of them and they accept the routine and go along with it." Most often, he explained, the men had their own "way of dealing with bad actors." "If a man had dirty personal habits or is objectionable for more serious reasons," he explained, "you can trust his bunk-house mates to deal with him. A persistent course of snakes in the bed is, I am told, highly efficacious." More specifically, for minor infractions of the rules, the offender was subject to a hearing or court-martial which meted out penalties ranging from demotions, loss of privileges, reduced allowance, to the most extreme penalty, return to the city shelter. For steady or more serious crimes the camp relied on the local authorities to deal with the guilty party.[19]

Another frequently expressed concern was about prevalence of drunkenness among the men. Some local communities envisioned camps filled with wild inebriates just waiting to be loosed upon their towns. While all participants in the camp projects recognized and admitted that drunkenness did occur, opinion varied as to the extent and seriousness of the problem. Ruth Lerrigo, who was herself a staunch supporter of the program, still had to report that from her personal observations the problem was widespread and "almost impossible to control." Robert Wilson agreed as to the seriousness of the problem and the negative effect that alcoholism could have not only on community relations but also on the individual and the morale of the men with whom he lived, but, after touring numerous transient centers and camps nationwide, he found the problem to be no greater than in any other isolated all-male environment such as an army camp or construction site.[20]

The director at Greenhaven recognized that some of his men had a problem with alcohol, but he did not see it as a particularly severe problem for the camp, and, furthermore, he understood it. "Think of the way these men have lived," he explained. "Liquor has been their only escape and God knows they still have enough to escape from." Most seasoned drinkers or habitual drunks stayed away from the camps. After all one could not get very far on one dollar a week. Those that did get drunk had to stay out of the camp until they sobered up. "We draw the line," however, "at the second offense." Such offenders had to leave. And they did go. "We lost a swell cook that way not long ago—used to be a chef in a Philadelphia country club—but he would get drunk and raise merry Cain in camp, so he had to go back to the shelter."[21]

Another concern related to the isolated, all-male camps was the incidence of homosexuality. Not many, however, addressed the question openly and publicly. Springer did not ask the camp directors she interviewed; Schubert did not include the question in his tablulations. Yet homosexual relationships were part of the hobo/tramp culture, and they did occur with apparent frequency in the very jungles from which these men often came. Both Box-Car

Bertha and Tom Kromer accepted this conduct as part of the culture within which they traveled. Kromer admitted to such a relationship himself. Thomas Minehan gave scholarly confirmation to their stories. Despite the promiscuity of their female traveling companions, he explained, the disproportionate number of girls and women on the road were not sufficient to the demand. Therefore, "boys and men denied natural sex outlets turn to other less approved ones," including homosexuality. Most often this relationship involved a younger boy, "the lamb," being lured into an illicit relationship by an older bum or "wolf". Sometimes these relationships were mutually enjoyed; other times they represented a form of slavery. Kenneth Allsop, in his comprehensive history of the tramp in America, *Hard Travellin'*, confirmed all of these contemporary accounts showing homosexuality to be a common feature of this subculture. He also implied that the fact that only 6 percent of the men registered in the federal program were married, and that even those were at least temporarily separated from their wives, perhaps had some bearing on the whys and wherefores of this question.[22] Contemporaries, aware of this persuasion in the hobo culture, feared its transference to the transient population. They were especially concerned about the effect on young men and boys. Robert Wilson studied the problem at the sites he visited and included a section on dealing with homosexuality in the Travelers Aid handbook that he was preparing at the time. As with alcoholism, Wilson pointed out, homosexuality can occur in any insulated, one-sex group. The fact that it occurred in transient camps, where the men are isolated from normal contact with women, should be expected. He did not find, however, through correspondence and conversation with camp directors and/or shelter supervisors, that it occurred with any "alarming frequency" or in any greater proportion than in construction camps or army barracks.[23] This final answer, for all intents and purposes, should have settled all questions about the transients' behavior. One could expect them to act like any other group of men would act in similar situations.

In return for the opportunities offered by the camps, the transients did what they could to express their gratitude and contribute to the local communities. The true test of the transients' gratitude was to come in mid-summer 1935. In July the southern tier of New York State experienced severe flooding. Farm lands in Elmira, Binghamton, Bath, Ithaca, and the surrounding areas were heavily damaged and in need of emergency relief, clean-up and rehabilitation. Terming the extent of the damage a disaster, Governor Lehman turned to the federal government for aid. FDR responded by informing the governor that twenty-five hundred persons currently on FERA relief rolls were being assigned to the area to assist in the emergency. In his telegram FDR explained that transient labor was to make up a large portion of this aid, rather than the Civilian Conservation Corps that had been requested. "In order to get around the difficulty of using persons in the Civilian Conservation Corps on private ground in the flood area," the president explained, "the Federal Emergency Relief Administration have worked out arrangements whereby transients and other persons on relief will be concentrated in that area."[24]

The fear of another disastrous flood, a flood of transients, set off immediate reactions in upstate New York. Sharp criticism was leveled against the plan by Congressman Bert Lord who complained to Roosevelt that his constituents were "thoroughly dissatisfied" over the failure of the federal government to give the stricken area the labor force it needed. By using transients rather than the CCC, he claimed, the government was creating "an unnecessary police problem." Republican State Chairman Melvin C. Eaton added that the use of transients would cause the influx of thousands of transients into the southern tier counties which would add to the "difficulties and unpleasantness" of the "harassed farmers." "To me," he asserted, "it looks more like an effort at colonization than anything else." A few days later FDR notified Lehman that CCC workers would join in the flood relief work; however, the transients had already willingly accepted the challenge to pay back the state for its faith in them and to prove their worth to the rest of the community.[25]

Without waiting for orders from Washington, the state transient director had placed the various district directors on alert as soon as the flood broke on July 8th. All facilities of the Transient Division were to be put at the disposal of the local community. By the early hours of the next morning old army trucks, vintage 1917, filled with transient volunteers from the surrounding transient bureaus and camps moved out toward the flood area. Within days their numbers topped five hundred as additional volunteers continued to arrive from as far away as Buffalo. Six camps were set up in the area in the two weeks following the flood — weeks before the controversy over their use began to stir. Makeshift tent camps, abandoned buildings, and empty factories were used as camp sites in Hornell, Bath, Smithville Flats, Montour Falls, Ithaca, Whitney Point, and Sidney. From these sites the transient labor force performed invaluable service to the surrounding communities working day and night "opening roads to traffic, constructing temporary by-paths where bridges had been washed out, carrying out wreckage, and removing debris and pollution from private property, thus mitigating a real menace to public health and safety."[26]

The hard work and heroics of the men did much to reverse the initial hostility of the stricken communities and won acclaim for the transient group as a whole. Under the title "Transient Services Volunteered On All Fronts During Disaster; Rescue, Feed, House Residents," *The Evening Tribune* of Hornell sang the praises of its heroes. "As muddy water swirled through Hornell streets to bring panic into many homes," the paper dramatized, "one organized force of men mustered to the emergency, doing rescue work and carrying food, water and other provisions into stricken areas." The group of which they spoke was a volunteer force of approximately two hundred transient men from the local transient center. The men manned their trucks to deliver the first food supplies to the stranded; they took to boats to rescue marooned citizens; they opened their barracks to house the homeless; and they even shared their food supply with the community. Individual stories of men wading through neck-high waters leading boats filled with refugees, climbing to second-story windows to rescue hysterical women and childen, and transporting the ill to medical facilities, filled the article. The mayor of the village of Montour Falls expressed the gratitude of his community in a letter to Thomas Cotton at TERA with a copy to the transient center in Elmira from which most of the transient contingent working in the village had come. He also expressed the hope that they would stay until the cleanup was finished. By August 13th Hopkins was able to report in good conscience to FDR that the work performed by the transients in the crisis was satisfactory; in fact, it had in many cases "assumed heroic proportion."[27]

Praise of the transient continued throughout the cleanup period that followed. In September 1935 the *Steuben Courier* recounted the rehabilitative work done by the residents of Camp Bath on the surrounding farms and the appreciation that their labors brought. When a representative of the Transient Division surveyed the area, he made informal inquiry as to the opinions and reactions of those persons who had been served. "In every instance . . . nothing but earnest praise has been given, both for the behavior of these men from the four points of the compass, and for the willingness and application they put into their efforts."[28] The police problem anticipated by Congressman Lord never materialized.

The appreciation for the flood relief work was mutual. Homeowners, businessmen, farmers and local officials were thankful for the help offered by the transient workers, and the transients were grateful for the opportunity to prove themselves and for the reception they received in the communities where they worked. The house paper at Elmira, named "Floodlite" in recognition of the relief work being done in Montour Falls by its clientele, reported that visitors from the site "have nothing but praise for the treatment they have received." "The men have comfortable billets and good wholesome food and are about as congenial a group of men that can be found on any job." Their help, added camp director Andrew Johnson, would not soon be forgotten by the communities they served.[29]

After the emergency passed, the transients remained at the request of Governor Lehman to assist the Soil Conservation Service in their long-term flood control and soil erosion program for the area. The task was given federal transient project status by FERA and a commitment of fifteen hundred to two thousand men was made to the site.[30]

Less than one year later the men were back to their emergency work as spring floods threatened to ravage the area once again. Approximately two-thirds of the enrollees at Elks Park answered the call of Port Jervis city officials and spent two days pumping out the cellars of residences and stores and clearing catch-basins in the city. The men, "visibly showing their worth as workers," received many compliments from businessmen, homeowners and organizations throughout the city. In Marathon, quick work by the men of the nearby camp prevented the collapse of the Cordland Highway Bridge over which Route 11, the main highway from Syracuse to Binghamton, passed. Against swiftly running water the men worked day and night for two days shoring up the bridge with sand bags and rocks. A letter from the mayor of Marathon was duly received commending the men for saving the bridge and highway.[31]

Even with such community service as exemplified in New York State by this emergency relief work and similar work performed across the country by transients in a nationwide network of camps, the camps did have their critics.

Among the critics were those who scoffed at the whole project as nothing but a string of government supported resorts for indigent "ne'er-do-wells." Such critical voices complained that the shelters, recreational facilities, and three square meals a day were nothing more than a government dole that supported and encouraged transiency at the taxpayers' expense. The men who utilized the camps, they claimed, were not the true unemployed looking for work. They were rather a motley group of fugitives, misfits, handicapped, bums, hobos and tramps. Among such critics was a former director from an unnamed camp who told his story in a two-part article for *The Saturday Evening Post.* Your chances of participating in the program, he claimed, would be "much enhanced if you are gorgeously tattooed, take food with your knife and use the double negative." The same individual likened his job to that of the man who ran an insane asylum, chain gang, or zoo. Describing the camp he directed as an Alice-in-Wonderland world, a glorified jungle, and/or a three-ring circus, he doubted there was any purpose behind the program other than the effort of the Democratic administration to remove these victims of the depression from the public eye. As to rehabilitation, such critics said there was none. Instead of rehabilitating the genuine unemployed, explained another disillusioned camp director, the camps were being used by clients as a convenient stopover where one could expect reasonable care while on the road or a place to hibernate during the winter.[32]

For every one of these critical reports, however, there came many more positive ones praising the men, their attitude, and what they had thus far accomplished. From Camp Frontier came word that the transients there were "willing and faithful" and capable of "accomplishing a great deal." "Their general behavior," reported the camp director, "has not been troublesome." The director at Camp Roosevelt with whom Springer spoke gave no indication of an Alice-in-Wonderland atmosphere at his camp. The men, he reported, were hard workers who appreciated the opportunity the camp afforded them. Revealing the secret of a good camp, he explained, "as long as we are fair they are fair." In Hornell, a painting of the flood-ravaged streets of that community, painted by one Otis Scott, artist-transient, hung in the City Hall as quiet testiment to, and appreciation of, what the transient was capable of.[33]

Some grumbling could also be heard from within the camps. Not all transients serviced by the program were duly appreciative of Uncle Sam's hospitality. Periodic complaints about food, work, discipline, and bad management were addressed to both Hopkins and FDR. Most complaints were easily answered by investigation at the local level. Mr. A. A. M., for example, complained to Washington about the quality and quantity of the food served at Camp Greenhaven. The men, he explained, had refused to work on the day he wrote because of the poor breakfast served them. "It is a pity for the government to abuse these poor unfortunates to such an extent as to make us go hungry day in and day out and then make us work at heavy labor. In the name of all humanity please help us all." The matter was satisfactorily explained a few weeks later in a report submitted by the supervisor of Greenhaven. The breakfast, in question, he explained, had followed an "imaginary" epidemic of dysentery" that affected several men. "As is customary in cases of dysentery, our chef furnished a lighter meal than usual the following morning." The "work strike" resulted when these men, prompted by agitators and an ominous-looking sky, decided not to work. The men were put on the prescribed diet and the agitators were asked to leave the camp. Apparently the men were not above goldbricking on a wet morning.[34] A complaint from Stony Brook received a similarly quick dismissal. The complainant informed Hopkins that he had been beaten and locked up and then forced to leave the camp without receiving the allowance due him. In reply to an official inquiry, the Stony Brook director explained that the complainant had been incarcerated to protect him from the wrath of the rest of the men in camp who wanted to impose their own judgment on him for shaving all the hair off the camp dog. He was later arrested for public intoxication in the town of Dansville.[35]

While most complaints could be attributed to chronic malcontents, each was investigated. Field investigators visited the camps without prior warning to see conditions for themselves. Sometimes they found the complaints legitimate. From Elks Park, for example, came a complaint that the chef and foreman were embezzling supplies and cutting rations to line their own pockets. The complainant appealed to Hopkins: "Please investigate so the poor men will get something to eat. It is a shame the way things are going in the camp. . . . Investigate Mr. Hopkins or there will be no camp." Hopkins did initiate an investigation, and it was found that the complaint was legitimate. The chef in question was subsequently arrested.[36] Some complainants did not wait around for a remedy. After trying no less than three transient camps and never receiving the suit of heavy underwear he requested, John M. informed FERA, "I am quitting my dollar a week job and am returning back to the road rather than freeze and starve in the F. E. R. A. camps."[37]

It is important to point out emphatically that complaints from within the camps did not reflect the typical response of the men nor should the complainants be seen as representative of the camp's population. The number of complaints is minimal compared to the number of men who participated in the program. FERA records contain a mere three file folders of complaints. Of these, only a fraction are from men in the camps or are in any way directed toward those projects. This number pales to insignificance when one considers that thousands of potential complainants were served by the program. The majority of transients who participated in the camp program were more than willing to endure the primitive conditions and to accept that supplies would be limited, personnel inexperienced, and, occasionally, the food bad in return for the opportunities afforded them by the camps to work and to prove themselves.

While conditions were primitive and the work was hard, the men generally appeared appreciative. Most camp directors reported in glowing terms about the attitude of the men and the rehabilitative effect of the new environment. Camp newspapers reflected this appreciation. After examining twenty-seven such papers from across the nation, William Weathersby and Emily Smith reported:

> Almost without exception the papers comment on the thankfulness of the men for having a means of living, a chance for a job, a chance for constructive education, appreciation of the new policy of allowing them to stay in a place instead of forcing them to move on as was customary formerly, and on the general improvement in transient camps.[38]

The director at Camp Greenhaven had a file full of letters of appreciation and gratitude from men who had been at the camp earlier and had now returned to work in the private sector. A number expressed the wish to return for a visit for old time's sake.[39]

For the individual men, the camp had decided advantages over the city shelters from which they had been sent. The impersonality of long lines and mass handling were eliminated. Turn over was less frequent; thus, more familiarity among the population was possible. The men could identify with their environment much more easily than in the city shelters. "While the city shelter tended to be only a place to eat and sleep, most of the men in the camp seemed to take a pride in the place and its improvement." Representatives of the Governor's Commission who visited the camps thus found the men "to be much more of a self-respecting, clean-shaven, alert, responsible, and hard working group" than their fellows in the city shelters.[40] Other visitors concurred.

When Dr. Schubert visited Camp Frontier in the rural environs of Erie County to collect more data to complement his study of the city transient, he found to his pleasure a picturesque scene complete with a large white main building set on the side of a hill, outbuildings scattered on the rolling hillside, and even a babbling brook to complete the picture. Within this environment Schubert found many factors to appeal to the men including

> the lure and peacefulness of the forest and open country with the opportunity to obtain plenty of unpolluted air and sunshine,' . . . activities which one is not able to engage in within the confines of a city, and . . . a chance to better one's health by wholesome physical activity.

Inside he found the camp to be "to a large extent a community within itself."[41] Gertrude Springer was equally impressed on her visits to Camps Roosevelt and Greenhaven. While she had reservations about the social services available at the camps, she was greatly impressed by the men and the work they were doing, by the facilities they built and maintained, and by the dedication and common sense attitude of the camp director. Lewis Hine brought back the pictorial documentation to confirm her observations and to illustrate the resulting article for *Survey Graphic*, "Men Off the Road."[42]

The easy dismissal of the foregoing handful of complaints and the evidence of good work and appreciation should not overshadow the fact that the camp experiment did have some serious inherent problems. A number of these were created by the very distance that separated city and camp. On the one hand, this distance was a positive feature of the program in that it removed the transient from the negative influences of the city with its "burlesque shows, flop houses, deteriorating buildings, cheap gambling-joints, and questionable diversions." However, it also tended to atomize the individual by removing him from the normal environment with its natural relationships and opportunities for reintegration into society and putting him in an artificial isolated one where standards may have been higher, food better, and idle time constructively occupied, but reabsorption into the community was further delayed.[43] Succinctly put by one participant: "They cared for us first in city shelters, raising the standard of physical care. Then they shunted us away from the cities into isolated camps on the fringe of civilization, when most of us were city workers and city dwellers." A survey of camp newspapers shows an oft-repeated question: "Why isolate us as a group and call us transients? Are we not citizens of the United States?"[44]

The distance also removed them from the key job markets in the cities which was what usually had drawn them to a given city in the first place. The reluctance of some of the most physically fit of the transient population to participate in the program made this problem glaringly apparent to the administration. Looking back on the camp experiment from a later date, Hopkins explained, "It was neither surprising nor to be regretted that the more enterprising remained in camp for a short time only and then set forth to try their luck again."[45] TERA statistics show that the average stay in a camp in New York State was approximately three weeks. At Camp Frontier most transients stayed between one and ten weeks, with older men staying significantly longer than the younger ones. Rumors of jobs usually lured away the youngest and most capable.[46] The dollar a week cash allowance promised by the camps provided little inducement for such men to tarry longer. Many more refused to leave the city and with it the last hope of finding employment.

It was also apparent that, while the optimistic, physically fit shunned the camps because of the distance from the city, others used the camp's isolation as an escape. For some, the camp, with its adequate shelter, substantial food, companionship, and security, could become a haven or a crutch which, in the long run, would make transition back into the community and the resumption of individual responsibility all the more difficult. In such cases, the philosophy of the camp experiment would be subverted with the camp becoming an end in itself rather than a bridge to reintegration. "It was the men who became so well adjusted to the secure, if limited, life of a transient camp," Hopkins explained, "who hoped, like certain soldiers, that the war would never end."[47] In such cases, the cure could be worse than the disease.

The Governor's Commission recognized similar problems. They found the same reluctance of the able-bodied to leave the labor market, as well as the same detachment from the community of those who did participate in the program. The main reason that Camp Frontier could not always remain filled, Schubert had explained, was because the large number of factory workers who came to Buffalo looking for jobs did not want to leave their places in line outside the factory door. In addition, the commission noted, the distance also severed the relationship between client and social worker. Once the transient was removed from the jurisdiction of the intake bureau, he could remain uncounseled for the duration. Thus, an important rehabilitative service was neglected. Part of the problem was due to the lack of trained personnel in the camps. Where such personnel was available, the multiple duties of camp supervision, record keeping, and registration left little time for a one-on-one social service program. As a result, men who came into the camp with problems were not always sought out and counseled. Instead, their problems persisted while the individual became more estranged from family and job ties and perhaps lost settlement elsewhere. To compensate, the commission strongly recommended that, if the state chose to continue this experiment, it must locate camps on the periphery of urban centers.[48]

Another problem of the camp experiment from the social worker's perspective was the lack of a constructive release policy that would ease reentry into normal society. "What of the day," it was asked, "when a man, his body sound and healthy, his initiative and self-confidence recovered, is ready to take hold of his own life again?" As the program was designed nothing was done at this point. "At present he just goes." It was left to the individual to make his own final adjustment after leaving camp, which, of course, was no guarantee that that adjustment would be made and that he would not simply take to the road once again.[49]

Another problem that plagued the program throughout was that community acceptance was never complete. While there are many good examples of how the men won over their neighbors, there still were pockets of resistance, often among the influential citizenry. Some communities continued to worry about their safety and the negative public image that came with having camps in close proximity. As late as the spring of 1936, an influential combination of residents at Saratoga Springs was requesting the closing of the camp there. According to Chamber of Commerce president, Paul McGirr, the camp was having a detrimental effect on the newly developed, multi-million dollar Saratoga Spa, despite the fact that the transients had contributed their labor to that very same facility. People who had used the park freely in the past, he explained, were curtailing their visits because they knew such a camp existed there and they did not feel the same security. "There is always the possibility of our guests being molested and if this should happen it would cause ill feelings toward Saratoga Springs." The Junior Chamber of Commerce, the Junior Civic League, and even the Girl Scouts seconded his concerns. The president of nearby Skidmore College added that his girls did not feel secure "going and coming in the environs of a town where a camp made up of strangers of unknown character is located." He promised to discourage students from traveling in that area as long as the camp remained. So as not to be mistaken or appear ungrateful, McGirr explained that they were not adverse to having a camp somewhere outside of the city "as long as it does not come in close contact with the public," that is, out of sight, out of mind.[50] Other communities worried about property values. Congressman James Meed, for example, explained to Hopkins that residents in the vicinity of a proposed Beckman Camp on the Hudson "felt that the establishment of the camp would be a serious injury to the value of surrounding real estate." Therefore, they were voicing their objections to the proposal.[51] Finally, many local county welfare commissioners resisted the idea of locating transient camps within their jurisdictions. Such hesitation was partially due to the traditional fear of strangers, and a natural reluctance to have such persons imported into their districts. More practical, however, was the ever present fear of added relief expenses. To begin with, the FERA had specifically excluded hospital or other institutional medical care from federal funding except in emergencies. If a transient required any such care, the local district was responsible for the expense. In addition, the local relief official realized that the federal government could withdraw from the program any time it chose, leaving behind scores of unsettled indigents who would then, according to the Public Welfare Law, once again become a local responsibility.

A final problem that was not usually addressed in the general jubilation over the camp experiment was the relatively small "drop in the bucket" that these camps represented. A few hundred camps nationwide could do little to assist a wandering population estimated to be in the hundreds of thousands. In New York State, where the program was heartily endorsed, a quick perusal of the statistics reveals the relatively limited nature of the experiment. As Table 8 illustrates, the peak number of persons served in camps was only 3,216 in September 1935, ironically the same month that orders were received to liquidate the program. (See Table 8, page 173). What these figures mean is that the great majority of the transient population was still huddled in the cities, being cared for in the same lodging houses, missions, and city shelters as before. The highly acclaimed camp program only aided a small minority of those in need.

A final evaluation of the camp program is difficult. The hopes were so high, the intent so laudable, and the undertaking so immense, that it is hard not to appreciate the planners and their product. Stories of men's heroics, lasting legacies of their work, evidence of the camaraderie they shared, the lifted spirits and restored bodies all attest to the success of the experiment. Yet, the critics, even friendly ones, cannot be easily silenced. The camps did have their problems. Perhaps the best final assessment should be left to a contemporary who knew the camps, their purpose, and their limitations intimately. In the final assessment, Robert Wilson wrote, "camps are not a panacea — social work has none."[52] They provided a much needed temporary expedient that relieved suffering and restored, if only momentarily, the bodies and spirits of men too long buffeted by rejection and a day-to-day existence. Like the city shelters, they were unable to provide what the men needed most — real jobs and real paychecks. The transient, like the rest of the country, had to wait for an end to the depression before the final solution could be realized. In the meantime, the camps were as good as one could get.

The final type of facility utilized by the transient program in New York State was designed to separate designated classes of transients from the general population and to remove them to sites where specified rehabilitation programs were employed — hence the name of the fourth and final facility, the experimental rehabilitation center. Again the word rehabilitation may be misleading. Those chosen to participate in the programs were selected specifically for their high degree of employability. Rehabilitation, in this case, meant preparation for reintegration into the same mainstream America from which they often came. The means of rehabilitation were often as simple as treating them as individuals and giving them the opportunity to restore their self-confidence, to freshen up their outward appearance, and to sharpen their skills. In other cases, retraining and educational opportunities were all that were needed. Two such

TABLE 8. Number of Cases Receiving Care in Transient Camps in the State of New York on the Last Day of Each Month*

Month	Number of Cases
1933	
November	0
December	15
1934	
January	82
February	148
March	288
April	318
May	373
June	456
July	708
August	936
September	1,149
October	1,305
November	1,384
December	1,377
1935	
January	1,392
February	1,410
March	1,357
April	1,377
May	1,393
June	2,211
July	1,973
August	2,907
September	3,216
October	2,650
November	2,562
December**	0

*(New York State, Governor's Commission on Unemployment Relief, *Public Relief for Transient and Non-Settled Persons in the State of New York*, Albany, 1936, p. 85.)
**Not all camps were liquidated at this time. Some were transferred to WPA and phased out within the next year.

facilities were operative in New York State during the Federal Transient Program: Hartford House, in New York City, and Hartwick Academy, located just outside of Cooperstown.

The select clientele served at Hartford House were white-collar transient men. The dual purpose of the program was to segregate this class of more employable men from the demoralizing atmosphere of the congregate care shelters, much as the Buffalo city project had done, and to provide them with the independence of private sleeping and eating accommodations and, when requested, vocational and/or personal counseling. Since the ultimate goal of the program was to facilitate a return to employment in the private sector, the project was specifically located in the city, in close proximity to the job market, thus distinguishing it from the camp program which segregated the men not only from the shelters but also from the city and its opportunities.

Men were selected to participate in the program at Hartford on the basis of their professional training and/or status before the crash. "We do not assert that every guest was an important personage," the editor of the house newspaper modestly conceded, "but a glance at the house records reveals a profusion of college degrees, colorful careers and impressive examples of adaptability in a competitive society."[53] These were, in other words, the most employable men of the transient population. A visitor from Travelers Aid concurred. On the day of her visit she found that, of the more than two hundred men registered, half had attended college, forty held college degrees (including eleven higher degrees), and all possessed special job skills. In this specific group there were ninety-one different job classifications represented ranging from accountant to aviator, from interior decorator to metallurgist, from wood carver to "soldier of fortune."[54]

The house itself, located in midtown New York behind the Ziegfeld Theatre, provided the nucleus around which this carefully selected grup congregated. The men lived in furnished rooms scattered in a six-block radius around the main building. Five or six men would be sheltered in the same hotel or boarding house; two or three would most likely share a room. In this way the men would retain some independence while taking the first steps back into the community. The men came to Hartford daily to receive their meals; interact with persons of similar background, education, and promise; receive vocational counseling and encouragement in their job hunting; or to simply enjoy a game of chess, read a book, or just sit back and relax in a friendly comfortable environment.

An important feature of the house was the positive attitude it generated. This was due in part to the concerted effort that was made by the staff to provide a pleasant, noninstitutional environment and a wide variety of diversions to fill in the idle hours between job interviews. The effort was appreciated. In the words of one Hartford client,

> The Lobby, with its bridge, chess and radio; the vaudeville shows; the dramatic performances of strolling actors; the cub Thespians rehearsing upstairs; the feverish discussion on art and literature in the library; the horseplay in the dining room when someone produces a Jack-in-the-box and lets it go pop; the mad scamperings of Teddy, the circus dog; the weepy glee clubs in dark places, especially on Saturday nights — these interludes go a long way toward reducing the strain of cornering a job in a big city.[55]

It was also due in large part to the positive attitude of the men themselves. The camaraderie they shared, the reinforcement they provided their peers, and their ability to laugh at each other and themselves all contributed to the therapeutically fresh atmosphere. This spirit still comes alive in the pages of the few surviving copies of the house newspaper, "The Hartford Huddle."

Written, compiled, and printed by and for the residents, the paper allows us a glimpse into the house and the lives of those it touched. The first issue of the first volume, for example, begins with an editorial on the philosophy of Hartford and a general appreciation of the efforts made to help each "to discover for himself his next favorable role in the changing order," euphemistically speaking, to find a job during the depression. The rest of the issue is filled with good natured banter, often at the expense of fellow residents; some not very good poetry; interesting little short stories based on the experiences of transient life, usually with a humorous twist; job notices and congratulations to those who landed the "big one;" and updates on the library collection, art classes, and the plans of the Activities Committee, all of which were contributed by the men themselves from the front cover cartoon to the theater review in back. The two page report by the Activities Committee reveals the surprising array of entertainment and recreational options available to the men. They could participate in handball, boxing, swimming, bridge and chess tournaments; join athletic teams; attend Broadway hits; take free dance lessons or dramatic classes; participate in choral groups or in the house play; or, if the mood struck them, they could even learn puppetry. All of these activities were designed, of course, not to provide a country club for transients but to allow the men some form of release from the rigors and frustrations of job hunting.[56]

What is probably most impressive about the paper is the sense of humor that permeates it from the opening editorial and its tongue-in-cheek cracks about procedures, interviews, and psychological testing; about coming down in life and what the bottom is like; and about each other's idiosyncrasies and pet peeves; to an illustrated Thanksgiving Day menu. Celery hearts én CWA, creamed chicken a'la Transient, roast turkey with TERA giblet gravy, local homeless potatoes, and cranberry sauce, NYC, may not be particularly witty or clever, but it is good fun. There is a sense of boyish pranksterism about the whole issue, a healthy, satirical quality that shows that the men had not lost their sense of humor and, more importantly, had not lost heart.[57]

Hartford House was classified technically as a rehabilitation center. The men, however, preferred and used the term reintegration. They were perfectly capable of solving their own problems by themselves. This was known by both the men and the staff. What they needed were jobs, and they looked for them daily. What Hartford provided was an interlude. The entire house invited a sense of optimism by creating a healing environment of security, comfort, and companionship, where past experiences of unemployment, lodging houses, and humiliating bread lines could be forgotten, and the temporarily discouraged man could work out his problems with a minimum of direction by staff social workers and psychologists. In short, the therapy of Hartford House was to "help a man help himself."

As to the effectiveness of the experiment, the Travelers Aid representative was informed that during the six months from April 1 through September 30, 1934, 386 men had secured permanent positions in the private sector. As to its overall success, the Governor's Commission reported a 50 percent placement rate. Considering that this was the depression, and that the preference for local labor remained, this was an amazing accomplishment. Attesting even more dramatically to its success was the disappointment and dismay of New Yorkers when it was rumored in 1935 that Hartford would be abandoned along with the rest of the transient program.[58]

In March 1935 the State Transient Division launched the second of its special rehabilitation experiments, Hartwick Academy, a school for transient young men and boys. Proponents of the project hoped that by separating this element of the transient population from the mainstream, removing them from city streets to a more secluded environment, and providing them with sound educational and vocational training in a familiar school setting, they could better prepare them for the job market and reintegration into society. Accordingly, the old Hartwick Seminary, near Cooperstown, New York, was selected as a favorable site and the admissions procedure began.

At full capacity the academy could enroll approximately one hundred students. All registered state and federal transients under the age of thirty were eligible to apply. Preference was given only to those applicants who showed "a sincere desire to learn and a willingness to work" and agreed to make a commitment of at least six months to their education. Once accepted students were offered a varied curriculum in vocational training including dairying, vegetable gardening, plumbing, stenography, typewriting, bookkeeping; common school subjects including reading, writing, and arithmetic; high school subjects leading to Regents' examinations; and college courses. In addition to their studies, the boys were also expected, as in all transient program projects, to contribute to the maintenance of the facilities. The students adhered to a rigorous schedule: up at 6:30 a.m.; classes morning and afternoon; and bed at 10:00 p.m. While school and work occupied a large portion of the daily schedule, planners did not forget the therapeutic value of recreation. Included in the original proposal for the school were plans for a clubroom supplied with ping-pong, checkers, chess and cards; for organized sports including baseball, volleyball, and track and field; for dramatics, music, and hobbies; as well as a library and a canteen. The program, schedule, and school activities at Hartwick, *The Survey* reported to its readers, bore "surprising resemblance to those of any well-organized 'prep' school."[59]

As an experiment in a decade of experimentation, Hartwick received more than its share of attention. The question of transient youth had been such a perplexing and disturbing one that any effort to combat the problem generated genuine interest. In the case of Hartwick, even the first lady was impressed and expressed an interest in seeing the operation for herself. Members of the Governor's Commission, after personally visiting the academy, commented favorably on the "important accomplishments" achieved in "developing individual and group responsibility, increasing morale, reducing turnover, and developing habits of mind which prepared the individual to find a job or to return to a former place of residence."[60] Unfortunately, Hartwick came late in the Federal Transient Program. Just six months after it opened its doors, the government announced that the entire program was to be liquidated. As he proceeded to comply with liquidation, Thomas Cotton confided to Elizabeth Wickenden, "to liquidate ordinary camps is bad enough but the closing of Hartwick . . . is really tragic." Despite the attempted intercession of friends like Cotton, the experiment at Hartwick ended in July 1936.[61]

Both the Hartford and Hartwick experiments represented individualized care at its best. Because of their specialized clientele and low client/staff ratios, they were able to provide the services that shelters, and even the camps, were incapable of. They suffered from neither the overcrowding and problems of congregate care that plagued the city shelters nor the isolation and artificial community that marred the camp experiments. But Hardford and Hartwick represented more than just better facilities; they also reflected an attitude. In both, the individual was treated with respect. His current status was accepted as an unfortunate consequence of the economic crisis and not as a reflection on the person, his character, or his abilities. The assistance the men and boys received was clearly not charity that required humble and humiliating submission. Each client knew, instead, that the objective of the program he was participating in was to provide him with the opportunity to grow and to succeed by his own volition. The only criticism that can be leveled at either is that more people could not share in the experience of these one-of-a-kind ventures. Hartford was only able to accommodate approximately two hundred men at a time while Hartwick could only enroll another one hundred, yet there were many more white collar men and trainable boys across the state who could have benefited from these highly individualized and amazingly successful programs. A second criticism is directed at the federal and state governments for allowing these short-lived, but highly advanced, experiments to expire with the Federal Transient Program.

The facilities and projects of the Federal Transient Program were used almost exclusively for unattached men. Families and unattached women were generally treated on an individual basis, often with little or no distinction being drawn between them and the local homeless. Even though this procedure, in effect, incorporated them in the general relief population, this aspect of the program still deserves a brief examination.

Families had presented a perplexing problem from the onset of the transient program. Families on the move, criss-crossing the country in broken-down jalopies, hitchhiking, and on foot, were already familiar when the FERA administrator first sat down to tackle the problem of transiency. Since it was not the intention of the lawmakers to further break down societal ties, it was apparent that a policy of separation and institutionalization would be more detrimental than helpful to these families and to the country. The chosen alternative, according to Hopkins, was to provide home relief, that is, outdoor rather than institutional relief, in cash or kind, to make up the differences between the individual family's needs and its income. "Shelter care for families," he emphasized, "was taboo." In the final analysis of the Federal Transient Division it was estimated that approximately 40 percent of the federal transient load, almost 250,000 people at peak, were cared for as family members.[62]

In New York State, with the exception of Buffalo, Rochester, and New York City, such care, consistent with federal policy, was given in the home relief divisions of the county departments of public welfare. The numbers of state and federal transient families cared for statewide ranged from a low of twenty-nine families in November 1933 when the program was initiated to 1,491 at the same time the next year, to a peak of 2,776 in September 1935, the month that liquidation began. In actuality, the statistical breakdown of costs of relief show that the transient family suffered little discrimination, if not some advantage, in the distribution of funds. In September 1935 the average transient family of 3.7 individuals in upstate New York received $29.95 per month while home relief families, averaging 4.2 persons, received $33.50.[63]

In the state's three largest cities separate branches of the local transient bureaus serviced both women and families. In Buffalo, the average daily load of families registered with this branch peaked in January 1935 at 240. According to Schubert's figures, most came from neighboring industrial states and were looking for employment in New York's industrial centers. Most would have settled down, he explained, but lack of legal settlement and family responsibility kept them moving. About one-half stayed in the Buffalo area at least four months before moving on again. New York City had a similar arrangement. A separate Service Bureau for Transient Families and

Women provided for family care. This arrangement was secured, however, more out of necessity than design. New York City had, long before the depression, abolished outdoor relief by local ordinance. Thus even local families could receive state relief under the Wicks Act only if they met the two-year state residency requirement. Therefore, it was legally impossible for the local welfare bureau to handle transient families as was being done throughout most of the state. Despite their segregation, however, transient families in New York City did receive adequate if not superior care. The Governor's Commission's report credited this branch of the city's transient program with providing "intensive service comparable to that of private case work agencies of high standard." The bureau, unrestrained by limited fundings, interagency conflicts, or legal settlement restrictions, could provide more for the individual needs than could the city's welfare system when it dealt with local homeless families. A transient family of 3.7 members, for example, received an average of $38.88 per month in September 1935 while the local family of 4.2 received $36.43 in home relief. The third city, Rochester, followed the example of her sister cities in providing special individualized assistance to this class of unfortunates. Overall, the treatment accorded the transient family across the state was comparable to, if not better than, that given the local homeless family.[64]

Next to the problem of roving bands of youthful transients, the second most common concern of the witnesses who appeared before the Cutting Hearings in early 1933, had been the plight of transient women, especially those under twenty-one. In his testimony before the Senate Committee Nels Anderson had expressed his belief that too little had been said to date about this 6 to 8 percent of the transient population. Their numbers were increasing proportionately more rapidly than those of the transient population in general; yet, he explained, there were fewer facilities available for them than there were for their male counterparts. Perhaps the lack of facilities explains why Dorothy Wysor was able to report to the same congressional representatives that "many young women and girls do not apply to the social agencies and therefore are without social protection." To remedy this situation most transient centers across the nation offered individualized care and outside relief for women transients. In New York State, with the same exceptions of Buffalo, Rochester, and New York City, women were referred to local relief bureaus for care comparable to that given local homeless women. In New York City each transient woman was provided with emergency shelter and interviewed by a trained caseworker. The caseworker determined whether the women should be placed in a public shelter, such as the women's annex of the city's municipal lodging house, or given home relief. "If there is a question of shelter versus home relief," she explained, "the woman is given the benefit of the doubt until the Bureau knows more about her situation." A handful of fortunate women received the opportunity to participate in an experimental camp program, Camp TERA, in Palisaides Interstate Park. This pet project of Eleanor Roosevelt served as a "rest camp for jobless young women in need of mental and physical rehabilitation." It was a much publicized venture. Pictures of girls swimming, picnicking, and playing decorated numerous pages of the media; yet, as with other experimental programs, its ability to reduce the problem of the homeless unattached woman was limited by its size and resources. Overall, the entire transient program for unattached females in New York State reached only 526 women in the peak month of September 1935.[65]

The various programs established for women and families suffered from many of the same shortcomings that beset the overall Federal Transient Program. Practice did not always conform with policy, and, despite the best of intentions, such programs were never able to reach all of the needy. These limitations, however, must be measured within the context of what the program was attempting to do and the short time it was given to realize its goals. Any program that attempts to meet an overwhelming social need, on a national scale, is subject to certain problems. Communications must be established, policy must be explained and tested, and local suspicions must be replaced with cooperation. In the process mistakes are made and errors of judgment occur. Experience often must become the guide. The transient program did indeed tackle a monumental task. It was not, however, given the time to "get the bugs out." Any assessment of the program must take this into consideration. The Federal Transient Program attempted to change attitudes and practices that were centuries old; yet it was only given two years to accomplish its task. In this short time, however, while all goals were not realized, the program did represent the federal government's recognition of its social responsibility for the nonresident needy, and a very healthy and mutually beneficial example of state-federal cooperation was provided as a precedent for the future.

Elks Park transient camp

Works Progress Administration print (No. 69N30101) in the National Archives

Rest and relaxation at Bear Mountain transient camp

Works Progress Administration print (No. 69N25189) in the National Archives

Elks Park transient camp baseball team
Works Progress Administration print (No. 69N25021) in the National Archives

Men from Stony Brook camp working on picnic site
Works Progress Administration print (No. 69N30101) in the National Archives

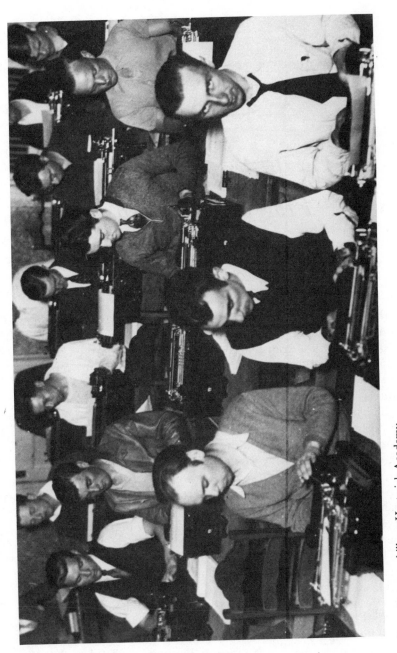

Learning new skills at Hartwick Academy

Works Progress Administration print (No. 69N30109) in the National Archives

$\wr 8 \wr$

The Federal Transient
Program Assessed

As the Federal Transient Program evolved, people wanted to know how many were being cared for, how much it was costing, and what sort of people these transients were anyway. By the time that the program was liquidated in 1935, these questions became more urgent because now the people are asking, the people of the states and localities, were the ones who had to face the problem—alone.

The question of how many transients were actually in need was a perplexing one in the early 1930s. Everyone had his own estimate. According to Anderson's 1933 testimony before the Cutting Hearings, estimates ran as high as two to three million homeless. The figure most commonly referred to, however, was that derived from the NCCTH January 1933 census. According to that admittedly imprecise tally, the number of dislocated people in the United States was estimated to be 1.5 million. It was virtually impossible to determine how many of this number were transient as opposed to the local homeless. With the establishment of a federal program for transients specifically, and the govenment's insistence on careful record keeping, a much clearer picture of the overall problem emerged. Table 9 reflects the final statistical overview of the program as compiled by FERA. (See Table 9, pages 184 and 185.) According to the official figures, the peak *number of persons under care* in federal facilities at one specified time was reached in February 1935 when 300,460 individuals were so cared for: 36,106 families, 155,519 unattached men, and 5,004 unattached women were included in this record breaking number. WPA researcher John Webb recorded a considerably higher number of individuals in his statistics on *all registered cases*. In this case, the peak was reached later that same year in August, when 395,384 unattached persons and 16,232 family groups registered with the federal service.[1] Webb's explanation of this variance was that the census methods used by the FERA statisticians underestimated the number because they did not include persons en route, while his method of tallying total registrations over-estimated the number because the more mobile individual was counted more than once in the same registration period. Neither method, it should further be explained, was able to count those persons choosing not to avail themselves of the program or ignorant of it. After a thorough compilation and explanation of both sets of figures, Webb conceded that,

> despite the steady improvement in reporting procedures developed by the Division of Transient Activities, it was never possible to determine with any degree of accuracy the size of the transient relief population. Actually, the transient unemployed were not a definite and fixed group in the total relief population. On the contrary, the transient unemployed were a relief population that changed its membership constantly, and was never the same on any two days in any one place.[2]

Despite the obvious problem of counting a highly mobile group, all of the final estimates on the number of people who used the federal program fell short of the conservative 1.5 million estimate. Webb attributed the original overestimation to the use of the term transient in such an all-inclusive manner as to include many of the local homeless; to the fact that estimates were taken in cities where the problem was observable and great; and, finally, to the zealous exaggerations of those who wanted federal aid. Harry Hopkins was probably more to the point when he explained the overestimate not as an overinflated idea of the original problem but as a testimony to the effectiveness of other federal programs that kept people at home or encouraged them to return home to brighter prospects. With the CCC employing some of the male youth and CWA providing four million jobs, there was "less need to move on in search of a place in the sun."[3]

The cost of the total federal program is much easier to assess than the number of people cared for. Plants, relief, and facilities for all types of transient care from January 1933 through March 1937,

TABLE 9. Midmonthly Census of Cases and Persons Under Care at Transient Centers and Camps*

Month	Total Cases	Families	Unattached Persons Total	Unattached Persons Men	Unattached Persons Women	Total Persons
1934						
February	92,104	13,303	78,801	76,460	2,341	126,873
March	105,293	14,791	90,502	87,891	2,611	145,119
April	118,381	17,162	101,219	98,196	3,023	164,244
May	124,138	18,515	105,623	102,746	2,877	174,138
June	134,990	20,142	114,848	111,152	3,696	187,282
July	138,071	22,149	115,922	112,799	3,123	194,051
August	148,293	23,822	124,471	121,038	3,433	206,173
September	154,997	26,877	128,120	124,050	4,070	221,734
October	165,492	28,703	136,789	132,660	4,129	235,903
November	184,568	32,760	151,808	147,423	4,385	266,790
December	196,629	36,106	160,523	155,519	5,004	288,955
1935						
January	198,534	38,657	159,877	155,305	4,572	297,058
February	198,612	40,259	158,353	153,683	4,670	300,460
March	196,854	40,125	156,729	152,086	4,643	299,509
April	192,017	39,638	152,379	147,558	4,821	293,676
May	178,077	37,271	140,806	136,252	4,554	273,824
June	169,273	36,831	132,442	127,711	4,731	263,668
July	162,910	35,267	127,643	122,962	4,681	253,340
August	156,502	34,484	122,018	117,273	4,745	245,266
September	141,290	30,509	110,781	106,862	3,919	218,722
October	100,837	21,771	79,066	76,218	2,848	157,634
November	77,056	13,342	63,714	61,847	1,867	112,277
December	43,456	7,678	35,778	34,692	1,086	64,409

TABLE 9. Con't.

| Month | Total Cases | Families | Total | Unattached Persons | | Total Persons |
				Men	Women	
1936						
January	19,383	5,434	13,949	13,073	876	34,650
February	14,130	4,081	10,049	9,401	648	25,109
March	10,058	2,723	7,335	6,805	530	17,467
April	8,082	1,968	6,144	5,662	452	13,445
May	6,544	1,538	5,006	4,568	438	10,837
June	5,121	1,159	3,962	3,591	371	8,336
July	4,113	972	3,141	2,792	349	6,691
August	4,225	979	3,246	2,868	378	6,879
September	3,865	1,020	2,845	2,406	439	6,653
October	3,844	1,016	2,828	2,387	441	6,789
November	4,441	1,325	3,116	2,695	421	8,357
December	5,482	1,847	3,635	3,210	425	11,207
1937						
January	3,656	333	3,323	3,050	273	4,726
February	3,611	382	3,229	2,937	292	4,824
March	3,206	350	2,946	2,690	256	4,504

*(Theodore E. Whiting, WPA, *Final Statistical Report of the Federal Emergency Relief Administration*, Washington, 1942, p. 71).

when the final phasing out of the program was completed, stood at $106,517,000. At peak the program was costing five million dollars per month.[4]

The state government in Albany was as zealous in keeping records and tallying and totaling its relief programs as was the federal government. From the mass of statistical data left from this three year feat of record keeping we can gauge, remembering and applying the same limitations explained regarding federal figures, the extent of New York State's transient program. Such figures were conveniently broken down, month by month, by the Governor's Commission and are included in Table 10. (See Table 10, page 187.) Before analyzing these figures, it is important to remember that this tabulation represents the *number of cases* cared for. The number of families can then be multiplied by approximately three or four, to reach the actual number of individuals so represented. Therefore, the total number of cases in the monthly survey represents a somewhat higher number of individuals. With this in mind, we can note that the peak number of cases was reported in February 1935 to be 16,457, of which 2,117 were families. By rough estimate, if we assume three members to a family, approximately 20,691 individuals were being cared for. Later this year a slight drop in the case load was more than made up by an increase in the proportion of families. In August 1935 the number of individuals stood at approximately 24,321. From these estimates it is safe to say that the peak New York State case load ranged from twenty thousand to twenty-five thousand individuals.* Another aspect of these figures worth noting is how rapidly the program grew from its inauguration in November 1933 until the liquidation orders were received in September 1935. Immediately thereafter the figures show a dramatic decline. Another interesting point is that the number of total cases fluctuated somewhat, yet the family cases show a steady decline until September. The total cost of this program, November 1933 to December 1936, including relief, buildings, equipment, work programs, administration and liquidation expenses, amounted to $8,385,042. Relief alone averaged three hundred thousand to four hundred thousand dollars per month at peak.[5]

Next to numbers and costs, the second most urgent question asked was exactly who was the transient? Once again the urgency of

---

*The New York State figures it will be recalled include both federal and state transients.

TABLE 10. Number of Cases Receiving Transient Relief in the State of New York on the Last Day of Each Month, November, 1933 to December, 1935, Total *Cases*, Federal and State Transients*

Month	Total	Families	Men	Unattached	Women
1933					
November	1,640	29		1,611	
December	5,367	134		5,233	
1934					
January	6,647	403		6,244	
February	5,677	674		5,003	
March	5,631	719		4.912	
April	7,087	784		6,303	
May	8,657	727		7,930	
June	8,440	768	7,484		188
July	9,192	915	8,043		234
August	11,476	1,065	10,146		265
September	11,717	1,163	10,323		231
October	13,096	1,294	11,653		149
November	13,256	1,491	11,508		257
December	14,579	1,728	12,547		304
1935					
January	15,821	2,012	13,471		338
February	16,457	2,117	13,982		358
March	16,157	2,213	13,567		377
April	15,802	2,213	13,201		389
May	15,975	2,203	13,360		412
June	15,777	2,277	13,086		414
July	15,512	2,524	12,500		488
August	16,226	2,701	13,016		509
September	15,465	2,776	12,163		526
October	12,194	2,003	9,804		387
November	10,730	1,833	8,592		305
December	1,678	1,433	--		245

*(Compiled from statistics found in the Governor's Commission on Unemployment Relief report, *Public Relief for Transients and Non-Settled Persons in the State of New York,* pp. 164–68.

the question was enhanced when the transient question was turned back to the local and state governments. A barrage of public relations material, as well as a good number of serious studies conducted by social workers and federal and state governments, repeatedly reiterated that the transient was no different from the proverbial you and me. Such material was needed to counteract the latent skepticism and animosity toward the stranger which was being simultaneously nurtured by a hostile press, negative profiles, and reports of occasional skirmishes with police.

On the most basic level, social worker and much-published expert on the subject, Robert Wilson, asserted that the fact that the "transient and homeless are people," is sometimes a forgotten notion. "Their human needs," he wrote,

> just as urgently require intelligent sympathy, are just as meritorious of intelligent, coordinated action, are just as full of possibilities as are the needs of those whose residence qualifications make them fit legal subjects for aid. The novel mode of life of such transients as the more extreme types of migrant, does not change the simple fact of a human being in trouble whose status as a stranger makes it especially imperative that intelligence and experience be focused on his problem.

From FERA director Hopkins came the often restated belief that the transients were not bums or professional hobos as feared, but rather, they were,

> industrial workers, artisans, laborers, who, after years of unsettled life, were forced by necessity to such employment in new places. They were dispossessed farmers, travelling westward with their families as their fathers had done before them. They were young men who had never had a chance to work, and who could no longer remain in dependence on their burdened parents. They were country people looking for work in the city and city people looking for security in the country, [and so forth].[6]

Over and over, it was repeated that transients were people looking for work, seeking the greener grass on the other side, not parasites and criminals. That their condition was not chosen by them was dramatically revealed in a *Survey Graphic* article, "Pea Picker's Child," and the accompanying photographs by Dorothea Lange. "This here was sort of pushed on me and Jennie Bell and the young ones," explained Joe Kane. "None of our folks — neither side — never lived like gypsies, and we sure never set out to." Forced off his Texas farm, like thousands of others in the Dust Bowl, Kane, his wife and seven children had set out "sure we was gon' where things were better." For five years they had been working their way around the country, taking whatever work they could find. "A body'll try any fool thing when he's up ag'in it." he explained simply. Now they had stopped only long enough to bury their youngest child. That people like the Kanes made up the bulk of the transient population was statistically confirmed in 1935 by John Webb. Looking at the overall figures of the FERA Transient Division in thirteen representative cities, he concluded that, "except for the fact that they were non-resident, there seems little reason for considering transients as a distinct and separate group." They were young, native white, only 2 or 3 percent had no formal education; two-thirds had some grade school or better; and 90 to 95 percent were willing to work. All things considered, Webb believed that they actually represented the more ambitious and hard working sector of the population.[7]

The Governor's Commission came to similar conclusions regarding the typical transient. Using Webb's study as a basis for comparison, they reported: "New York State transients were on the whole not radically different from transients in other states." Regarding their ages, they were not much different than the national average for transients. The majority of unattached men fell in the twenty-five to forty-four age group; most unattached women were between twenty-five and fifty-four. As with the national average, therefore, the transient was generally young. With their youth usually went some formal education and a large instance of employability. Educationally, the level of a group of transients under care in Buffalo as compared to those in the thirteen cities studied by Webb show them to be typical. Just over 60 percent had some formal grade school education; approximately 35 percent attended some high school; but, only a small percent, 2.5 percent in the unattached group and 5.9 percent heads of families, ever went beyond high school in any type of educational training. Perhaps due to the stamina needed to survive on the road, the great majority of transients, including all ages and both sexes, were classified as employable: 71.3 percent employable; 20.3 percent semi-employable; and only 8.4 percent unemployable. Male heads of families were 86.9 percent employable. Not only were the transients physically rated as being capable of work, but, through the observation of bureau directors and the supervisors of the various shelters and camps, they were reported to be "ready and willing." According to the same sources, they worked as hard for their one dollar per week as any relief labor in the state.[8]

Looking more closely at the Buffalo group, Schubert attempted to profile the unattached male transient. After reviewing their registration cards and interviewing representative transients, he established the following profile. The majority of the group was white, 80 percent; their median age was 29.98; they came to Buffalo from every state in the union, but usually from large cities. Occupationally, approximately three-fourths were unskilled factory workers. About 70 percent of the whites in the group had completed eighth grade, but only 13 percent had made it through high school. Blacks accomplished proportionately less. When intelligence tests were administered, 40 percent were judged average while as many as 20 percent were above average. Schubert took this to mean that there was within the group a segment worth "salvaging." The health of the transient was of real concern to the communities through which they passed, but, contrary to popular belief, Schubert found that three-fourths were in good health and capable of performing work. Only one-tenth of the population passing through Buffalo had communicable diseases. As to their character and willingness to work, Schubert accepted the word of nine-tenths of the men, that they were on the road looking for work, on the basis of their responsiveness to the call to work in the centers. Asking the question, "Are they bums?" Schubert answered, as did Webb, "Not unless one wants to classify a goodly section of the remainder of the country's population as such."[9] Putting aside his registration cards and tabulations and looking at the human side of the men with whom he had worked, Schubert offered this subjective profile:

> The transient largely wants a job but cannot obtain one. He has tried at home, he has tried here, and tried there. He is weary and disheartened. His clothes are shabby and he has no car fare to carry him around a city or nickels with which to make telephone calls. He wants to 'go on dates' with girls but again has no money. He would like to have his own home, even if it were just a room or two, to consider his castle. Again and again he meets a stone wall, no money. Getting started is so hard.[10]

In profiling the women who applied at the Buffalo center, Schubert found much the same characteristics and reasons for wandering as with their male counterparts. Only approximately one-quarter of the women were unskilled and most had a "goodly amount of schooling," 90 percent having completed the eighth grade, 15 percent high school, and 5 percent had some college training. One thing that he did find that was different about the women, however, was that a large number of them, more so than the men, were married. Of these, most were separated or divorced; some were widowed. While most of the women were on the road looking for work, this latter fact reflects the second most noted reason for wandering, conditions at home.[11] Box-Car Bertha concurred with most of his findings. While hitchhiking through the East, she stopped at the various transient centers to see for herself how her sisters of the road were faring in the new program. She found that "their stories are very much the same — no work, a whole family on relief, no prospects of marriage, the need for a lark, the need for freedom of sex and of living, and the great urge to know what other women were doing."[12]

The sample from which Schubert drew his profile was admittedly small. While Bertha claimed that the number of women on the road was increasing dramatically, the Buffalo center only registered thirty-five in an entire year.[13] Schubert could only interview those women who sought out the program and, for many of the same reasons that kept them from seeking the assistance of the private and municipal agencies before the federal program, many women stayed away. The preferred solution for dealing with women was still to establish settlement and return them home if it was in their best interest. Preconceived notions about women's place in the home often tempered one's judgment about best interest. A study of the treatment of 131 transient women at the New Orleans Transient Center by social welfare student Esther Hachtel effectively illustrated the inadequacy of this treatment.[14]

The final profile is that of the transient family. It is important to remember that the Joads were not yet on the road in full numbers; in other words, the migrant Oakie family that was thrust into the national limelight by John Steinbeck was not yet a highly visible factor in the transient population. In fact, it was not until well after the federal program was terminated that the exodus from the Dust Bowl reached its peak. Through the program, the largest case load of families in New York was reached in September 1935 when 2,776 families were on the rolls. (See Table 10, p. 187.) This number would be dwarfed by the experience of California within the next few years. Yet transient families were noticed as early as 1930. In an October article in *The Family*, Robert Wilson reported that some families were already making their "third and fourth trip across the country." Even at this early date, he noted that it was unemployment that started them on the road. "Anything," they felt, "is better than staying around to eke out a marginal existence or be forced to ask for relief." Their wandering was not casual, and, while they might temporarily resort to seasonal farm work to get by, what they were looking for was the opportunity to reestablish themselves with jobs, homes, and community. "If they then do find a permanent job," Wilson explained, "the family is ready to settle down." But, he warned, the habits of the road were infectious, and there was the danger that their wandering might become permanent. He was especially concerned that the children would come to accept as normal their parents' unconventional behavior and adopt it in their adulthood.[15]

When the transient family turned to the federal program for relief it was profiled more formally, but the conclusions were generally the same. In Buffalo, the largest daily load of families was reached in January 1935, when 240 cases were registered. Of that number 86 percent were looking for work. Only 4.7 per cent of these fell into the category of seasonal workers. For the vast majority, therefore, migrancy was not a normal experience. The families, furthermore, came generally from the surrounding industrial states and were, more often than not, headed by men who had previously been factory workers. The families were also generally small. Over one-quarter of the families registered in Buffalo were childless couples; the majority of the rest had one to two children. Again this predates the scenes of extended families spilling out of dilapidated automobiles that characterized the Dust Bowl migration. There were also many more traveling by paid transportation on buses or trains, or hitchhiking, than there were traveling by car. Schubert also noted that most registrations occurred in winter, when resources were most strained and need was greatest. In other words, they would make it on their own for as long as possible. Interestingly, Schubert found that many of the families, approximately 20 per cent, had formerly had residence in Buffalo and thus were simply returning home. In the final analysis, Schubert concluded, "the general picture of the families traveling around the country is much the same as that of the unattached men. The family heads are looking for work, are largely factory workers, and have had a goodly amount of schooling. What they need is a job or at least to settle down in one place."[16]

To draw any final conclusions regarding the Federal Transient Program and its operation in the state of New York, it is necessary to pause for a moment and ask a few questions. First, while it is clear that both the federal and state governments went to great pains to formulate a humane program and provide adequate facilities, just how extensively was the program implemented locally? Did local officials accept the funds, but not live up to the rules? Secondly, how did the local community accept the program? Did it cooperate and thereby enhance its overall success, or did it present obstacles? Finally, did the federal programs indeed correct the problems so apparent in the pre-1933 period, that is, passing-on and removal? In answering these questions, we should be able to come to a final evaluation of governmental involvement in the interstate migration of destitute citizens.

The answer to the first question was sought by the NCCTH. Throughout the period of the federal program, the committee adopted the role of watchdog, carefully following the progress of the program and monitoring its standards of care from the social worker's perspective. As chairperson Potter explained, the federal government needed a group of people like theirs, experts in the field from the public and private sectors as well as concerned laymen, to offer constructive criticism of its activities and to furnish suggestions as to possible direction it should take. Consistent with this philosophy, the committee undertook an evaluative survey of the transient program in action. There was also, it must be admitted, an ulterior motive behind the project. Anxious over the program, they hoped to use the resulting study to influence friends from the past, Senators Costigan, Cutting, and LaFollette, and to gain new allies, namely the sympathetic first lady.[17] Accordingly, in early 1934, whether for pure research and fact finding or for propaganda value, the committee solicited funds from their generous benefactor, Tracy McGregor, to engage Ellery Reed to direct a twenty-state survey of transient centers and to produce an evaluative report on his findings. Included in the states selected for review was New York. The final product, *Federal Transient Programs, An Evaluative Survey*, was ready for distribution later that spring.[18]

The stated purpose of the survey was to measure exactly how closely the operation of the Federal Transient Program conformed to the standards of care established by Washington. The rules set down by FERA in Rules and Regulations Number 8 called for a "fairly good program for care," but, as yet, the survey concluded, no one had been able to fully attain them. The fact that congregate shelters outnumbered camps was disheartening, but the situation, Reed felt, would be corrected with time. The shelters that were investigated were clean and had sufficient facilities. Criticism was expressed about the continued lumping together of all ages, races, and characters. Food was substantial, three meals a day; clothing, though meager, was clean and available. Medical care for emergencies and to provide protection against communicable disease was acceptable but limited. As to leisure time, it was found that the primary activity, work, was limited by the lack of appropriate projects, but most shelters did provide recreation to occupy some of the idle hours. Casework was found to be marginally adequate, in light of the limited staffs. In presenting his overall ratings, Reed concluded that 45.7 percent of the transient shelters were "good," 35.4 percent were "fair," and 18.9 percent "poor."[19] While this was not a glowing report card, it was enough to show that the program was addressing a real need and, given the circumstances, was performing a respectable job.

In New York, the Governor's Commission performed a similar evaluative task with, it should be noted, the NCCTH serving in an advisory capacity. What they determined was that despite setbacks, the program had marked a decided improvement over what had preceded it. They did note, however, that when care was administered outside the controlled environment of center or camp standards varied. They also noted that, due to a lack of statewide supervision and the failure to accept the philosophy behind the program in some locales, passing-on and overnight jailings did continue in some small communities.

The second question is a very important one. Governmental programs can be well formulated, meticulously organized, and well funded, but the bottom line to their success or failure generally lies in local community approval. As to the transient program, the attitudes described at length in chapter one were still very much alive when the government instituted its programs. Hopkins was well aware of such attitudes. To him, hostile unwelcoming feelings were indicative of a hate/envy relationship. "To the stay-at-home confronted with unescapable problems of his own," he explained,

the life of a transient, free from the responsibilities of settled life, frequently appeared at once glamorous and reprehensible. This romantic attitude obscured an understanding of the economic and social problems in which the transient was involved. So long as he was regarded as a cross between a carefree gypsy and a fugitive from justice, a reasonable approach to his quandary was impossible.[20]

Reaction to the federal program in the host communities in New York followed lines consistent with this appraisal.

The Governor's Commission reported an initial hostility to the program rooted, they believed, in pre-depression attitudes toward the bum. Communities feared that the presence of transient centers in their neighborhoods would attract ne'er-do-wells, carriers of communicable diseases, and/or criminals; therefore, they often presented organized opposition to proposed transient shelters. Health and safety concerns were enhanced by economic considerations. Local public welfare commissioners, quite rightly, were fearful that the transients being imported into their districts could eventually become their responsibility should the federal government choose at any time to withdraw from the program. Except in areas where long-standing and severe transient problems persisted or where services were desperately needed, as in rehabilitating the southern tier, communities were reluctant to see transients drawn into their communities. Such suspicions were confirmed and fears fed whenever a transient stepped out of line. "The arrest of one transient for vagrancy or alcoholism," Reed explained, "did more to shape community attitudes than the behavior of 100 men working 30 hours a week on community projects." In Hornell, for example, barely two weeks after the dedication of Otis Scott's painting, the evening paper carried the story "Put Transient in County Jail as Shoplifter." In Saratoga Springs the story of the theft of a Skidmore student's car by a transient camp resident and the wild early morning police chase that followed was used by the Chamber of Commerce president to support his request for the removal of the camp. Community concern was further aroused when it was found that the thief had a prior prison record. Much more menacing was the murder and mutilation of a thirty-six-year-old Elmira man by "train hobos" as reported on the front page of *The Canisteo Times*.[21]

There was a recognized need from the beginning of the program for positive publicity to counteract these fears. An entire session of the National Conference of Social Work in 1935 was devoted to a Travelers Aid presentation on such publicity. An excellent paper, "How Do We Interpret 'Problems on the March?'" by J. Arthur Flynn, highlighted the need for publicity and gave the assembled social workers constructive advice on how to use that publicity to interpret for the public both their role and the needs of their transient clients. "Most transient workers know that transiency is something to be understood rather than condemned as a nuisance," he explained, "but this premise is not accepted by the public generally." It was then up to the workers to inform the public that the problems of the transient were as worthy of their attention and sympathy as were those of their unemployed, impoverished neighbors with whom they sympathized so greatly. This, he charged his audience, was their greatest challenge. To accomplish the above, he suggested nationwide publicity campaigns utilizing "national magazines, syndicated newspaper articles and feature stories, national radio broadcasts, talking pictures, speakers' bureaus, and other educational and publicity media." Because the transients were part of the inarticulate masses, he called upon his audience to pass the message on.[22]

Positive publicity was forthcoming. A Warner Brothers release, *Stranded*, went a long way to portray to a national audience a sympathetic picture of Travelers Aid and the people it served. In addition, valuable press publicity was generated when reporters visited transient facilities and saw for themselves the worthiness of the men and the value of the various programs. In New York, in an effort to enhance community relations, visitors were frequently invited to observe the camps and participate in their entertainment programs. In Elks Park the transient's gymnasium became a virtual community center. Time also proved to be a positive factor. Attitudes toward the transients mellowed as time passed and personal contact showed them to be no different than local victims of the depression. The most valuable piece of publicity, however, proved to be the work attitude of the men themselves. Their contributions to community projects and the way they rallied to the call during the floods went a long way to reverse the initial hostility they had faced. With the precious ingredient of time and constant public relations reinforcement, community attitudes gradually changed. Perhaps the most illustrative example of a changing attitude was the manner in which communities reacted to the ending of the program. Very few voiced any pleasure in its liquidation. Instead, Washington was inundated with petitions from across the country objecting to the closings.[23]

Finally, what of the overt problems of the pre-1933 period? On the positive side, the federal program did cut down greatly on the traditional passing-on practice. But what of the more civilized practice of official removal? Now that the federal government had assumed responsiblity, had this practice also ceased? According to Hopkins, this was precisely what was to happen. Familiar with the agonies of forced removal, Hopkins stated that "there was to be no passing-on of transients from place to place." Leaving the option open, however, he explained, "Families and individuals might be returned to their homes or sent to relatives only with the consent of the authorities in the locality to which they were being sent."[24] According to Reed the option was not forcefully used:

> It may fairly be said that transients, except those less than 16 or 17 years of age, or mental cases, were not commonly being forced to return to their place of legal residence, irrespective of whether or not they themselves wanted to go. Only a few case records revealed this outgrown attitude of desiring and attempting to engineer other people's lives.

"Theoretically, at least," he explained,

> the attitude of the client himself was commonly consulted, and he was not forced to go to destinations contrary to his own desire. In support of such policy, it was contended that the client would probably not stay at the point of destination if sent there against his will, would move on again to the detriment of both himself and society.[25]

In New York State, it was the considered opinion of the Governor's Commission that "the philosophy of both the Federal Transient Division and the State Transient Division . . . tended to emphasize *care for people where they are*. Resettlement and local assimilation, rather than removal, were emphasized." The assumption of all expenses by the federal government made "it seem more reasonable to let the family or individual reside where he wished." In addition, the time and effort involved in verifying residence and seeking authorization prevented any wide-scale removal policy.[26]

In the annual reports of the State Board of Social Welfare, however, the number of persons removed from the state continued to rise, even after the implementation of the federal program. The rationale of the commissioner and assistant commissioner remained basically unchanged. In the years during which the program was operative, removals did increase. The rise is especially dramatic when compared to preceding years. (See Table 11, p. 198.) From these figures it is obvious that removals continued their upward trend. Two years after the inauguration of the program Harry M.

TABLE 11. Removals in New York State*

	1929–30	1930–31	1931–32	1932–33	1933–34	1934–35	1935–36
State Poor	217	259	352	511	574	641	1,029**
Non-Resident Poor	1,357	1,658	1,715	2,557	2,257	2,712	3,170**

*(New York State, Board of Social Welfare, *Seventieth Annual Report of the State Board of Social Welfare for the Year Ended, June 30, 1936,* Albany, 1937, p. 30).

**These figures most likely reflect the liquidation activities of that year.

Hirsh reported that the activities of his division had reached a new peak with a record breaking volume of removals. Since 1929 there had been an increase of 195 percent in the number of state poor removed and 100 percent in nonresident poor. By 1936 the figures were 374 percent and 134 percent respectively.[27]

Both categories, state poor and nonresident poor, by the definition of the State Department of Social Welfare, fell within the eligibility range of the federal programs. That the division received one-half fare transportation cost from the federal government also reinforces the belief that such persons did indeed come under the federal transient plan and thus should have been cared for where they were. Nevertheless, both the commissioner and assistant commissioner held that removal remained an essential part of their program. "Unless this procedure is followed," Hirsch explained,

> it is quite obvious that in the event the Federal Transient program should be terminated and Federal relief discontinued, the respective counties would find themselves with a case load probably beyond their control and with insufficient funds to take over their care.

This concern over a possible federal pull-out was reiterated each year as the chief reason for removals. Again, as in the pre-1933 period, it was also stressed that the cost of removal was far less than maintenance expenses. "All those removed," it was explained, " were persons incapacitated by disease or disability, [or] others who, because of infancy, old age, or other reasons, were likely to become dependent either for a long period of time or permanently."[28] This belief was confirmed by a sociological follow-up study of six hundred removal cases. Tentative findings showed that "a prolonged period of dependency would have been inevitable had they continued to live in the State." Only 33 percent of persons within the group were readjusted to the places to which they had been removed. The conclusion was that such persons would have remained unadjusted, that is, on relief, even if they had stayed in New York. This was interpreted as evidence that it was best that they had been transported out of state. It was not seen, as we may see it now, as a haunting suggestion that removal diminished any hope that such people had had for establishing themselves in the place of their choice.[29]

From this brief survey of the figures and rationale of that very state agency with whom responsibility for removal ultimately rested, it is apparent that the positive statement of Hopkins, Reed, and the Governor's Commission were seriously undermined in practice.

In the final evaluation, it must be conceded that the Federal Transient Program, both nationwide and within the state, suffered from severe problems. On the national level, critics scoffed at its coddling of the bums while more serious studies raised the question of whether or not the program was encouraging transiency. As one such skeptic noted:

> The shelters established in many towns and cities adjacent to railway terminals and highway intersections afforded to migrants many snug harbors of refuge where they could eat, sleep, get cleaned up and be on their way. Here was a degree of security never before experienced by itinerants.[30]

In New York, as we have seen, there were many problems inherent in what seemed to be a well-constructed program. One such problem was the limited numbers that the program could reach. While the most publicized and highly praised experimental programs did provide definite rehabilitative service and adequate standards of care, the sheer magnitude of the transient problem made it impossible for any but a very small proportion of the total population to share in such experiences. As late as July 1934 *The New York Times* was reporting that the number of nomadic boys living in vacant lots and empty buildings in New York City was increasing at an alarming rate. For every one boy cared for, it was estimated, ten went without care.[31] The majority who did receive aid, regardless of age, were still relegated to congregate shelters where many of the pre-1933 conditions still could be found. The stabilizing influence of the program was also jeopardized by continuing adverse publicity, such as a report of the Welfare Council of New York City claiming that the city's "army" of beggars presented a menace to public health.[32] Finally, as Schubert repeatedly pointed out, none of the programs, no matter how innovative, individualized, or rehabilitative, could give the transient what he really needed, a real job and a real pay check. "As in the case of any other difficulty or malady affecting humans," he wrote, "the cure can only be achieved by following the general principle of treating the cause and not the symptoms." At present the program could only deal with symptoms; the country had to work on the cause—the depression.[33]

Despite these important shortcomings, it must be remembered that the Federal Transient Program, as all the New Deal programs, represented a bold new experiment into uncharted waters. As with any such experiment, time was needed to develop facilities and lines of communication, to devise an adequate system to regulate standards, to train a staff, and, most important, to change the consciousness of the people. Yet the program was given only a brief two years to correct a problem that was centuries in the making and was literally impervious to cure while the depression stubbornly persisted. "Transiency and homelessness are not simple phenomena to be readily resolved by spectacular feats," Dr. Ellen C. Potter exclaimed with exasperation. "We cannot expect transiency to be eradicated nor can we condemn a program because it has not performed miracles and turned a hideous sore spot into a Garden of Eden."[34]

Even though the experiment was cut short just as it was beginning to have a positive impact, it did represent a precedent-setting assumption of government responsibility, and, as such, it held great promise for the future. In the final analysis, Dr. Reed conceded that the program, "although having much room for improvement, was one of the greatest and most significant achievements in the field of social work in recent years." After many years of being passed on, the transient was finally having his basic physical needs "fairly well met." Looking back upon the program, Hopkins was also pleased to write that it had "isolated the problem of transiency and showed it to be a legal problem whose solution must lie in rewriting of laws that arbitrarily excluded the non-resident from benefits of protective legislation." "No less important," he added, "it pulled men and women by the hundreds of thousands from the despair of aimless wandering, misery, and the complete neglect of health, back to self-respect and their place in the world of working people." As *The Transient* had jubilantly proclaimed in its maiden issue: "The transient has become a person, not only to the social workers but to many people in the 47 States where the Federal program is operating. His problem has emerged as one quite worthy of our sincere attention."[35] Even in its early developmental stage, the program gave the transient an alternative to his constant wandering. More importantly, it gave the recipient the *right* to relief. He no longer needed to be a person without a country—one of the forgotten of the Great Depression.

Specifically, the program went a long way in just meeting the physical needs of the transient. According to Potter, the program helped abolish jungles, lessen petty crime, and maintain men and families on a new "level of decency." In New York, the Governor's Commission concluded that, while the program "did not stop transiency any more than the unemployment relief program stopped unemployment," it did definitely and materially raise the standards of physical care given transients. Standards of congregate care improved for the first time under the stimulus of federal guidelines as evidenced by the improved rating of New York City's municipal lodging house. From the mayor's office came the congratulatory message:

> While the former administration aimed merely to care for as many cases as possible through lodging and two meals a day . . . the present administration is not only endeavoring to provide more varied nourishment, but also adequate recreational facilities.

Communities were more adequately protected from contagion and the annoyance of beggars. The evils of passing-on were almost completely mitigated. And, finally, the transient was given the opportunity for physical rehabilitation. "The inability of the State Transient program to control transiency," the Commission concluded, only "reflects the inadequacy of all relief."[36]

In the conclusion of his evaluative report of the program a foreboding prediction was made by Reed. "The study left no doubt," he explained, "that if federal funds for the transient program should be discontinued the program would almost completely disappear and conditions would revert promptly to the pre-program status."[37] Yet, word went out from Washington in the late summer of 1935 that, as of September 20, the states were to cease the intake of transients into the federal program, and liquidation was to begin. The announcement was exactly what state and local welfare officials had long feared. The federal government was abandoning the transient, and they would now be expected to resume their old responsiblities. The experiment was over. The transient was once again to be the forgotten man of the depression   .

₰ 9 ₰

Liquidation

TO ALL STATE RELIEF ADMINISTRATORS:

AFTER MIDNIGHT SEPTEMBER TWENTIETH NO MORE
PERSONS SHALL BE ACCEPTED FOR SERVICE AND RE-
LIEF FROM SPECIAL TRANSIENT FUNDS stop SUGGEST
YOU POST NOTICE TO THIS EFFECT AT ONCE AT ALL
TRANSIENT CENTERS AND RELIEF OFFICES WHERE
NONRESIDENTS MAKE APPLICATION stop INSTRUC-
TIONS MODIFYING PREVIOUS RULING LIMITING
CERTIFICATION TO THOSE WHO WERE REGISTERED
BEFORE JULY FIFTEENTH WILL BE SENT IN ORDER
TO FACILITATE PLACEMENT OF ALL EMPLOYABLES
NOW REGISTERED WITH TRANSIENT SERVICE stop
THIS ORDER IS NECESSARY IN ORDER TO AN-
TICIPATE LIQUIDATION OF TRANSIENT RELIEF PRO-
GRAM BY NOVEMBER FIRST.

So read the September 6, 1935, telegram from Aubrey Williams at
WPA that marked the beginning of the end of the Federal Transient
Program. "After Friday midnight,' *The New York Times* reported, "the
doors of 595 lodges and camps, where a quarter of a million persons
have been receiving food and shelter, will be closed to future guests."
Henceforth, employable transients already registered in the federal
program were to be assigned to WPA rolls while the estimated 7 percent unemployables were to be either returned to their places of
settlement or else turned over to the local community wherein they
presently resided. Newcomers were to be directed to the bounty of
state and local governments and/or charitable agencies. "To the

habitual knights of the road," the paper predicted, "the approaching winter may be the toughest since 1932."[1]

Liquidation of the transient program, in hindsight, should not have been surprising to anyone. It was merely part of an inevitable retreat by Washington from direct relief that affected the entire relief population. Roosevelt had made it quite clear when he signed the Federal Emergency Relief Act that he did not favor the idea of a federal dole, but rather that he had resorted to it reluctantly as a practical necessity. Gertrude Springer had recognized this back in 1933. While celebrating the initiation of FERA, she reminded her readers that "President Roosevelt is not 'relief minded.' He sees relief . . . as a necessary evil to be gotten rid of at the earliest possible date."[2] That date had apparently arrived. On January 4, 1935, FDR instructed Congress: "The Federal Government must and shall quit this business of relief." Fearing that the dole was "sapping" the vitality of the people, he asserted, "We must preserve not only the bodies of the unemployed from destruction but also their self-respect, their self-reliance and courage and determination."[3] To accomplish this, he proposed a massive federal work program that would substitute work relief for direct relief for some 3.5 million people, a permanent social security system that would provide for an old age pension as well as categorical aid to specifically defined dependents, and a system of unemployment insurance to assure that emergency relief measures like FERA would never again be necessary. The needy who did not fit into the specified categories or were unable to participate in the works program were to be once again, as tradition dictated, returned to the responsibility of the state and local governments. This was, in effect, the second New Deal.

Response from the social work community to the demise of FERA and the substitution of the Works Progress Administration and Social Security in its stead was immediate. Social workers had not been completely enamored of the outgoing FERA themselves. The initial elation that had been recorded by Springer in 1933 had lasted only about a year along with the rest of the New Deal honeymoon. Differing philosophies between New Dealers in Washington and social workers back home became apparent as early as March 1934 when one of the favorite programs of the social work community, the Civil Works Administration, was abruptly terminated. Dissatisfaction with the inadequacies of the FERA added to the growing alienation. An activist splinter group of more radical social workers, the rank-and-file, was even more vocal and extreme in its criticism of the program that it saw as a sellout to the old order. The FERA was regularly criticized in the pages of the movement's journal *Social Work Today*. William Bremer also comments on a growing rift between New Yorkers and New Dealers during the tenure of the FERA. On the whole, however, despite their watchdog criticism, the mainstream had stayed with FDR. By 1936, with the liquidation of FERA complete, relations were so strained that social workers found it difficult to give the president a hearty endorsement in his reelection bid.[4]

It was not that the profession did not appreciate WPA and Social Security. What alienated them was the price that was paid in the deal. Addressing his colleagues in the pages of *The Survey*, Russell Kurtz of the Russell Sage Foundation articulated this sentiment. Applauding the new work relief program as a "long step away from the evils of direct mass relief," that "recognizes the claim of the unemployed for work rather than a dole," Kurtz gave credit to its humanitarian interest. However, while work relief was a preferable alternative to direct relief, it should not be won at the expense of the latter. For if the federal government does quit this business of relief, he asked, "who will hold the net under the new works program to catch . . . [those] unfortunates who are bound to slip through the gap? Who but the federal government has the strength to hold it?" It was highly conceivable, even at this early date, that individuals meeting all the criteria of need, and being strong of body and capable of employment, might not find a place in the works program. The federal government might pass responsibility for them, as well as the unemployables who were automatically excluded from the works program, on to the state and local governments, but there was no guarantee that they would or even could accept the burden. A general federal relief program, therefore, was not expendable. The NCCTH agreed: "The 'dole,' i.e., unearned direct relief from government funds, will continue to be needed for the unemployed 'until' the works program has absorbed them all, if ever." Social workers, Kutz concluded, appreciated the works program but "deplore the price that is being asked for this program."[5] One of those first called upon to pay was the transient.

Harry Hopkins was more optimistic about the transient's place in the second New Deal. According to the now WPA director, the transient population fit well into the new direction being taken by

Washington. Through their admirable work efforts, they had shown themselves to be little different than the rest of the relief population. Now, for their own psychological benefit and to end the discrimination inherent in separation from the general population and specialized care, they were to be mainstreamed into the general working population. WPA, Hopkins felt, would be the ideal vehicle to complete the transition. By "working side by side with the local man," the transient would be known "simply as a good workman worthy of his hire." This, Hopkins contended, would be the final victory for the transient. "to be recognized as being no different from the rest of the un-employed except for the accident of residence."[6]

Few outside of Washington agreed with his assessement of the liquidation of the Federal Transient Program. Even before the deadline date, public officials on the state and local level and social workers in both private and public service flooded FERA headquarters with protests. *Public Welfare News* reported "an avalanche of protests in letters and wires" from social workers, interested lay persons, public welfare officials, advisory committees, health departments, congressmen, and even a few from transients themselves. In the months to come there were added petitions from state conferences of social workers, governors, and mayors, all calling on Washington to continue its support of the program.[7]

While most did agree in theory with the transition from dole to work relief, for the very reasons stated by FDR and because of the overwhelming expense involved in supporting the needy, local and nonresident, what was objectionable was applying the new philosophy to one of the most vulnerable relief groups. "The federal government wants to cut down on its vast relief expenditures," *The New York Times* editorialized, "it is necessary that it should do so. The only question is whether it could not more wisely make the reduction in some other category than this, which involves a responsibility that is hardly fair to place on the locality alone." The point was reiterated early the following year when Dr. Ellen Potter, speaking for the NCCTH, expressed surprise and indignation over the turn of events. "In the early days of the establishment of the transient program, Mr. Hopkins said that in his judgment this was one of the portions of the relief program which was distinctly a federal problem and that it would, of course, be the last unit to be liquidated if liquidation came about." Yet on September 20, 1935, "the 'unthinkable' had happened." "In issuing this edict," Dr. Potter charged, "the federal government was abandoning its commitment to a policy which seemed, in the light of our knowledge of poor laws and their restrictions, to mark a great advance in social and political thinking."[8] The NCCTH would spend the remaining years of its tenure lobbying for the resumption of that commitment by Washington and keeping the public mindful of the transient.

For some, the hostile reaction to liquidation was one of self-defense. With the government abandoning the program, local and state governments would inherit the transient problem, and local communities would once again have to cope with the dark stranger lurking in their midst. Thus fearful of the added expense and dangers involved, public and private officals urged the federal government to continue with the burden it had so wisely assumed. Robert P. Lane, executive director of the Welfare Council of New York City, speaking for eighty-two public and private agencies in that city, made an impassioned plea to Hopkins. Reminding him of the conditions that had preceded the federally sponsored transient program, he asserted, "the Federal Relief Administration assumed its proper responsibility for state-to-state transients in response to widespread demands from communities unable to bear this burden alone and it should not now throw this burden back on localities." Local communities, it was reiterated across the state and nation, could not and would not assume a burden already recognized by Washington to be a federal responsibility. In Syracuse it was estimated that the combined resources of all the existing public and private agencies could not duplicate the care given by the federal program to eight hundred to twelve hundred transient men who sought relief each month in that city alone. Those communities housing transient centers or in the vicinity of federal camps were especially concerned. Once the program was finally liquidated, it was feared, the transients that had been drawn into the community by the federal program would remain behind as a local burden. *The Albany Evening News* pointed out that more than one thousand transients and unsettled were already in the capital, and they anticipated that many more would be attracted when the camps in Schenectady, St. Johnsville, and Saratoga were closed.[9]

In addition to the self interest of the local community, there also was a genuine concern for the fate of the transients. Editorializing once again about the injustice of the federal government's decision, *The New York Times* explained that in New York City alone ten thousand transients and three thousand transient families would soon be on their own. With little prospect of employment, ineligible for relief under the Wicks Act, and unable to turn to private agencies who simply did not have the funds, "for the men transients . . . it is a night or two in the Municipal Lodging House and then no place to go. With women and children it is even worse. The family must be broken up and cared for in different institutions—otherwise only a night or two in a shelter." With winter approaching, the editors warned that the government must do something about these people. Predicting that liquidation in New York City would bring about "untold suffering among individuals and families," Lane hinted that their desperation "will lend great impetus to the activities of radical groups." *The Syracuse Post-Standard* summarized the plight of the transient in that city with a picture of transient men sitting around the local shelter pondering their fate. The picture was captioned very simply: "They don't do much, but they need shelter." Yet, "we can't take care of you" was the only reply available to those men who approached the transient registration office in the days following the federal order. For them the only choices left were "police shelter, panhandling or thieving."[10]

Despite the pleas and warnings, liquidation proceeded apace. In September 1935 New York received and complied with the federal orders to discontinue the acceptance of new cases into the program. By October 7th, Stanley Davies, general director of the Charity Organization Society in New York City, was warning that the city was already facing a crisis.

> Since Sept. 20 there literally has been no place where transients in need and not already receiving care can go with assurance of receiving service. Private agencies have been able to do little because of lack of funds and because they are already taking care of as many transients as their budgets and functions will permit.

Only good weather, he explained, had prevented a serious problem up until then. "Unless there is some change in Federal policy," he predicted, "the situation will be disastrous."[11]

Others from his profession agreed, and they were taking action. "We find it practically impossible to hold our people in leash on this matter of transients," Robert Lane warned Aubrey Williams. Social workers were moving quickly to intercede and try to reverse federal policy before the impending deadling. The New York Welfare

Council contacted its members soliciting an immediate letter-writing campaign to New York's senators and representatives. The October 16th letter outlined present conditions. Since September 20th, "mendicancy and vagrancy are increasing. Hobo towns are again springing up. An increasing number of men and boys are sleeping in subways, parks and hallways. Families are being broken up due to lack of facilities. . . . We are rapidly reverting to the old order when there was no adequate care and the city was faced with a constantly increasing burden." Warning that neither the city nor the private agencies had the wherewithal to meet the need, the council made its pitch: "DO YOU WANT this problem dumped on the city. DO YOU WANT to pay an increased cost of care through the increase in begging, panhandling, crime and all the by-products of a floating population?" If not, then write your congressmen, or communicate directly with Harry Hopkins for the continuation of federal funds for the care of nonresidents "who logically are the responsibility of the federal rather than the municipal governments." The COS did its part by circulating "The Inside Story" in the October issue of its weekly bulleting. Inside the small pamphlet was the complete text of Davies' speech and COS recommendations that the government continue to recognize its responsibility, accept new applicants into the transient program, expedite the placement of employable transients on WPA projects, and continue its responsibility for those not absorbed into such programs. COS had obviously come a long way since Mrs. Lowell's advocacy of anti-vagrancy legislation and an end to outdoor relief.[12] Despite these efforts, on November 1, 1935, the end of federal care for transients in New York, including men, women, and children then under care, was announced.

Response again was immediate. From Syracuse came the protest of the county welfare commissioner: "If ever [the federal government] had a responsibility it is now, just as winter is about to set in. It is not fair to drop 250 men on the community at this time. If nothing more, it should be continued through the winter." From Westchester came the vow of the Board of Supervisors to fight the closing of nearby Camp Elmsford because "discontinuance of the camp would throw the burden of providing for an increasing number of transients upon county municipalities." A few days later Mayor Fiorello LaGuardia announced that New York City was terminating transient relief, explaining that, "this city cannot assume any responsibility for any people coming into this city in need of relief." At the same time TERA chairman, Frederick J. Daniels, explained that, under state law, state funds could not be used for transient relief.[13]

On December 4, 1935, responsibility for the transient was officially returned to the local level. In New York, the State Department of Social Welfare set up a transient camp liquidation project. Social workers were assigned to transient camps and centers to take the history of every one of the approximately twenty-nine hundred individuals involved in the now defunct federal program. Each case was then to be sent to Albany where the Division of State Aid would determine whether those with definite settlement outside of the state, approximately 33 percent of the cases, should be returned in compliance with the Public Welfare Law, classified as state poor, or certified for WPA employment. Emphasis, as in the past, was upon removal. It was for that reason that such detailed histories of each case were taken. Eventually one-half of those with definite settlement were returned. For those persons who refused removal or who had lost settlement outside of the state while they were in transient facilities, and thus had nowhere to be returned, the state, in accordance with federal guidelines, was to certify them for WPA.[14]

In New York Sate the promise of a smooth transition to WPA was repeatedly offered. On November 27, 1935, it was reported that twenty-two transient camps had already been approved by Washington as WPA projects. More than four thousand upstate transients, it was estimated would be shifted to such projects where they would receive monthly wages of fifteen to twenty-five dollars, along with maintenance and medical and dental care. In December, upstate WPA administrator, Lester Herzog, further assured local communities that transients set loose by liquidation would not become a local burden. "All these men—and we have estimates varying from 2,500 to 9,000—are relief cases and eligible for WPA jobs," he confirmed. On paper the plan promised an easy transition from one form of relief to another. In actuality, however, serious problems were inevitable.[15]

To begin with, to be certified for WPA was one thing, to be chosen for specific projects by local boards over local candidates was quite another.* In other words, as Harold Winchester of the Albany

---

*The law specified that residency was not to effect eligibility. The states, however, openly flouted this directive. In a number of states, including New York, this was done by requiring applicants for WPA to first qualify for state relief, i.e., fulfill residency requirements.

Travelers Aid Association told delegates at a conference of New York state social workers, "with ten million at least out of work and a WPA program that plans to take care of only 3,150,000 at the most, it takes no expert to figure out where the transient comes out in this program."[16]

Those transients who preferred to return home, if they still had a place to call home, could very easily find that, while taking advantage of the federal program in one state, they were losing settlement in another. Consequently, upon their return, they would continue to be viewed by local WPA boards as transients. This was to be the case for one Peter C., former transient camp resident. Upon returning to New York, after a year and a half at federal transient camps in the southwest, Mr. C. was informed that he had lost his New York settlement and with it eligibility for the WPA in which he now sought to enroll. Since his original reason for leaving home had been to relieve his parents of the added financial burden of an unemployed son, and finding the financial situation at home unchanged, Peter was on his way again. "I want to stay home," he explained "but with the circumstances as such. . . . I cannot impose any longer on the meager resources of my father, and feel inclined to resume the riding of the freight train, etc."[17]

Even in those cases where settlement was not lost, returning transients could still find difficulties with WPA. If another member of the immediate family was already employed on a project, for example, it was highly unlikely that a second position would be allocated to the same family. Therefore, in families with a number of able-bodied, employable men, just one would have to spread a thin WPA paycheck to support the whole.

It was not only participants in the now defunct Federal Transient Program who faced difficulties securing promised WPA jobs. The newly unsettled also found this avenue of relief blocked when they turned to the federal government for assistance. Shortly after the dissolution of the transient program, a distraught woman from Brooklyn appealed to Roosevelt for help. Because of a temporary absence from the state, her husband had been refused WPA work in the city. Now, after selling most of their furniture and with an impending gas shutoff, she made her appeal—"we are not fakers"—we are desperate. Others shared similar stories. World War I veteran Martin H.'s frustration was compounded by the fact that he had never even left the state, yet he too was denied WPA because of a short move from a small town outside of Buffalo into the city proper.

In the process, he was told, he had lost his eligibility for local relief and with that WPA. The logic of the situation eluded him. Why should he, a family man with a wife and three children, who wanted desperately to work, who tramped the streets "day after day," be denied the opportunity to work on WPA just because of residence? "Am I forced to accept charity," he asked, "when I positively do not want it, for that reason alone?"[18]

Five years later, with quite enough time having elapsed to implement the planned transition to WPA, Nels Anderson was to report that, due to local preference for their own, "cases of migrants who are assigned to WPA employment are so rare as to be conspicuous." The Governor's Commission confirmed this to be the case in New York. Except for a limited number of cases in New York City, the shift to WPA for the unattached transient usually meant a shift to WPA camps. While the camps did provide subsistence for approximately thirty-five hundred persons in the first year after the liquidation of the program, these camps would not accept applications by people stranded after the fall of 1935, and WPA followed a policy of closing the camps as quickly as possible.[19]

By June 1936, Thomas Cotton, now New York director of camp management, WPA, was able to report to Hopkins that he had thus far decreased the transient camp population to about one thousand, closing thirteen camps. The remaining nine camps continued to operate, but, he predicted, we "shall be forced to close all camps by September or October." Anticipating future problems, he attempted to persuade Hopkins to convert the abandoned transient camps to facilities for the local homeless, whom he saw as transients in the making. His suggestion was rejected as inconsistent with the current philosophy of the administration.[20]

The current philosophy was, as we have seen, to treat the transient as part of the general relief population. If they were employable, they would be eligible for WPA, regardless of settlement, and would thus have the opportunity to prove themselves and, more importantly, to shed the stigma of a separate transient designation. The philosophy was fine. Translating it on the local level, however, as we have seen, was less than effective. Thus, one of the twin pillars of the second New Deal proved ineffective. The second pillar excluded the transient per se. To qualify for any of the benefits of Social Security, the applicant had to have worked under the plan or be the dependent of someone who had. Unemployed transients, obviously, need not apply. In the transition from early New Deal to later New Deal it becomes increasingly apparent that the transient was one who needed the "net" referred to by Russell Kurtz, but general relief was no longer in place. In the last analysis, therefore, rather than offering the transient a final victory, as Hopkins believed, the new direction of the administration once again left the transient as the "forgotten man" of the New Deal.

Not only were the New Deal programs incapable of absorbing the transients left over from the federal program, but the tide of that population continued to swell as the depression refused to subside. Industries continued to collapse leaving stranded employees faced with the choice of inadequate local relief or migration. For example, when the largest single employer in Manchester, New Hampshire, was forced to close in 1935, one-half of the city's labor force became jobless. In New Castle, Pennsylvania, the results were similar as iron and steel mills closed down leaving a 64 percent drop in employment in their wake. In Illinois coal country the closing of still-productive mines in the face of declining prices and the competition of oil meant unemployment rates as high as 42 percent followed by a steady population decline.[21] These experiences were being repeated nationwide as industries cut back, closed down, or relocated.

Not all of the unemployment that fed the resulting exodus, however, was due to the collapsed economy. A good deal of it resulted from the immediate effects of potential recovery. Despite the depression, technological development proceeded apace, resulting in many new work-saving devices and techniques which would eventually help business and the economy to recover. With every such development, however, workers found themselves unemployed, their particular hand skills becoming obsolete. By 1939 approximately one million fewer persons were employed in nonagricultural pursuits than had been a decade earlier, yet industry was still capable of producing as much without them. Railroad employment, for example, decreased 57.4 percent between 1923 and 1936, yet those employed were able to perform more man-hours of work due in part to increasing mechanization. "In 1923 they rode the trains as workers," commented Nels Anderson. "In 1936 they ride the trains as hobos." Accompanying such technological accomplishments, there often came a "trickle-down" effect on other suffering industries. The greater efficiency of railroads, for example, was in great part due to the use of oil. This had a devastating effect on its former chief supplier, the coal industry. In 1936 coal employed only about 72 percent of the number of workers it had in 1920. At the same time, the growing petroleum industry was so man-hour efficient that it could not absorb the displaced miners.[22]

What was happening to industry was also happening in the agricultural sector. During the late nineteenth and early twentieth centuries, the urban areas of this nation had enticed labor off the farms and from across the seas to feed the growing industrial machine that was bringing prosperity and greatness to the nation. With the depression these people were no longer needed, yet the rural population continued to need the cities to absorb its excess labor. The city's welcome, however, was no longer extended. In addition to the pressure of the natural increase, those already employed in agriculture also faced technological displacement. Dropping farm prices in the 1920s had necessitated that farming become more efficient — larger tracts of land had to be farmed to produce enough to show a profit. Mechanization and concentration provided the efficiency and the profit. Small farmers and tenants, bankrupted by debts accumulated in the "good days" of World War I, were bought out by owners or investors with capital enough to convert inefficient small holdings into mechanized farms, or "factories in the fields." The result was modernized farming, but along with it came the displacement of hundreds of thousands of small owners, tenants, and sharecroppers.* Government attempts to rehabilitate agriculture only hastened the process. If was only natural that owners, given the option by the Agricultural Adjustment Administration (AAA) to plow under a portion of their land in return for much needed subsidies, would choose the most unproductive parcels of their holdings, that is, those farmed by tenants and croppers. Finally, adding to the economic effects of the depression and the natural tendencies of modernization, Mother Nature also conspired against those hundreds of thousands of croppers and small

---

*Larger farms also meant the replacement of farm hands with farm machines. The real culprit was the tractor. Anyone who has read John Steinbeck's moving epic of the Joad family, will surely not forget the farmers' encounter with these unfeeling "monsters." As the tractors plowed over the land, the farmers stood by watching, rifles in hand, wanting to fight for their land as they had in the past, but not knowing who or what to fight. "Who can I shoot," Steinbeck's farmer pleads. "I don't aim to starve to death before I kill the man that's killing me." Yet they did stand by helpless as the tractor plowed under their fields, pushed over their houses, and uprooted them from their past. (John Steinbeck, *The Grapes of Wrath*, New York, 1958, ed., p. 52).

farmers who tried desperately to hold onto their land and livelihood. Severe drought and harsh windstorms which turned the center of the nation from the Texas Panhandle to the Canadian border into a Dust Bowl during the years of 1932–1936, followed by grasshopper plagues, destroyed the hopes of thousands.

The exodus from the Dust Bowl was so great that it literally changed the composition of the transient population and usurped the place of the lone transient in most depression histories. As large and extended families like Steinbeck's Joads took to the road, they began to outnumber the lone unattached men that had preceded them in the public mind and in statistical profiles as the typical transient. From their numbers rose the image of the Oakie who is still readily identified as the depression migrant.

The combined effects of continued unemployment, industrial and agricultural displacement, and the ravages of nature added to the numbers of uprooted who might be looking to New York state for jobs. Buffalo, a port city of the Great Lakes and a railroad center, had for a long time attracted transient seamen and laid-off railway and factory workers. Once again they came hopefully in search of work. Adjacent farm lands in Western New York also attraced a flood of agricultural laborers in season. Nearby Lackawanna, with its industrial base, similarly was a Mecca for the displaced factory worker. Industrialists in both Lackawanna and East Rochester complicated the transient problem in their areas by encouraging workers into the area when their labor was required and then abandoning them when no longer needed. In the Rochester area such abandoned factory workers mingled with migratory agricultural workers attracted to Monroe County fruit farms in summer and into the city for jobs in the winter. New York City, traditionally attractive to persons looking for excitement and opportunities, continued to draw migrants who could not help believe that a city of that size must have either jobs or relief for them.[23]

The dismantling of FERA had been done with the assumption that it was part of a transition to recovery. While the following year, 1936, appeared to justify the optimistic belief that the depression was indeed ending, the recession of 1937, in large part the result of that transition itself, showed that the economy was not ready for a government withdrawal. In order to facilitate the transition, FDR not only ended FERA, but in June 1937 he attempted to cut government deficit spending by drastically curtailing WPA. In effect, he stopped priming the pump, and the pump ran dry. In August 1937 industrial activity experienced the "most brutal drop in the country's history." *The New York Times'* business index went from 110 to 85 wiping out all gains made since 1935. As a result, between Labor Day 1937 and the end of the year, two million more people were thrown out of work, all becoming potential transients, once again accelerating the problem that the government had considered all but resolved. The situation did not reverse itself until the spring of 1938 when FDR resumed multi-million dollar spending. By that time many more had already joined the swelling ranks of the indigent transient class.[24]

While FDR did reconsider the cutting of WPA funds when he saw the results of his actions, he did no such thing when the effects of the liquidation of the transient program were brought to his attention. The federal government did not again become actively involved in the issue of transient relief until 1940 when a House panel, convened under the chairmanship of Representative John H. Tolan of California, began a series of hearings in cities from coast to coast on "the interstate migration of destitute citizens." The hearings were to collect 12,400 pages of testimony before United States involvement in World War II put the surplus population back to work in factories or in fatigues. In the intervening years, 1935–40, the government confined itself to studying the problem through various agencies. Numerous such efforts were conducted by the WPA. *Depression Pioneers, Migrant Families, Migratory Casual Worker, The Transient Unemployed,* and *Problems of a Changing Population* were but a few of the finished research projects that traced the consequences of life after FERA for the relief population. Jacob Fisher points out "the irony of the executioner making public the suffering of his victims," that is, the irony of the WPA studying the effects of the demise of its predecessor. "The more cynical said it was cheaper to study the effects of the end of the FERA than to restore the program." He also questions the impact of the studies upon the policy makers, believing that few, if any, read the reports, and even fewer took them into account in formulating new policy.[25]

In 1936 Congress did authorize the secretary of labor to "study, survey, and investigate the social and economic needs of laborers migrating across state lines," in order to aid Congress in enacting remedial legislation.[26] Pursuant to the resolution, Secretary Frances Perkins conducted a remarkably comprehensive study and reported her results to Congress. Despite the obvious need apparent in the report given one year later, nothing was done to enact the contemplated "remedial legislation." Several bills offering a variety of solutions to the problem were presented to Congress, but nothing became of them. All other efforts to aid the transient were conducted by individual agencies including the Department of Agriculture, the Department of Labor, the Public Health Service, the National Youth Administration, and the Civilian Conservation Corps. The most significant such effort was the establishment of some forty-five camps for migratory workers by the Resettlement Administration. After living in hoovervilles, company camps, and on the roadside, these sanitary, self-governed, well-organized, and well-protected government camps provided many transients with their first taste of decency and dignity since leaving home. Unfortunately, this relatively small number of experimental camps, only housing approximately 150 people each, must be regarded as insignificant compared to the overwhelming number of people in need of such services.

The effect of the economic changes and the government's reluctance to become reinvolved was the creation of an army of dispossessed — "America's own refugees." Normally stable families traveling with all of their worldly possessions perched precariously atop dilapidated jalopies, or piled high atop push carts reminiscent of the dispossessed of imperial Russia of old, met on the road with tens of thousands of other hitchhiking or walking across the country in search of jobs and homes. Together the uprooted family and unattached individual met with the seasonal laborer who had long been roaming the country, creating numbers impossible to absorb. What to do with this human suffering was once again to be the responsibility of the individual states.

How the states accepted this responsibility varied greatly. Some states continued to operate the temporary emergency relief administrations that had been set up under the now defunct FERA. Some transferred relief responsibility to permanent state welfare agencies, while others liquidated state relief altogether and passed the responsibility on to the localities. Consequently, the quality of relief varied drastically from state to state, while the loss of federal funds invariably meant lower standards, no matter which of the above was resorted to. In some states constitutional limits on debt and tax rates prohibited them from doing any more than setting up committees to study the problem.[27] The universal reaction, however, was the logical one — to revert to past practice. What this meant was a vigorous application of pre-1933 state welfare laws; that is, settlement and removal laws. During the federal program, Washington had assumed responsibility for all persons without one year's state residency, regardless of the state and its laws, thus alleviating some of the previous obsession with settlement. As long as the federal government was paying the bills, settlement lost some of its urgency. With liquidation, however, the states quickly scrambled back behind the protective barriers of strictly interpreted settlement laws. Once again eligibility for relief was gained only by state-specified residency requirements.

Complicating the situation even further was the fact that a uniform settlement law had never been developed by the states. Some kind of uniformity had been imposed from above during the federal program, but after its liquidation the states reverted to forty-eight different variations of what settlement was, how it was gained, and how it was lost. In 1935 the time required to gain settlement varied from six months in four states, to one year in thirty-two states (including New York), three years in seven states, four years in one state, and five years in five states. Even this great variation was further complicated by how the time was to be calculated. Depending upon the state, residency was to be measured by time spent "prior to" or "immediately proceding" application, by a determined amount of "continuous" residence "without interruption," or by "consecutive years." In Colorado, so as not to confuse what continuous meant, 350 days physical presence out of the preceding year was specified. Many states added that a specified amount of time must be spent in a particular city, county, or town to qualify for settlement. For example, Oregon and Texas required one year residency in the state and six months in a particular county; Ohio required twelve months' residency in the state and three months in a township or municipal corporation; Nevada law provided for three years in the state and six months in one county. In addition, most states, including New York, specified that the applicant must have been "self-supporting," or maintaining himself and his family "without receiving public aid," or, in some cases, private aid or even family help, during the required residency period. In many states specific sections of the settlement laws excluded time spent in public or private institutions, including hospitals, poorhouses, jails or prisons, homes for the aged, veterans homes, or military bases, from the final calculation of residency. Parolees, employees on Indian reservations, and former tuberculosis patients were also excluded from gaining settlement in some states. New York put specific prohibitions on persons living in counties where TB sanatoriums were located.[28]

The attempt to deny settlement to paupers and other undesirables was even more rigidly pursued in other states. In North Carolina, for example, the settlement law required one-year residence for the self-supporting, and three-years residence for paupers. In Pennsylvania applicants were required to establish a permanent residence and demonstrate that they had "sufficient mental ability to make a bargain," before being recognized as settled. Paupers in Vermont were susceptible to a ten dollar fine and ninety days' imprisonment if they should apply for aid after having once been denied it for lack of settlement. Statutes in Virginia and West Virginia determined settlement by the ability of the applicant to maintain himself at the time he entered the state. Iowa and North Dakota even retained and utilized the warning system, denying settlement to any paupers who had been duly warned to leave the state.[29] Each one of these statutes was of dubious constitutional validity. Each was a denial of the legal right of U. S. citizens to cross the borders of the various states at will. New York, New Jersey, and California, however, shared the dubious distinction of encompassing one of the most blatant abuses of this constitutional right within the legal system. The culprit was the pauper law.

Pauper laws prohibited the importation of known paupers into the state. In New York this meant:

> Any person who knowingly brings, or causes to be brought, a destitute person from out of the state into this state and leaves him or attempts to leave him for the purpose of making him a public charge, shall be guilty of a misdemeanor punishable by a fine of one hundred dollars, and shall be obligated to convey such person out of the state or to support him at his own expense.

Though not well publicized, the law was not obsolete, and it was used in at least one case in an attempt to remove a family of Oakies from Buffalo. In November 1938, Mr. and Mrs. Austin Walker were arraigned in city court on charges of bringing destitute children likely to become charges into the state. The paupers in question were their five children. The Erie County Welfare Department explained that they chose to prosecute this case because this was the second time that the family had hitchhiked to Buffalo from Oklahoma. The first time they had been removed from New York at the expense of $122 in railway fare. "We want to put a stop to this," explained the prosecutor. Judge Clifford McLaughlin adjourned the case while the husband attempted to find a job by which to support his family; thus a test of the constitutionality of the law was not to come from this case.[30] On the other side of the country, however, a similar law in California was to receive court testing all the way to the U.S. Supreme Court where it was declared unconstitutional.*

The individual states jealously guarded their interests through a variety of settlement laws. Equally complicated and diversified laws meant to determine how settlement was lost show just how eager they were to terminate that relationship whenever possible. Very few states provided that settlement remain in effect until the individual acquired a new settlement in another state. The common sense of this approach was overshadowed for most states by the obvious fact that they could find themselves supporting out-of-state past residents virtually for life. This led an increasing number of states to either not specify how settlement was lost, and thus leave it up to the welfare officials to determine, or else to resort to vague clauses regarding intention to leave. Both depended on an interpretation of the individual case and thus left a large loophole by which settlement rights could be denied to indigents who had left the state but still required financial support. Other states were more

---

*The law in question was an obscure section of the 1901 anti-migration law of California which had been revived in the 1930s when more stringent laws to restrict migration had failed to pass the state legislature. By its language, the importation of any known "pauper, poor, indigent, or incapacitated or incompetent person into the state" constituted a misdemeanor. The unconstitutionality of this law and the pauper law concept was decided by the Supreme Court in the appellate case of *Edwards v. California*. The case involved a California man who had been convicted under the state statute for bringing a destitute relative into the state. The attorney for the appellant argued that the prohibition of movement in and out of a state threatened to cause a condition of peonage by which people would be chained to one area by the accident of birth. Legally, he argued that the California statute invaded the power of the national government to regulate interstate commerce, deprived the appellant of equal protection under the law, and violated the Fourteenth Amendment of the Constitution. John Tolan, then chairing the House Investigation on Migration, offered an *amicus curiae* argument for reversal. While the attorneys for California claimed that the statute was within the jurisdiction of the police power of the state, the court reversed the lower court's decision and held invalid the California statute as an unconstitutional burden on interstate commerce.[31]

precise in seeing to it that their responsibility not be abused. In South Dakota, Utah, and Mississippi loss of settlement ranged from thirty days' to four to six months' absence from the state. Many states, including New York, compromised between these two approaches by specifying that settlement was both gained and lost by the same period of time.[32] Not understanding the intricacies of settlement laws, many people unwittingly lost settlement and, with it, all claims to relief back home as they roamed the country in search of employment. They became, as Secretary Perkins put it, "stateless."

Without such a variety of settlement laws, it is easy to anticipate the chaos that was to result when the transient again became a state and local responsibility. Not only did such laws affect the individual, but the more complex and prohibitive the laws became, the less chance there was that indigent persons entering a state would have any place of settlement responsible for them or, consequently, any place to which they could be returned. Thus the laws of one's sister states could and often did increase the welfare burdens of any one state. This was especially true in the case of states such as New York which assumed legal responsibility either on the state or local level for all nonsettled persons within its borders. For example, if a person were to leave South Dakota and come to New York in search of employment, a search which extended over one month, he or she could lose settlement in South Dakota and become the responsibility of a public welfare district in New York. Each state and its laws provided a different variation of this predicament. The situation was further complicated after 1935 by the fact that many persons who had sought refuge in transient centers outside of their home states had in the intervening weeks, months, or years lost by their absence all claim to settlement back home. Once again this was to complicate the situation in New York because of its wholehearted implementation of and cooperation with the Federal Transient Program.

The state and its problems aside, the effect of this system on the individual could be devastating. The same person traveling from South Dakota, Utah, or Mississippi, if he lost home settlement, would have to wait from a few months to five years to acquire it again *anywhere*, least of all back home. If the same person were to have had settlement in New York, but lost it by an absence of one year, and sought to settle in Maine, Massachusetts, New Jersey, New Hampshire, or Rhode Island, it would be five years before he or she would acquire settlement and be eligible for any form of public relief. The variety of laws thus subverted the centuries-old concept upon which local relief had been founded, the belief that everyone belonged somewhere and that that someplace was responsible for his/her care.

As the nation's transient crisis worsened, many states sought additional protection against the indigent by further raising their legal barriers. Between January 1938 and October 1939, eight states increased their residency requirements. In New York a bill was proposed in the legislature raising settlement to five years. Although defeated, the proposal revealed a growing fear that the state needed more protection against "relief floaters." During the same period more states were changing their laws to eliminate specific regulations regarding the loss of settlement. Along with this, *The Transient* noted a stricter interpretation of the laws. "Rulings that settlement has been lost by intent," it was reported, "are more and more frequent in certain states." Some states began a system of double protection, specifying that settlement alone was not enough to qualify for relief. In Pennsylvania, for example, one years' residency was required for settlement, but two years were necessary to receive public assistance. In Illinois it was three years.[33] As the states withdrew responsibility through such measures, the localities more and more were forced to find immediate solutions for the now twice-abandoned transient. Regardless of whether local laws prohibited care as strictly as the state and federal governments now did, the practical reality was that the people were there on their doorstep and something had to be done.

By all accounts, contemporary and historical, the reception received by the transient seeking local relief was not welcoming. The year of transition that followed liquidation, according to social work historian Josephine Brown, "stands out as a time of confusion and near chaos in the history of public relief. It was a time of uncertainty, insecurity and even terror for the relief client who could not get work relief jobs and who had no sure niche in the developing categorical programs."[34] The transient surely was one such person without a "niche." In many cases when transient programs were liquidated by federal order, nothing was done by the states to assume the responsibility. As a result, the transient was forced to turn to local relief agencies which were totally unprepared, incapable, and often unwilling to pick up the responsibility. A full five years after liquidation Nels Anderson was to report that transients did not, in fact, receive equal consideration with residents in local public relief agencies. In order of priority, he found that the limited relief funds available were distributed first to local unemployables, then to families, and then, if funds were still available, to the resident homeless. At the end of the line came migrant families followed by unattached transients.[35] Public relief, by and large, still followed the dictates of local responsibility. Thus, in practice, public relief was not forthcoming for the majority of transients.

Private agencies, less restricted by legalities, generally accepted applicants to the limits of their resources. Approximately one-half of those cared for privately were to be found in mission houses. Such establishments usually accepted all who applied, on the condition that they remain sober and attend religious services. Other agencies, the Salvation Army, Travelers Aid, YMCA, and the like, usually limited the amount of time a transient could stay with their agency to anywhere from twenty-four hours to a few days, or they limited their services to specific categorical groups, such as families, juveniles, or emergency cases.

In many communities the private agencies provided the only assistance available to transients. In Norfolk, Virginia, the Salvation Army provided the only services, and those were severely limited. Not far away in Richmond the private agencies were their only recourse. In Nashville the men were sent to the Salvation Army and women to Travelers Aid. "High class fellows" were sent to the YMCA "where they have a high class environment." In Omaha, Nebraska a poor Community Chest campaign denied Travelers Aid's request for funding. Since the city's other private agencies did not include allotments in their budgets for nonresidents, there was no agency that would assume responsibility for transients. Another Nebraska agency reported that "non-residents and transients are treated as if they did not exist." In Minneapolis limited budgets meant that the agencies could provide only one night's lodging and two meals for transient applicants. In one town in Illinois the work test was resurrected by a local agency to determine which transients would receive food or aid. In this case, the test was administered at the woodpile. The plan was reportedly working well "as the man who is transient rather by force of circumstances than desire is very glad to give some labor for decent food and clean lodging, while the bum or pure tramp . . . stays away from here because if he will not work willingly he is promptly dealt with rather harshly."[36]

In some cases the valiant efforts of these few agencies were circumvented by restrictive Community Chest policies. Rationalizing that monies donated to their drives were contributed by the public to meet resident needs, and that the dispensing of aid to transients would not only violate this trust but might also attract outsiders, some chests withheld funding from agencies that cared too liberally for the transient. Some agencies capitulated; others stubbornly resisted the intimidation. The local Travelers Aid in Los Angeles, for example, continued to service transients even though the Community Chest had cut off their funds for that very reason. Travelers Aid was, by the way, the only agency in the city attempting to meet this need.[37]

With such limited means of support, various methods, both innovative and revived from the poor law past, were used to deter transients and to keep them on the move. "The hospitality of the police station, the 'two meals and a flop' in a municipal lodging house or second rate mission, the curt 'move on, you!' of the sheriff at the county line, or actual arrest and sentence to the workhouse or chain gang," Potter reported, "have been and still are the penalties too frequently exacted from the victims of misguided migration."[38] Another serious student of the transient problem, Dr. Eric Beecroft, enumerated more specific examples:

> In Spokane, Washington, single men transients asking for relief have been sent to the police department for fingerprinting before being referred to a relief agency. Norfolk, Va., has provided food and shelter for transient men at the city prison farm; and a welfare agency there reports that 'they naturally do not relish this kind of care, and this probably discourages transiency in Norfolk.' In Salt Lake City single men transients have been housed at the police station, while the police department has attempted to discourage transients from coming into the city. After 50 cents in cash is given to a single man transient in Hartford, Conn., three people look at him, and if he is seen again in the city he is arrested for vagrancy. In Akron, Ohio, the male, nonfamily transient who applies for assistance is given meals for the day, a night's lodging and breakfast, and instructed to move on.

Such community hostility had various tragic effects on the transient. According to Beecroft, the arbitrary treatment of transients as criminals by the local police tended to assume criminal or other undesirable qualities to innocent individuals. Mislabeling and misconceptions also resulted from such treatment. When so received the migrant could never become established; he lost pride and dignity and became a constant wanderer. Another result predicted by Beecroft but which never materialized was the radicalization of this frustrated but, as yet, unrevolutionary and unpolitical people. Beecroft's comments were shared with the U.S. Congress when the preceding article was read into the *Congressional Record*.[39]

Other more physical means were also used to either remove the transient or prevent his ever entering a particular community. The "hobo express" proved effective in a number of places. Transients were physically loaded onto trucks and dumped over county or state lines. In other towns near railroad crossings or depots, armed guards would meet incoming trains and prevent transients from disembarking, or they would round up the transients and put them on freight cars heading out of town, despite the loud protests of the railroad companies. The most blatant abuse of civil rights to prevent transients from entering city limits was the infamous border patrol of the Los Angeles Police Department. Testifying before the Tolan Committee, Governor Culbert Olson of California described the patrols as a force created by the Los Angeles Chief of Police to patrol all highways along the state border watching for vagrants and to "discourage" such people from entering California. Olson stressed the ambiguity of the term discourage and added that the patrol was established despite the opinion of the state's attorney general that it was illegal. According to Olson, it eventually proved ineffective and was discontinued, having turned back "only" fourteen hundred persons from November 1935 to April 1936.[40] Carey McWilliams, then Commissioner of Immigration and Housing of California, showed the obvious outrage that such actions deserved. In his book *Factories of the Field*, he referred to the "power drunk" patrols as being created in "flat disregard of constitutional provisions."[41] Such treatment was extreme, and its blatant violation of the rights of U. S. citizens to move freely from state to state brought loud protests from across the country. *The Chicago Daily News* referred to the force as a "foreign legion" violating both the Constitution and its own city charter; the *News-Telegram* of Portland, Oregon, called it an "attack upon vital American principles"; while the *Evening Gazette* of Reno, Nevada, related the anxieties of those states bordering California which would be left with those indigents denied access to the state. Yet, in New York, it is interesting to note that the *Buffalo Evening News* was editorially sympathetic with Los Angeles due to the fact that 40 percent of the city's population was already on relief.[42]

Despite the clamor and generally adverse public outcry, Colorado's Governor Edwin Johnson followed the California example calling out the National Guard to protect the state's borders from Utah to Kansas from "alien laborers." The guards were under executive order to stop all cars, buses, and trains in search of "undesirables." Governor Dave Sholz of Florida followed suit in late 1935 and organized a road patrol of state police to prevent undesirables from entering that state. The patrol was disbanded by the new governor in January 1937.[43]

Such extreme measures as border patrols and hobo expresses mirrored a growing prejudice toward and fear of the indigent transient. The depression had already taxed the dwindling number of the local citizenry that remained employed to unbearable limits in their efforts to support their less fortunate neighbors. Helen and Robert Lynd, for example, found one-fourth of the Muncie, Indiana, population supported on relief by the rest of "Middletown." Under such conditions, available sympathy was spread thin. In addition to competing for relief, impoverished transients undercut local wages and thus threatened resident jobholders. As summarized by Philip Ryan:

> The community at large feels little or no responsibility for aiding the migrant and fears the consequences of extending help. The newcomer doesn't 'belong': he had made no contribution to the community; he may become a permanent charge and a drain upon its resources. If aid is given him, it may mean that less assistance can be granted to local needy persons; other migrants may be attracted; and not only may the burden of relief become excessive but community standards may be threatened.[44]

No one in the latter days of the depression needed these constant reminders that the corner around which prosperity was to be found had not yet been turned. Travelers Aid's general director, Bertha McCall, hinted at this attitude in testimony before Congress when she explained that the greatest problem faced by private organizations was the "unwillingness of communities to accept the very fact that there is any problem." The Lynds found in Muncie a similar attitude of trying to take the depression lightly so as to convince oneself that it was temporary. The idea also existed that giving outright charity was against the American Way; it was demoralizing to the recipient. Concurrent with this belief was the continued faith that, in this land of equal opportunity, any man could get a job "if he really wanted to." Signs of hostility were also found in Middletown editorials with titles such as "Let's Take Care of Our Own."[45]

As a result of the ending of the federal program and local reaction, the transient's living conditions reverted to pre-1933 levels. "Men have gone back to park benches to sleep, back to the back door handout, back to the hobo jungle. 'Brother, can you spare a dime?' promises again to become our national appeal. The soup kitchen and the bread lines seems imminent," was the assessment of one contemporary observer. "From New Jersey to California," wrote another, "reports pour in of new 'jungles' springing up in the fertile soil of abandoned excavations under bridges, along rivers, dumps and railroads. The origins of many of these colonies is traceable to the discontinuance of shelters and work camps." As Secretary of Labor Perkins reported to Congress in the recession year of 1938:

> Living conditions for most migrants are deplorable. Families with as many as six children are traveling in old cars and trucks. At night they sleep by the road-side, in squatter camps, or crowd into one-or-two room cabins in low-priced tourist camps. Unattached men live, for the most part, in congregate shelters maintained by relief agencies or in 'jungles.' Even labor camps provided for migrant agricultural workers are frequently crowded, inadequately equipped and unsanitary.

Such conditions, she reported, were of danger to the transient and to the communities through which they passed. In general, she felt, the whole situation represented a threat to "the development of good citizens."[46] All of these conditions were to be dramatized by John Steinbeck a few years later.

While some observers felt that the migrant's life style was of his own choosing and used this to justify their attitude toward him, most transients, when someone bothered to ask, despised what the nomadic life was doing to themselves and their children. When asked by Anderson if he would stop moving if he could, one migrant replied: "As far as I'm concerned, I'd rather go to war if I knew my kids were eating than to be up against what I have to face now. . . . Going to war would be a lot easier than seeing your kids hungry and not being able to do anything."[47]

Despite loud protests, the Federal Transient Program did end with the year 1935. For all intents and purposes, the new year saw the burden of transient relief once again turned over to the states and local communities. Yet, very little had happened between the years 1933 and 1935 to assume that the transient would fare any better in the years after the program than they had before it. Circumstances, in fact, seemed to conspire against them. The combined effects of technological displacement, recession, and the ravages of Mother Nature was swelling their numbers. The states, which had for the most part been cooperative while the federal government was paying the bills, once again scurried behind the protection of their anti-quated settlement and removal laws. The concept of a universal one-year settlement was replaced with the chaos of forty-eight separate and conflicting state relief laws. Complicating the situation further, many states proceeded to increase the restrictive features of those laws while local communities often resorted to extra-legal methods such as border patrols and the hobo express to guarantee their pro-tection. As state and local governments scrambled to protect them-selves, they in turn complicated the situation in neighboring states. The more effective they were in preventing transients from mi-grating into their states or in passing them out of the state, the more the burden increased in those states that attempted to meet this new crisis with responsible action. This was precisely the case when New York State attempted to cope with the transient problem in the years following the liquidation of the federal program.

₹ 10 §

"On Every Town's Doorstep"

THE situation in New York State immediately following liquidation closely paralleled the confusion and chaos that reigned nationwide. In New York City private agencies, straining to take care of their own, could not absorb the transient. At the same time, public relief to nonresidents was limited to a single night's care at the municipal lodging house. A one-night census of the city conducted by the Emergency Relief Bureau found six thousand men sleeping in subways, parks, abandoned buildings, terminals, and similar makeshift shelters. An acute situation in Albany caused the private agencies to announce in November that the problem was beyond their resources, and, with the exception of Jewish assistance agencies, all private aid for transient men was to be discontinued. At that time there were already almost one thousand transient or unsettled people in the capital district and hundreds more were soon to be released from nearby camps. While attempts were made to reopen the Salvation Army's Lyon Lodge to accommodate those left homeless by the closing of the federal camps, all that was currently available were two local missions or "accommodations" at the police precincts. According to the local representative of the NCCTH, the efforts of that group to secure shelter and aid for the homeless had thus far been fruitless:

> There isn't any public agency where these men can be taken care of
> . . . .We've sent telegrams to the President, to H. L. Hopkins, to
> the governor, and we talked to Lester W. Herzog, administrator,
> WPA, but we haven't accomplished anything. Private agencies
> haven't funds to take care of these people. The government won't

and relief officials say they are trying to give WPA jobs to all employables. But nothing has been done so far, and the fellow who wanders into Albany or the homeless man is simply up against it, except what help he can get from the Salvation Army and the missions — and they haven't funds enough.

On January 10, 1936, the *Albany Evening News* reported that the "hundreds of penniless, homeless and wandering men on Albany streets are the 'forgotten men' in the present relief situation." From Schenectady came reports that transient men could only expect to receive overnight care in the City Mission in the months that followed liquidation. In Syracuse the unattached man received a bed for one night, two meals, and orders to move on.[1]

Similar situations were occurring across the state, especially in those areas where transients had been congregated between 1933 and 1935 by the federal program. The care of unattached men, the Governor's Commission reported, had "reverted back to jails, county homes, local missions, and other private agencies — and the lodging given is again limited to one or two-day periods, thus fostering a continuous movement of this segment of the population." Overall, they concluded that "the cessation of the former transient relief program has left many persons, who were formerly cared for without aid," and that, with the precarious nature of WPA and the questionable stability of private agencies, the problem was indeed severe.[2] Municipalities facing the imminent release of the present occupants of the federal transient camps agreed. Although New York did, by the terms of the state's Public Welfare Law, accept responsibility for those classified as the state poor, technicalities within the law and conflicts with the state's temporary emergency relief measure, the Wicks Act, served to exclude many needy non-settled persons during the period following liquidation. By the terms of the Public Welfare Law, the state assumed full financial responsibility for all persons without settlement in any welfare district in the state who had not resided in any such district for sixty days. Persons who had remained sixty days or more were then the responsibility of the locality. Under the Wicks Act localities were reimbursed 40 percent of the cost of all relief cases they financed for persons with two years' residence. The provisions of these laws left a large gap into which a majority of the unsettled population fell. Unless applicants were in a district less than sixty days or more than two years, the localities could not expect any state reimbursement for relief funds allocated to them and were understandably reluctant to assume the burden alone. WPA should have filled the gap, but, as we have seen, it did not.

Those people caught between the Wicks Act and the terms of the state's Public Welfare Law found themselves in a "no man's land." The frustration of this situation is evident in the protest of one Guy M. Mr. M.'s problem, as explained to him by the relief officials in Rochester, was that the office could not document a residence of twelve months for him in any place, in-state or out. Therefore, he was a man without settlement. This meant that he could not be transported, as he requested, back "home" to Birmingham, Alabama. "Regardless of the ruling of Monroe County . . . and of the N. Y. State departments of relief," he wrote Hopkins, "I know that I am entitled to relief. I am a citizen of the United States irrespective of where I might be in the U. S. Relief funds are for the relief of destitute citizens." Unfortunately, for Mr. M., this commonly held belief, that a citizen of one state is a citizen of all states and share equal rights, as stated in the Constitution, did not take the fine print of the states' settlement laws into account.[3]

The fine print of settlement was especially frustrating for people who considered themselves New Yorkers, yet were informed when they applied for relief that they were in fact transients in their own home towns. The search for a job, as we have seen, took many people far from their place of birth. Some considered the move permanent and looked for homes and communities as well as jobs. For many more, however, traveling around the country was only a temporary expedient in a crisis situation. They had no intention of severing their ties with home. It was only when they returned that the full consequence of their job hunting became known. Donald C. of Hornell, New York, was one who found this out the hard way. After spending four years at temporary jobs in the western states, Mr. C. returned home to his wife and children in 1935 to find that he had lost his settlement and was now legally a transient. "I can't see how they can possibly figure that I am not a resident of this state having never moved from the state only to go out to work," he protested in disbelief to the president. "I am," he wrote, "a man without a country."[4]

One way of dealing with people caught in the gap between the terms of the Wicks Act and the Public Welfare Law was to determine the place of their legal settlement and return them. Not all, however, appreciated the suggestion. Mrs. Tony Q., for example, wrote to Roosevelt to intercede on behalf of her, her husband, and their four children. The Q family were New York natives, but they had lost their settlement rights when the family moved to New Jersey to care for Mrs. Q.'s elderly parents. After losing two children to the "bad air" in New Jersey, they returned home. When her husband was unable to find work, they turned to the relief offices but were denied. In Mrs. Q.'s words, they were told that they would have to "go back in Jersey or starve." Convinced that the move would threaten her remaining four children, she wrote Roosevelt, "What good is it to be a citizen when they have to treat us like slaves. . . .I don't want to go back in Jersey. I have nobody there . . . for the sake of my children . . . please . . . do something for my children." Appealing to his paternal instincts, she pled, "Dear President just look at your children and then just think of my four children. What would you do in my place?"[5]

Ada S. confided a similar problem to the president. "I shall have to tell you my trouble," she wrote. "I have not wanted to do this, but am driven to it." Mrs. S. had made what she considered to be a permanent move to New York City in 1935 because she felt that there were more career opportunities open to her there than in her home in Tulsa, Oklahoma. While she was able to remain self-supporting for a year, she finally was forced to apply for relief. Not having two years' residence, however, her request for state-reimbursed relief was denied, and none of the city organizations would assume responsibility for her. "All the help I can get," she explained "is a ticket back to Oklahoma." However, having broken her ties with Tulsa she did not want to return. "I do not want to go back," she protested. "I have nothing to go to." Being "above begging" she was now making a personal appeal for assistance to the president.[6]

The situation for married women who were separated for one reason or another from their husbands, was particularly distressing. According to the Public Welfare Law, the legal settlement of a married woman followed that of her husband until such time as the marriage was legally dissolved. Therefore, women who left their husbands, were abandoned by them, or who were for other reasons living apart, were still considered legally settled wherever that husband happened to be. Similarly, if he lost his settlement and with it his rights to public relief, so did she. A number of actual cases from the state's attorney general's office illustrate the precarious position this put many women in.

In one case, for example, a woman who had lived fifteen years of her married life with her family in Vermont before leaving her husband and moving to New York was denied relief in Rochester even though she had supported herself and her children without public assistance for over one year. Since she was neither legally separated nor divorced from her husband, her settlement remained with him in Vermont, and she had no legal claim on the state of New York. Relief was also denied to a woman who had returned to her father in Jamestown, New York, after being deserted by her husband in Pennsylvania. Almost seven years after the desertion, having maintained unbroken residence in New York for the entire period, her settlement remained with her husband in Pennsylvania. In another case of abandonment a woman in New York continued to receive state relief for herself and her children after her husband left because his whereabouts were unknown and it could not be determined if his settlement had changed. After two years, however, it was learned that the husband had been living outside the state for the entire period. Consequently, he had lost his settlement and she lost her relief status.[7]

Mrs. Neil M., mother of four and native New Yorker, told a similar story to the first lady. At the time she wrote, her husband was serving a six to eight-year sentence in the Massachusetts State Prison, which was to be followed by another lengthy term in Arizona. She had four small children under the age of seven at home, and, therefore, could not work to support her family. Because her husband's settlement was in Massachusetts, she had been receiving care as a transient during the federal program, but now the program was terminated, and with it her only source of assistance was gone. Relief officials told her that Boston was responsible for her and offered to send her there. But, she explained, "I do not want to go to Boston to live as I know no one there, and the sixteen months I did spend in Boston were the most unhappy time in my life." Her ties were in New York where her family was close by to offer her "the encouragement and cheerful advice I sure do need." She ended with a final appeal, "I am pining [sic] all my hopes on what you might have to tell me. I have looked for advice and help everywhere I could think of and am writing you as a last recourse." Moved by the appeal, someone in Washington made inquiries to New York, which in turn made inquiries to the New York City Department of Public Welfare. The response: "We will try to convince her that it is best for her to return to the State of Massachusetts where she is entitled to widow's pension for the support of herself and her children." Apparently, the officials at the relief bureau either failed to recognize or could do nothing about her true problem—New York offered security while Boston was only an unpleasant memory.[8]

The legal quagmire in which these women, and the many others with similar stories, found themselves has a nightmarish quality about it. All the efforts on their behalf to determine legal responsibility were being done "in their best interest," but not according to their own wishes. The end result was that women were being wrenched from the security they desperately needed in times of crisis to satisfy a legal definition of belonging. While the intent was humane, in many instances the result was cruel, as these letters attest. Not only did enforcement of such laws severely limit the independence and mobility of many women, but it also caused undue suffering and an addded burden to already troubled lives.

Two more stories that were brought to the attention of the White House bear repeating in their entirety to fully appreciate the impact of settlement on human lives. The first is the story of Raymond W. He was young, thirty-two years old, married, and the father of three small children. Both he and his wife considered themselves New Yorkers, having both been born and raised in the city. When the depression threw Mr. W. out of work, he decided not to sit around and be a burden on his family, friends, or community, and went out looking for a new job. His efforts took him just across the Hudson, not far from home, to Newark, New Jersey, where he did find a job as a hotel clerk. Four years later that job was gone and he returned to the city where he was able to keep his family together "doing any kind of work I could secure," for awhile. Finally, in April 1935, he was forced to apply for relief. That was when he found out that the short trip across the river to Newark had cost him his settlement and, with it, his claim for relief. He also found that the only assistance for "nonresidents" like himself was at the Federal Transient Bureau, but that had been dismantled by this time. Like many before him, he was told that the only assistance available was temporary lodging and fare to return to Newark. He protested: "I have lived 28 years of my 32 in the City of New York and consider myself a New Yorker." He did not want to be returned to New Jersey. "As I have no connections in New Jersey, I see no reason for my returning there." Furthermore, even if he returned, he would not be eligible for relief in New Jersey because that state had a five year residency requirement, and he had only been there four years. The full extent of his situation was upon him. "They tell me," he explained, "mine is a borderline case. . . .In other words, I am not eligible for relief in any state in the United States."

After being refused relief at the Emergency Relief Bureau, he began the rounds of the private charities. None of them would accept his case either because they lacked funds or because of his lack of residency. Others simply told him that they were taking no new cases. "I have been chased from one Agency to another, on an empty stomach . . . and in the end have been able to receive no assistance, except one month's rent, supplied by our church." As that was now running out, and his children lay ill in the next room, fed this night on only coffee and bread, he made his last desperate appeal to the president.[9]

The second story is that of Mrs. Adys J. who appealed to Eleanor, "as I have read about the nice things you do for poor folks." In a lovely hand, she explained her plight. "My little family is *very much* in need of help, and I am too much of a mother to stand by and not try to help or ask for help." Her husband had only been able to find part-time work, on and off, for the last two years. Consequently, the family was separated. He looked for work and got by as best as he could, while she and the children stayed with relatives "here and there." In December 1935 the family was reunited and tried to make a go of it in a small twelve dollar per month flat which they bartered from the landlord in return for cleaning and painting it. "We could be happy [now] if only we had enough to eat. We hardly know what it means to have enough to eat." Her husband had applied for relief to try to keep the family together, but had been denied because of lack of residency. Now she appealed to the president's wife as a last resort. In a postscript she assured the first lady that any assistance would be held confidential. What happened to the family after this point is unknown.[10]

Throughout all of these letters and stories, and the many more they represent, there is not only an impassioned and poignant plea for help, but also a pervasive ser se of injustice that this could be happening to them, citizens of the United States. "I am a citizen," Guy M. kept repeating. They also share a surprise and disbelief over their present situation. For the most part, these were people who under normal circumstances would be self-supporting. It was the depression—lost jobs and hard times—that was the cause of their present problems and that put them into the awkward and uncomfortable position of having to ask for relief. "This is the first time I've had to ask for aid," Ada S. explained to the president. Donald C. cashed in his life insurance and made due with temporary jobs for almost a year before approaching the relief offices. Thus, it was for many a courageous act to put pride aside and apply for relief. Now they found, at first to their amazement and later their consternation, that their earlier attempts to find jobs, to be self-supporting, had cost them their eligibility for relief when they most needed it. Most had no idea of the complications of settlement laws as they started out looking for jobs to support their families or for opportunities for relocation and advancement. Raymond W. and Donald C. were looking for ways to support their families. Ada S. wanted to advance her career. Now they found out what it meant to be transient.

Another striking feature about the letters is the very personal tone of their appeals. Each, be it directed to Hopkins, the president, or his wife, was written on a personal level asking for direct intervention. Donald C. wrote Roosevelt as if he was asking for a personal favor between friends, "I will appreciate it if you will straighten out this mistake." Mrs. M. appealed to Mrs. Roosevelt as one parent to another. They were also very polite and apologetic for having imposed upon another with their troubles. "I am sorry to bother you with such," prefaced Mrs. S.'s request. "I sincerely hope I have not taken too much of your time with my lengthy letter," Mrs. J. apologized. Finally, they were appeals of last resort based on human compassion. "I am pining [sic] all my hopes on what you have to tell me," Mrs. M. wrote Eleanor. "You are my last recourse." Unfortunately, the responses were not offered in like tone. All letters were directed to the state TERA for further action. The situation for those lacking residencey in New York City was further complicated by a restrictive city charter that prohibited the city from supplying any outside relief, that is, home relief, out of municipal funds. This provision left the transient with the choice of institutional care, which meant splitting up the family, or no care at all. This situation was clearly on the mind of Raymond W. as he contemplated the fate of his family. Having inquired of the city's Emergency Relief Bureau what ultimately would become of him should he be evicted from his apart-

ment, he was informed that, in that case, his furniture would be con-
fiscated, his children would be placed in homes, and he and his wife
would be sent to shelters. In classic understatement, he protested, "I
hardly think that this is a way to help a man keep up his morale, be
clear-thinking, and helpful to himself."[11]

In addition, the refusal of the city to assume the initial financial
responsibility for persons who may have been eligible after examination for state relief as state poor automatically disqualified four hundred families from the state program. By April 1936 the Governor's
Commission was able to report that of the 9,455 families and unattached persons receiving transient relief on August 31, 1935, less
than one-half had been absorbed in WPA, "while other care at
public expense has been almost wholly discontinued." What became
of those not so absorbed, as well as the 22,511 transients and 540
transient families who had been refused aid by public and private
agencies in the month after liquidation, was hinted at by a survey
taken on April 1, 1936, by the New York City Police Department.
Over two thousand persons who admitted to being transients were
found sleeping in railroad stations, subway cars, in abandoned
buildings, under bridges, in public parks, and in other make-shift
shelters. Another 3,668 persons who were found to be in similar
destitute situations claimed residency; however, it was believed that
many of their number were also transient but were reluctant to admit it. Even this number was considered low because of the limited
nature of the search.[12]

For those persons denied public relief, the next recourse was
private charity, by tradition the mainstay in times of crisis. As Raymond W. learned, however, private agencies were not able to accept
all of the cases brought to their attention. Furthermore, the care they
were able to afford, especially in the area of casework, was limited
by their own standards. A field study conducted at the Buffalo office
of Travelers Aid from October 1935 to September 1937, by social
welfare student Janet Hirt, provides some insight into the difficulties
faced by one such agency as it attempted to serve its clients.

Hirt looked first at the community's reaction to the transient
and its effect on the local Travelers Aid in Buffalo. Obvious dangers
to the mental, physical, and moral well being of the transient resulting from a life "on the road," hitching rides, living in jungles,
and associating with hardened tramps and fugitive criminals, were
recognized by the community. However, the positive action that

could have alleviated the pain of the transient, as well as the resulting social problems for the community, was not taken. Hirt, as many a concerned social worker before her, could see that the causes of the transient's distress were often the same as those of the community's destitute:

> It is when the unhappy individual seeks to establish himself in another setting that the onus of being a transient is added to the already heavy burden which the unemployed, financially disabled individual carries. It is here that the new community steps in and shakes its head in vigorous disapproval of the transient's arrival.

Such community reaction had a decidedly negative effect upon what the agency could accomplish. To illustrate her point, Hirt gave the example of a twenty-year-old transient, Jane, who came to Buffalo for employment. She applied to Travelers Aid for assistance in making an adjustment in Buffalo and demonstrated the ability to make that adjustment "given proper treatment." The agency felt that returning her to her place of settlement, where she was unwanted by her family, would not be in her best interest, but "because she was a nonresident the existing services [in Buffalo] were not available to her." She was returned. The community thus failed to provide the proper agencies or care necessary to help such a person. Jane showed her determination to leave home when she again ran away to Buffalo. This time, however, she did not seek aid.[13]

A second insight provided by this study is a look at the agency's methods in handling transients. According to Hirt, when a transient man applied for a meal or a flop, an attempt was made to discover his legal residence, but nothing was done investigatively or in terms of case work beyond that point. If he wished to return home, an attempt was made to verify residence and to gain authorization for return. If successful, he was referred to the Department of Social Welfare which furnished transportation; otherwise, the applicant would most likely be sent to the Erie County Municipal Lodging House. Women were treated in the same manner, except that they were referred to the Erie County Emergency Relief Bureau for accommodations. Quick dismissals such as these were the key in most of the cases reviewed by Hirt. The most common resolutions were: "Applicant returned home," "Applicant referred to another agency," and "Applicant left or made plans of own." Runaways were simply returned home after settlement was established. In a few cases, however, the applicant did not want to return and either refused the aid of the agency or else ran away again as in the earlier case of Jane.[14] Such "treatment" was unsatisfactory from the viewpoint of the positive rehabilitative action desired by Hirt.

While referrals seem to have been blind alleys for many applicants, the most tragic cases were those in which no aid whatsoever was provided. This could be the result of the applicant's simply refusing to go to the referred agency, or it could be the neglect of severe cases of need merely because of the lack of facilities for treatment. Take for example the case of a fifteen-year-old runaway who was returned home to Buffalo by a Travelers Aid in the West. The brief five sentence abstract on his case ends:

> On returning he was beaten by his father who also took him out of school and insisted that he go to work until the money spent for transportation was paid back. Boy extremely unhappy in job found for him by his father, and threatening to run away again. No facilities for treatment.

A similar example is presented in the case of an eighteen-year-old boy referred to Travelers Aid by a clergyman for return to the South: "Since authorization to return him could not be secured [from the home community] and since there were no resources for assisting him in the city the boy was forced to make his own plans.[15]

While Travelers Aid's emphasis on referral is understandable, considering their lack of facilities, other private agencies followed the same procedures. Referrals and removals were not problem solvers; they were temporary delaying tactics. One can only wonder how the transient in need was able to accept this system with such apparent patience. Why did he not lash out, and, if he did rebel in his frustration, what eventually became of him?

The initial instruction of Governor Lehman to the Governor's Commission on Unemployment Relief had been issued in the midst of this crisis situation. The urgent pleas of the New York State Association of Public Welfare Officials for state relief and the pressure upon the legislature to act demanded a response. Being reluctant to assume the added financial burden that transient care entailed, the governor resorted to delaying tactics and, in the spring of 1936, referred the matter for study by the commission. Four months later, on August 3, 1936, their report, confirming earlier local reports and reinforcing the need for a comprehensive state program, was presented to the governor.[16]

The conclusions the commission offered were five fold: first, the end of the federal program left a gap in the financial care of the needy that the current state system did not fill; second, the localities either would not or could not handle the burden; third, New York's program as it existed would not reduce the transient problem, for people would continue to move and continue to remain without relief; fourth, controls on the transient population were necessary, for both county and state protection, to stop disease and panhandling and to prevent such people from being forced into "unsocial action as a means of livelihood"; fifth, that transiency was an interstate problem requiring renewed federal financial assistance. Until such aid was forthcoming, eleven recommendations were offered. The first five had to do with reorganizing the Department of Social Welfare, inter-agency cooperation, and better statistical recording. Next, they recommended a revision of the city charter of New York City to allow outdoor relief. Regarding standards of care, they recommended relief policies for unattached men that provided acceptable standards of "health, decency, and well-being"; whenever possible that work to be provided the able-bodied; and that care given for any length of time be of the "normal and noncongregate type, such as home relief." Where congregate care was necessary, it should meet certain standards. All warehouse types of congregate shelters should be replaced by small shelters housing fifty to three hundred individuals, and even they should only be used for temporary care. Finally, they recommended the adequate restriction and control of any relief beyond temporary and emergency care and suggested the use of qualified and experienced personnel to make decisions regarding transient cases based on full documentary evidence and the cooperation and willingness of the applicant.[17]

Following the recommendations of the commission, a bill was proposed to amend the Public Welfare Law in such a way as to transfer the burden of responsibility for the care of the unsettled from the local public welfare district to the State Department of Social Welfare. As such it received the hearty endorsement of organizations such as Travelers Aid and the State Charities Aid Association. On July 1, 1937, the resulting amendment became effective.

The 1937 amendment was significant in a number of ways. First of all, Albany now assumed the total cost of relief for "any per-

son who has no settlement in any public welfare district in this state."
Significant was the absence of the previous specifications that such
persons must not have resided for less than sixty days in any one
welfare district. Such persons were now referred to as *state charges.*
This provision was very similar to legislation vetoed two years
earlier by Governor Lehman as being too costly. Expense not-
withstanding, the state now assumed that burden. The care to be
provided was to be, "insofar as practicable," home relief. When institutional care was necessary, the law specified that it must meet
state standards. The liberality of such changes was tempered by the
virtual verbatim repetition of the section on forced removal, the addition of three more counties to the list of those in which tuberculosis
patients were required to have five years' residency for settlement,
and the inclusion of a new section authorizing the New York State
Department of Social Welfare to enter into reciprocal agreements
with corresponding agencies in other states in order to facilitate the
interstate transportation of the indigent.[18]

A second important change in the Public Welfare Law resulting
from the amendment was the deletion of the two-years' residency requirement from the Wicks Act, thereby allowing 40 percent state
reimbursement for home relief expenditures made by the localities
on *all* relief cases, settled and nonsettled. Other minor changes in the
law were accomplished by further amendments. In 1939 a relatively
important change was made when work relief wages were deemed
public relief, thereby prolonging the amount of time necessary for
persons on WPA to acquire settlement.[19]

The 1937 amendment created what was to be known as the
State Charge Program. The program did not create a separate
welfare program for transients; rather, it allowed all needy, settled
or nonsettled, to participate in existing state social welfare programs, that is, home and veteran relief, old age assistance, assistance to the blind, aid to dependent children, and so on. All
such aid was to be administered to the transient under the same
methods applied to the settled. The local welfare unit was to determine the settlement of each applicant, provide documentary proof
that such person or persons did not have settlement in any public
welfare district in the state, and submit such for review by the State
Department of Social Welfare. While such cases were being processed,
the applicant was classified as a presumptive state charge and cared for
at local expense. When the case was approved, the applicant would
become a state charge and the locality would be reimbursed.

At a time when many other states were making their laws more rigorous in an attempt to eliminate potential relief cases, New York was actually assuming a larger responsibility. This recognition of social responsibility, with all due credit given to its liberal and modern thinking, was a very extravagent undertaking. To assume 100 percent financial responsibility for a population with little chance of finding immediate recovery was a significant burden by itself, but the potential flood of indigent into the state that this policy could have attracted could have been overwhelming. The state was also making itself susceptible to local officials trying to drop questionable cases upon Albany. By designating questionable cases as unsettled, the local welfare district could collect 100 percent reimbursement from the State Charge Program, rather than the mere 40 percent from general relief. For these reasons, the state was forced to apply certain control devices to the implementation of the law, devices which, in many cases and for all intents and purposes, abolished the very relief it sought to provide.

In the fall of 1938 the State Department of Social Welfare engaged Philip Ryan, executive secretary of the NCCTH, to conduct a special study of the State Charge Program in operation. Ryan was an apt candidate for the task. Not only was he currently chief administrator of a group nationally recognized and respected as expert on the transient question, but he had also served his time in the field, in New York, working for TERA at Camp Roosevelt and Hartwick Academy. The conclusions he reached in *The New York Program for Non-settled Persons* are consistent with the above appraisal. While Ryan was impressed with the progressive and humane intent of the law, and appreciated the state's need to maintain certain controls over the program, he could not ignore the human price that was paid in the process. The controls were, he found, quite effective.

To begin with, all applicants had to first be screened and accepted by the local welfare unit and the State Department of Social Welfare. The state was quite specific in defining which applicants would be accepted. Very precise instructions were laid out in the *Public Welfare Manual* distributed to local districts. The burden of proof that a person did not have settlement in the state rested solely upon the commissioner of public welfare to whom the application was made. To ascertain this, the manual prescribed the preliminary interview format. The caseworker was to determine the place of residence for the last five years and the name and address of family members, former employers, and landlords. The method of inquiry to be used in verifying such information was also outlined. Finally, a list of all materials required to be on file for each case (narrative records, financial reports, settlement inquiry, and so forth) was specified. Every piece of information used in assessing nonsettlement had to be documented or the case would not be accepted.[20] Determining settlement had been a difficult enough task for the caseworker in the past; now the determination of *nonsettlement* proved to be even more complicated and tedious. Because of the difficulty of providing documentary proof of nonresidence and the administrative cost involved in such an investigation, the transient man was, according to Ryan, "almost entirely eliminated from the State Charge group." The single man, remember, represented the majority of the transient population, yet he was virtually eliminated from the program. Social Welfare Commissioner Adie readily admitted the failure of the program to reach these men. The single man, he conceded, was still given meals and shelter for a day or two and then passed on. The practice of passing-on had been carried over into the new State Charge Program "largely because it is difficult, time-consuming, and expensive for local districts to obtain documentary proof of the nonsettled status of these single men. Rather than go to the considerable expense and trouble involved, the local district assumes their care for one or several days and urges them on their way."[21]

Another effective control, purportedly necessary to protect the state, was an emphasis on removal. The state felt justified in returning individuals to their place of settlement, out of state, even if the resources in that state were inferior to New York's. According to Ryan, "if New York were to accept such cases for long-time care, it would only be subsidizing the lack of an adequate program in other areas," and subjecting the entire state public welfare program to ultimate bankruptcy. Thus the state removed 3,781 persons in the year ending June 30, 1939, at a cost of $68,451, and 2,048 the following year, at a cost of $34,273.[22]

The aspect of removal that Ryan found to be most difficult to justify both on legal and humanitarian terms was the use of the courts to forcibly remove those persons who refused to leave. In a practical sense, should this avenue be overused there was the possibility that a removal case could be lost in court, and thus a precedent would be set which would severely limit its effectiveness. Furthermore, there was nothing to prevent a removed person from returning to the state at a later date. Consequently, only seventeen cases across the state were brought to court by the State Department of Social Welfare from July 1, 1937, to December 28, 1938.[23]

It is necessary to pause for a moment here to regain perspective. Only seventeen cases were taken to court to force removal. Out of the thousands that passed through the files of the social welfare offices, that number seems insignificant. However, these are seventeen cases in which the constitutional right of citizens of the United States to freedom of movement, freedom to choose their place to live, was being challenged. Take for example the case of sixty-year-old Emanuel Fragael and his three sons who had lived in Buffalo for seven years without gaining settlement, and then, refusing attempts to be removed to Butler, Pennsylvania, found themselves taken to court by Erie County welfare officials. Or consider the highly publicized case of Fiore Battazzo and his family of six. When his two eldest sons moved from their home in Pittsburgh, Pennsylvania, to New York in 1935, he, his wife, and their four other children followed, living first in Webster and then settling in East Rochester. During this time, the family periodically applied for and received relief. In 1937 the Public Welfare Department of Monroe County determined that the family's place of legal settlement was in Pittsburgh. When Pittsburgh officials confirmed this fact and authorized their return, the department informed the family that they must go back where they "belonged." When Battazzo refused to go willingly, the county welfare office resorted to the courts to authorize the sheriff to forcibly remove the family. In a hearing marked by "frequent verbal clashes," Battazzo's lawyer argued that, as a United States citizen, his client had the right to live in any community he chose. The judge, however, saw things differently, and, after expressing his lack of patience with "squatters" who moved to New York for greater relief benefits, ordered the family removed. While his lawyer went through the necessary appeals procedures, Battazzo decided to take matters to FDR himself. He reportedly left Rochester with his wife to hitchhike to Washington.[24] In both of these cases the courts had been used to deny persons their freedom of choice. Another New York case in which the question of constitutional rights was applied to a forced removal was to find its way to the U. S. Supreme Court and bring national attention to the problem. This was the case of one Rosario Chirillo versus the county of Westchester.

Coverage of the Chirillo case began on December 29, 1939, with a front page notice in *The New York Times*, "Westchester Wars on Relief Floaters." As part of its campaign against "floaters" or nonresident poor, who supposedly were attracted to New York because of its generous relief, Westchester County officials filed court proceedings to have the family forcibly removed to their place of legal settlement in Wooster, Ohio, from which they had migrated three years earlier. The Chirillos refused to return, so the state proceeded with a test case of section 71* of the Public Welfare Law. The next day the Chirillo side of the story was told under the caption: "59 Relief Floaters Defy Westchester." The sixty-four-year-old patriarch of the family denied moving to New York for relief; rather, he claimed he had come to set up a cobbler shop but was forced to seek relief because of poor business. He did admit that he was unwilling to return to Ohio because of the low relief rate there, and he announced that he planned to fight the eviction in court. Stories on the judicial proceedings in the Chirillo case and in additional evictions by Westchester County continued for almost two years under such headlines as: "Chirillos Plead to Stay in State"; "Westchester Bans Relief 'Floaters'"; "County Judge Orders Widow and Two Children to Go Home to NJ"; "Westchester Wins War on Floaters"; "Chirillos Must Go Westchester Says"; and, finally, on May 20, 1941, "Cobbler and Sons 'Deported' to Ohio from New York State."[25]

During these months, the Chirillos had resorted to the New York State Court of Appeals, and, failing there to gain an injunction against their removal, they appealed to the U. S. Supreme Court claiming that the New York statute "interfered with 'a most basic right of the individual, that of free movement throughout the land.'" The constitutional question drew national interest with both the American Civil Liberties Union and National Lawyers Guild providing *amicus curiae* opinions.[26]

Chirillo's attorney, Morris Shapiro, argued that section 71 of the New York Public Welfare Law was unconstitutional, under article 4, section 2, clause 1, "the Citizens of each State shall be entitled to all Privileges and Immunities of Citizens of the several State," in that his client was not being allowed the fundamental rights of a

---

*Section number of the removal clause changed from the original section number 73 of 1929 law, to section number 71 by the amendment process in the later 1930s.

citizen to select a place of his own choosing, in whatever state, to establish a home. Furthermore, it was in violation of the Fourteenth Amendment which provided that, "No state shall make or enforce any law which shall abridge the privileges or immunities of citizens of the United States," in that the terms of the Public Welfare Law discriminated against the Chirillos because of their economic condition; as well as the due process clause of the same amendment that guaranteed due process and equal protection of the law, for much the same reason. If all else failed, the deportation of the Chirillos was still unconstitutional, he claimed, under article 1, section 8 which reserved to Congress the power to regulate commerce among the states. Shapiro's commitment to the case was not only due to his obligation to his client. As he saw it, he was attempting to stop a dangerous precedent from being set. Today settlement was being used to determine relief eligibility; tomorrow it might be used to exclude the same people from the vote.[27]

The state attorney general, John J. Bennett, Jr., and county attorney, William A. Davidson, quickly dismissed the issue of citizenship stating that a citizen does not have the right to place the financial burden of his support on any community he chooses to reside in. Furthermore, they contended that removal of the Chirillos was in actuality a humane gesture. If the Chirillos were to remain in the state, they would inevitably lose their settlement in Ohio while not being able to gain another in New York unless they were able to prove to be self-supporting for a period of one year. Turning the question of citizenship around, they asked, "Is it a privilege . . . of a citizen of the United States to starve free, if he will, in any State of his choice?" Furthermore, the state had a duty to protect its taxpayers from the influx of destitute persons seeking the largess of New York's liberal social welfare policies. This was not, they explained, a merely theoretical point. The State Charge Program had cost close to $3 million for the fiscal year ending June 30, 1939. Removal of the Chirillos, therefore, was well within the guidelines of section 71 of the Public Welfare Law. The plaintiffs did "belong" to another state which was willing to receive them, and the interests of both the family and the state, by their interpretation, would be served by removal. As to the constitutionality of the law, it was, according to their opinion and an impressive array of legal precedents, well within the sovereign police power of the state to remove the Chirillos. In answer to the claims of the defense attorney, they concluded: "The fundamental fallacy of the plaintiff's position is the failure to recognize that there is not inherent in citizenship a constitutional right to be supported at public expense; to live where one will and be a menace to society. Nor does the constitution make it mandatory to starve or guarantee the right to starve where one wishes."[28]

After all of the impressive constitutional and humanitarian arguments were drawn, and the legal footwork was complete, the Supreme Court refused to rule on the constitutionality of the law; rather, they sustained the lower court, leaving the ultimate status of the Public Welfare Law in a legal limbo. Mr. Chirillo responded to the decision with emotion: "I just work and behave myself and now they say I must quit and get out of the State." The county then made arrangements for removal despite the fact that Chirillo now claimed to be self-supporting and experiencing a "new prosperity," and despite the fact that he offered to pay back the $116 he had received from the county while on relief. The actual removal proved to be merely a comedy of wasted motion, or, as Chirillo put it, "a pleasant trip at state expense," for the family only remained in Ohio long enough to have a short visit with relatives and then returned to New York State. Westchester County officials, however, claimed victory in their "war" pointing out that the Chirillo case had induced a hundred more relief families to leave voluntarily.[29]

The rationale behind removal remained the same that it had been through the decade under review. Removal, when in the best interest of the state and the individual, was considered a service. In addition, it saved the state literally millions of dollars and the possible bankruptcy that may have resulted if such dependent persons had been retained by the state. Commissioner Adie made it perfectly clear that the state felt it was doing more than its share in trying to help these people and that the procedure was completed as humanely as possible on a casework basis. Stinging from all of the adverse national publicity focused on New York due to the Chirillo case, Adie offered a resounding denial that the state "deported" people. "Such persons," he explained, "are only removed to their respective places of settlement after a careful social consideration is given each case." Since New York's high relief standards acted as an incentive to attract indigent persons to the state, "the State must protect itself against the cost of maintaining such transients by arranging for their removal under proper safeguards to other places where they have settlement."[30] Nevertheless, cases such as that of the Chirillos reveal that, despite the opinion of the state, not all willingly accepted the conclusion that removal was in their best interest.

Another device used by the state to limit the transient load was the unwritten policy of denying relief to those who refused to be removed. This alternative was used most extensively in New York City where 808 cases of acknowledged need were dropped from the relief rolls for this purpose. What happened to them is unknown. They apparently joined with their peers in the streets, parks, and missions of the city. Philip Ryan found it particularly difficult to reconcile this practice with the letter of the Public Welfare Law which read that: "A person in need of relief and care which he is unable to provide for himself shall be relieved and cared for by and at the expense of a public welfare district of the state." His dilemma can be well appreciated. By stretching the spirit of the law, he could contrive the explanation that authorization to return represented a resource available to applicants, and that, if they did not use it, then, technically, they had not exhausted all known aid and were not eligible for relief. Even more difficult was the attempt to justify another practice used by the city. From July 15, 1938, through December 31, 1938, approximately seven hundred applicants were rejected at intake for refusing to consent at the time of application to future removal. It was impossible to rationalize this practice within the context of the Public Welfare Law. Yet, a committee of leading social workers set up by the Welfare Council of New York City to review cases affected by both types of controls approved of and endorsed the principle as a necessary safeguard. Without controls, they concluded, the entire program would be seriously jeopardized.[31]

The new devices did accomplish the desired ends. The state's case load was kept reasonable and fewer removals had to be made. It is important to keep this in mind when examining the statistics of the State Charge Program. When compared to overall state home relief, state charges represented approximately 2 to 3 percent of the total cost of relief, or approximately $3 million annually. The number of cases under care ranged from 2,770 in July 1937 to a high of 9,072 in November 1938.[32] Had the state not removed another three thousand per year, and withdrawn aid from those who refused removal, the numbers and the percentages would have been considerably higher and the program much more expensive.

Despite the very effective controls attached to New York's liberal public welfare policies, people continued to be attracted to the state. The possibility of industrial or agricultural employment and the lure of the cities with their superior hospitals, educational facilities, and excitement, continued to draw them to New York. When and if they became destitute and in need, they could apply to the State Charge Program, but, as we have seen, the loopholes were large and many. For those who slipped through, it was the same old rounds of lodging houses, missions, and making due.

In the state's largest cities — New York, Buffalo, Syracuse — the transient could still expect the customary one night's care in the municipal lodging house. According to the public welfare officials in each city, their lodging houses offered the men the most complete care possible. Mayor LaGuardia was so confident of the quality of care provided in his city that he invited a congressional panel to make a surprise visit and see for themselves. The annual reports of the New York City Department of Welfare echoed the mayor's evaluation of their performance.[33]

In Buffalo, the annual reports of the Erie County Department of Social Welfare showed a similarly positive self-evaluation of the building at Wells and Carrol Streets. The lodging house, while used mostly for the local homeless, was also used to house state charges and to give temporary relief (one night) to transients. As described in the annual report, "the Shelter has complete facilities, including a modern kitchen, showers, bath, sterilization plant, medical clinic, barber shop, shoe repair shop, tailor shop, check room, recreation and smoking room, with a stage, radio, library, and games."[34] Like the other lodging houses across the state, it received periodic inspections by the State Department of Social Welfare.

Despite the seemingly adequate facilities and consistently humane policy, controversy did stir over the conditions in the lodging house. Hints of trouble began to surface in sporadic newspaper articles in 1937–38. The story of twenty-five-year-old Ignatius Rakochi who was sentenced to six months in the county penitentiary for setting off two false alarms in the lodging house, revealed the frustration of someone who claimed to have "not received prompt and courteous service." A little more than a week later charges were leveled by William J. McMahon, supervisor of the fourth ward, that the men at the lodging house were being improperly fed. An investigative panel was formed to look into the allegations. Later the next month, the same supervisor, still dissatisfied with the condition of the house, proposed that three hundred local homeless men lodged there be taken out of that institution to be placed in private homes and small hotels. Continuing complaints the following year by stranded transient seamen brought Commissioner Adie himself to Buffalo to make a personal inspection. After touring the house "from top to bottom," Adie declared it to be a "high-grade congregate shelter." Giving it a "clean bill of health," he declared, "the food is excellent; the management is good; the place is clean and well maintained. I could eat off the floor." The people of Buffalo, he explained, had been "racketeered" into believing that the house was a terrible place. "It's high time they know that it is a fine organization." Nevertheless, he did agree to compromise with the Seamen's Union and remove a selected number of unemployed seamen from the lodging house into other quarters. Ever cognizant of the possibility of attracting more problems by being over generous, he demanded in return a promise from the president of the union to see to it that Buffalo not be swamped by seamen from other Great Lake ports seeking special treatment. The refusal of the county welfare commissioner to implement Adie's decision resulted in the picketing of the building by thirty seamen carrying placards protesting conditions in the house. Commissioner Jeacock explained his refusal to comply with the state plan: "I don't feel I should take responsibility for discriminating against single Buffalonians who are inmates of the shelter in favor of seamen who are transients." The same story of complaints, denials, and a secret inspection was played out again the following year.[35]

Whichever of the above perceptions of the lodging house was correct, and probably both were in part, the basic problem being faced was congregate care itself. As Robert Wilson had been repeating from the earliest days of the depression, such treatment in and of itself was inhumane, disheartening, and debilitating. Yet, after October 1939, even this inadequate service would be severely restricted in Rochester. Under the caption "County Halts Free Lodging to Transients" the Rochester *Democrat and Chronicle* reported that new and stricter policies were to be implemented regarding drop-in aid given to transients at the city lodging house, Hotel MacSweeney. "No longer will Monroe County play Lady Bountiful to transients," was the way county welfare commissioner Jesse B. Hannan explained the change in policy. In the past Monroe County had paid for every "overnight guest" who was "about to put up a good story, or even one not so good"; hereafter, he promised, the county would be more "hard-boiled" about such matters. There would be no more casual overnight stays. The move was necessary, he said, because the hobo's "grapevine" had brought a flood of transients to the city.[36] In Rochester, therefore, as in smaller cities and towns across the state, the jail might again offer the only substitute.

His one night up, the single man could try the mission houses for food, shelter, and a sermon. Again this service was usually limited to a few nights for transients. It has been estimated, however, that 50 percent of the unattached transients cared for privately in New York were cared for in religious missions. People's Rescue Mission of Rochester provides a typical example. During the year 1937 alone, it had provided the city's homeless and transient population with 8,340 free lodgings and 54,426 at a minimal cost, as well as 21,900 free meals and 2,191 paid. The primary purpose of the mission was to save souls; the primary purpose of those who sought its services, however, seems to have been more basic. The impressive attendance at religious services on "feeding night," as compared to the low attendance at regular services, was a clear indication of the transient's attitude toward the mission. "If 205 of the 261 persons on feeding nights could have had their physical needs supplied by another agency such as the state, very likely they would not have been present," was the conclusion reached by the sociology department of the University of Rochester which had been commissioned to write the history of the mission.[37]

In addition to the mission houses, other agencies, the Salvation Army, Travelers Aid, and the like, continued to strain their budgets to provide some limited service to the transient. In New York City the internationally recognized model lodging house, the Gold Dust Lodge, was gone. After serving over 75,000 men (not counting repeats), supplying 3,377,986 beds and 8,779,904 meals over the course of six years, the old flour factory was returned to its original owners in August 1937. The Salvation Army continued, however, to offer the transient three nights and four meals at its lodge on Forty-eighth Street. By 1940 this facility was servicing approximately thirty-five hundred to four thousand men per year, about one-half of whom were from out of state. Despite more than two hundred beds the lodging house was limited compared to the numbers that Gold Dust Lodge had been able to service. A small number of women were also provided for in the Salvation Army house on Twenty-second Street. As always, the Salvation Army continued to provide similar services across the state. In Syracuse, the Army bragged, its facilities on the third floor of the Citadel were "the only place in a city where a homeless woman and her children may be welcomed and housed in a real homelike atmosphere."[38]

Travelers Aid offices also continued to provide emergency assistance to friendless travelers in New York in time of need. A number of transients testifying before a federal panel in New York City in 1940 were only able to give the address of Travelers Aid as their residence.[39] In addition to their work in the field, the national organization continued to serve as advocate for the transient, publicizing his plight and lobbying for a revived program of government assistance. Executive director, Bertha McCall stayed with the transient throughout the decade. In the summer of 1939, when a lack of funding forced the NCCTH to cease functioning as an independent committee, McCall welcomed the group into Travelers Aid where a new committee, composed of much the same membership, was able to carry on its advocacy work.[40]

Thus the private sector had not abandoned the transient. What was supposed to be the first line of defense, the "private agency," had become in many instances the last. But the years were now starting to add up for their clients, and time was taking its toll. Speaking from five years' experience counseling men at the Salvation Army's Forty-eighth Street facility in New York, J. Fletcher Agnew noted the effect:

> Many of the men who have been traveling for a long period of time — that is, for 5 or 6 or 7 and 8 years — they have got so into the habit of it and have been so unsuccessful in finding steady employment that they have almost given up hope of finding steady employment. If they can just get something now and then to keep them alive, that is all they expect. As long as they expect nothing more, it is pretty hard for them to find more.[41]

The next logical question was whether even a revived economy and job opportunities could fully restore their spirits.

The lodging houses, missions, and private agencies could not serve everyone, and those they did serve knew that time was limited. For those who were unable to avail themselves of these limited services, or who had used up their allotted number of meals and nights, for the women and minors who continued to avoid such agencies for fear of being returned home, for the families who discovered the technicalities of the State Charge Program the hard way, there were still cheap louse-infected flophouses, doorways, bridges, shanty towns, and parks.

Easily lost in the resulting mass of migratory and seasonal labor, the transient's trail becomes more difficult to trace here. Too easily were they lumped together with Dust Bowl refugees or classified as casual laborers. Even contemporary students of migration, overwhelmed by the Dust Bowl exodus, began to use the terms migrant and transient interchangeably. But there is a distinction. Today the term migratory labor connotes a permanent economic status. The "job" of the migratory worker, according to the current definition, is to follow the crops or industry in a regular seasonal pattern, providing necessary labor during the times of peak need. The transient and the Oakie only resorted to such employment as a temporary expedient. They did not consider their present status as a permanent job classification—they did not consider themselves migrant workers. The James Miller family, for example, spent the entire decade of the thirties traveling from city to city, mill to mill, and shipyard to shipyard, from Gary, Indiana to Pittsburgh, Pennsylvania, from Boston to Chicago, working three months here and six months there. Still Mr. Miller did not consider himself to be an itinerant worker. He was a skilled operator and electrician who had worked for the Edison Company for twelve years before being laid off.[42] What he was looking for, as were the rest, was a permanent job in a stable community. The labor they performed on the way was but a temporary expedient.

As the transient was forced to share with the migratory labor force the dubious distinction of being referred to as migrant, so too was he forced to share their problems. For one thing, when they did work, pay was low, especially in agriculture. With a surplus of labor eager for jobs, the employer had a decided advantage. On the farms of New York, for example, it was estimated that a family of 3.1 members earned only $127 seasonally for nine to ten hours of work per day. At the same time, the United States National Resources Committee estimated that an income of one thousand to twelve hundred dollars was not enough for a resident family to live on without borrowing.[43]

Such limited resources translated naturally into a poor standard of living. Shelter was primitive and food basic. For many, "home" could be found in any one of the shanty towns that still dotted the landscape and lined the highways. Here the basic necessities of a decent life, clean water for washing and bathing, sanitary facilities, sewage treatment, garbage collection, an adequate place to cook and sleep, were all missing. Company housing might also be available especially in those farming regions that had relied on migratory labor before the depression, but it was little better. A New York State Department of Labor investigation of farms in Erie County found conditions in the company camp to be unsanitary and demoralizing. "If the code for factory camps [established by state law] had been applied, inspectors would have issued orders for the correction of 1,117 violations."[44]

Under such conditions good health was precarious at best. Improper diet, constant movement, hard work, and exposure all contributed to lower resistance, increased susceptibility to disease, and a higher risk of accident. A United States Public Health Department report confirmed the vulnerability of the migrant poor to "the ordinary communicable diseases and filth born diseases." In all areas except for degenerative, nervous, and rheumatic diseases, the survey showed that the medical problems of the migrant exceeded those of the resident. There was an especially high proportion of rickets, scurvy, and pellagra, which were due to dietary deficiency, and a significant incidence of epidemic disease such as tuberculosis, gonorrhea, syphilis, and malaria. At the same time that they were more prone to illness, migrant people were less likely to receive assistance. Medical care was generally provided for them only in emergency situations. Most of the time even the state and charity hospitals would not open their doors to nonresidents, even in cases of communicable diseases. Out of the 129 tuberculosis clinics nationwide that would admit indigents, for example, only eight would consider the nonresident. The only choice left for infectious migrants was to continue traveling, spreading his germs as he went.[45]

Where children were involved, the effects of the migratory life multiplied. Their small bodies were even more susceptible to the crippling effects of malnutrition, ceaseless labor, and accidents. Yet labor they did. According to a New York Labor Committee investigation, a "very considerable" number of the twenty to thirty thousand workers employed on commercial truck farms in New York were children. Interviewers in the Rochester, Syracuse, and Utica areas found that out of 764 workers, one-half (374) were under sixteen years of age, more than one-fourth (225) were under fourteen and not quite one-fifth (101) were eleven or younger. Almost a score of parents stated that their children had suffered from bad water, heat, back-bending work, or plant poisoning.[46] In addition to the physical dangers, contemporaries questioned the lasting psychological effect of a migratory existence on young minds. Many feared that the experience might breed a whole generation of habitual migrants out of children who know no other way of life. Some hoped that schooling would reverse the process, but few migrant children were afforded the luxury of education. The day-to-day existence of their families and the real need for their labor to supplement the family's income meant that schooling was sporadic at best. The children thus had little opportunity to escape from the future that was being set for them. As one father put it: "My kids will be dumb—just like me."[47]

With the last avenue of recourse available to the transient explored, we have completed our look at the years following the liquidation of the Federal Transient Program in New York. To recapitulate, the state responded positively, albeit slowly, to the situation that resulted from liquidation. When the overwhelming need of the transient became apparent, and the inability of public and private agencies to assume the burden adequately became undeniable, the Public Welfare Law was appropriately amended. The state, in assuming the total cost of the new State Charge Program, disbursed $1,700,000 in aid in the year ending June 30, 1938; $2,571,000 the following year; and by all expectations, were to top $3,000,000 annually by 1940. Yet, despite the liberality of the law and the large price tag that came with it, the State Charge Program did not solve the transient problem in New York State. Unattached men were openly overlooked on the local level without complaint by the state, while a set of unfortunate but necessary administrative controls initiated to protect the state were, in practice, eliminating the most needy from the State Charge Program. The majority of the homeless and transient were handled by temporary expedients, that is, a few days in public or private institutions, and then, as in the poor law past, they were passed-on. Little effort at individualized care or rehabilitation was made at any of their stopping places. The consequent effect on the transient did not bode well for the future.

Unsanitary living conditions eroded health and contributed to the spread of communicable diseases; especially to be feared were venereal diseases and tuberculosis. The pressure of constant rejection and an unsteady future threatened the mental well being of the individual while unsavory companions of the road threatened their moral fortitude. For the children especially, crowded and unsanitary living conditions and an absence of educational facilities were stepping stones to future disaster.

Despite the effect that transiency was having on the individual, the community continued to be hostile and fearful. In Westchester County, for example, the commissioner of public welfare reported a growing hostility toward the nonsettled:

> The fear of the community of an increasing burden of nonresidents on relief has led to a growing resentment of them. . . . Efforts have been made to secure restrictive legislation to hinder the movements of migrants and nonresidents, and to find ways of prohibiting relief to them; the lowering of standards of relief, including medical and hospital care, over the entire area in order to discourage the migration of nonresidents into the area has been suggested.

Such attitudes had already culminated in the introduction of a bill for a more stringent residency requirement in New York.[48]

Despite the best intentions of Albany, the transient problem was more than any one state could handle. The financial resources needed, the interstate nature of the migrant problem, the national scope of the economic depression and the tenacity of long-held attitudes toward the stranger demanded federal participation.

⟨ 11 ⟩

Knocking on Washington's Door — Again

In 1940 Bertha McCall presented a paper to the delegates of the National Conference of Social Work entitled "Migrant Problems and the Federal Government." Instead of asking the oft-repeated question, "What can the government do for the transient?", she suggested that a better question might be, "What *is* the government doing for the transient?" In answer to her question she offered a very optimistic review of current federal activity that was, either directly or indirectly, related to transiency.[1]

Included on her list were a multitude of government studies on migration including the long-awaited report by the Secretary of Labor, Frances Perkins, and the many monographs written by WPA researchers. The U.S. Public Health Service, she noted, was also presently conducting studies on the transmission of communicable diseases by migratory people. In addition, she was able to cite various departmental and inter-agency conferences in which related problems had been discussed. More concretely, she referred to the very positive work being done by the Farm Security Administration in its establishment of a network of labor camps for migrants. Most of the progress she was reporting, however, other than the camps, was in the field of study, discussion, and recommendations. Little of it actually served to alleviate the immediate problems faced by the transient citizenry. The federal government had, for all intents and purposes, followed FDR's dictate to "quit this business of relief." The last item on McCall's list, however, showed definite promise.

To provide the necessary element of "coordination and cooperation" to make the most of the aforementioned efforts, McCall looked
optimistically to the newly created House of Representatives' Committee to Investigate the Interstate Migration of Destitute Citizens,
familiarly referred to as the Tolan Committee after its chairman and
chief advocate, John H. Tolan of California. McCall gave the panel
a hearty send off encouraging her fellow social workers to "lend every
aid to the members of the committee." "I cannot plead too strongly,"
she asserted, "for an understanding cooperation with this group,
then an understanding acceptance of whatever conclusions are arrived at."[2]

The committee that elicited such enthusiasm from a long-time
advocate of federal responsiblity for the transient population was
established by House Resolution 63 of the Seventy-sixty Congress:

> Resolved, That the Speaker appoint a select committee of five
> Members of the House, and that such committee be instructed to
> inquire into the interstate migration of destitute citizens, to study,
> survey and investigate the social and economic needs and the
> movement of indigent persons across State lines, obtaining all facts
> possible in relation thereto which would not only be of public in-
> terest but which would aid the House in enacting remedial
> legislation.

The resolution, introduced by Tolan in 1939, one month before the
publication of *The Grapes of Wrath*, passed the House unanimously in
1940, just after the premiere of the film adaptation. The nation's
conscience had been touched and Congress wanted answers.*
House Resoluation 491 appropriated twenty thousand dollars to
cover expenses.[3]

The committee opened its hearings in New York City on July
29, 1940, with Mayor Fiorello LaGuardia as its first witness, and
closed its last session in February 1941 in Washington, D.C. with a
round-table discussion of the Federal Transient Program by Elizabeth Wickenden, Philip Ryan, John Webb, and Charles Alspach.
The New York opening was intended, according to chairman
Tolan, "to show [the people] that California was not the only State

---

*The five man committee consisted of: John H. Tolan, California; Claude V.
Parsons, Illinois; John J. Sparkman, Alabama; Carl T. Curtis; Nebraska; Frank C.
Osmers, Jr., New Jersey.

in the Union that had this migrant problem."⁴ In the intervening seven months between New York and Washington, hearings
were held in Montgomery, Chicago, Lincoln (Nebraska), Oklahoma City, San Francisco and Los Angeles. By February the committee had accumulated 4,245 pages of testimony, resolutions, and
prepared statements, complete with accompanying charts, graphs,
maps, and photographs, from over three hundred witnesses. The
committee heard from governors and mayors; social workers and
public welfare officials; lawyers, physicians and educators; statisticians, economists, and psychologists; farmers and businessmen;
and over one hundred transients. Virtually every agency and organization, public or private, that had anything at all to do with
migrating people was represented. Virtually every individual with a
role to play in transient relief either testified personally or was
spoken for. Even the name of the first lady, Eleanor Roosevelt, was
added to its impressive roster of witnesses.

In the course of their investigation, the panel learned about settlement laws and their inequities; discriminating relief policies;
inadequate assistance; communicable diseases; municipal lodging
houses, missions, and jungles; disreputable employment services
that led migratory labor astray; drought, soil erosion, and conservation. They also came to a better understanding of the subject of their
study—the indigent migrant. In the words of John Sparkman, "We
began to see the average migrant as a fairly typical American whose
misfortune had been a little heavier than his neighbor's. For many, a
temporary helping hand would enable them to go on alone."⁵ By the
time they returned to Washington, they could say with complete
confidence that they had conducted the most comprehensive investigation of the interstate migration of destitute persons ever
undertaken in the United States. They also returned with specific
suggestions from the more than three hundred witnesses on just
what should be done.

Much had been learned since Congress had last considered the
problem of America's transient citizenry. Thinking about transiency had evolved significantly between the time Bertha McCall
had addressed the Cuttings Hearing back in 1933 and her appearance now before the Tolan Committee. A federal transient program had come and gone. It had been a grand experiment, a
humanitarian gesture to meet the needs of the most forgotten of the
forgotten citizenry, and there was still a sense of loss that it had been
given only a brief two years to correct a situation that was generation

in the making. But few of the witnesses at the Tolan Hearings wanted a return to the Federal Transient Program. Those closest to the problem recognized by then the weaknesses and limitations of a program that singled out transients for separate, and sometimes, preferential, treatment and segregated them from the very communities into which they sought reintegration. They preferred now to see transiency in a broader context, as a normal and healthy element in the nation's economic and social life, and the relief of those who found themselves in trouble while en route as part of the general relief burden.

This changing perspective was articulated as early as 1937 in *The Survey* in an article entitled "Transiency—Mobility in Trouble." The author of the article, Elizabeth Wickenden, had served as Assistant Director, Transient Activities, FERA, and was presently Assistant to the Deputy Administrator, WPA. By virtue of the former position, she had been integrally and actively involved in the setting up and administration of the Federal Transient Program, and, by virtue of the latter, she was privy to and influenced by Washington's changing attitudes. By virtue of both, she was in an excellent position to provide "seasoned consideration, a re-analysis and a re-evaluation of the whole experience."[6]

Wickenden began with a frontal attack on what she termed the misconceived sympathy that had initiated the Federal Transient Program. "Transients," she wrote, "have suffered too long at the hands of their friends as well as of their enemies from the hazy thinking and unrestrained emotion which a romantic heritage inspires." In other words, in trying to counteract a negative popular image, the transient's friends had romanticized the plight of the "footloose adventurer," the heir of our pioneer heritage, and, in the process, had separated him from the rest of America's needy. This was a mistake that was to plague the transient population from that point forward, especially during the federal program when the government participated in the segregation of the transient in the Federal Transient Program. "Obviously," Wickenden explained, "the fact that an individual has either from choice or necessity moved from one place to another does not make him either better or worse, either more commonplace or more romantic than any other," and certainly neither more or less deserving of special attention. Yet, by treating the transient as a separate class set apart from other victims of the depression, the program "tended to brand men, once and for all, as 'transient'—a breed apart," reinforcing in the public mind the belief that transiency was a "social evil requiring corrective 'therapeutic' measures," and adding to the stigma they already bore. Furthermore, the fact that the federal program was often more generous than local relief created a resentment that further alienated the transient from the local community. All of this was complicated by a camp system which physically removed the men from the very community into which they sought reentry, separated them from "all possible contact with private employment, from normal society, and from contact with women and normal family relationships," and encouraged in them a false sense of community—a "cult of transiency" —that contributed to their maladjustment.[7]

Now, Wickenden advised, it was time to discard distracting romantic notions about the transient and see him for what he was—a part of the general relief population. To do this she urged a new appreciation of mobility. Rather than looking at transiency as a problem in and of itself, it was time to recognize that "mobility in itself is a desirable and necessary phenomenon if our present day economy is to function smoothly and efficiently." Mobility, in other words, is healthy and welcome in good times, and it even continues to be so in bad times when and if the job seeker is successful. It is when the migrant person has trouble finding that job that the problem occurs, hence, the title, "Transiency—Mobility in Trouble." Having defined the real problem, she went on to recommend long-range, "sweeping readjustments in our social and economic structure." In the meantime, the process of reintegration had to begin by including the transient in the general relief population and treating him accordingly.[8]

By 1940 even the most sympathetic advocates of the transient and one-time supporters of the defunct Federal Transient Program realized the need to view transiency in this broader context. Philip Ryan, past executive secretary of the NCCTH, argued convincingly against all proposals for transient relief that would once again separate the transient from other needy persons "on the arbitrary standard of residence status." "Transients are people," he explained in a rather obvious fashion. "If we treat them as people we shall do away with many of the difficulties that result from regarding them as a special and peculiar breed who must for some reason be treated differently from the rest of us."[9] Secretary Perkins agreed that mobility was a normal and healthy process: "Mobility has always been and still is a normal and vital feature of American life. So long as our economic and social patterns continue flexible, this will be true, and it is sound and wholesome for it to be so." Therefore, it was not necessary to create special institutions and programs for migrants, "if we recognize these people as part and parcel of the whole community of the 48 States, and [referring to archaic settlement laws] take down some of the barriers in the way of their getting the same treatment as those who stay at home."[10] The friends of the transient were, in fact, coming around to a better appreciation of Hopkins' position of 1935. This recognition was belatedly acknowledged by Nels Anderson in the dedication of his 1940 book, *Men on the Move:* "To Harry L. Hopkins . . . who recognized the migrancy problem in its proper relation to the larger problem of unemployment."[11] Wickenden, Ryan, Perkins, and scores of others of like opinion, shared their feelings candidly with Tolan and his committee.

Finally, the changing terminology used in reference to transients/migrants seemed to catch the spirit of the new perspective that was articulated by the witnesses. While the terms transiency and migrancy were by this time being used interchangeably, the balance was shifting to a more common use of the latter. The terms transient and transiency were increasingly associated with narrow questions of relief, while contemporaries seeking to broaden the common perception of the issues involved tended to adopt migrant and migrancy as more inclusive terms that could apply to the employed as well as the unemployed and could encompass larger questions of health, education, and welfare. Bertha McCall made the switch, as is seen in the title of the article referred to earlier, "Migrant Problems and the Federal Government." She did, however, lapse into the old, more comfortable terminology in her text. Perhaps the best indication of the significance of this changing nomenclature can be seen in the evolution of the NCCTH, specifically in the adoption in 1938 of a new name, the Council on Interstate Migration. Speaking of the decision, Ryan explained to the Tolan panel:

> We began to see the problem as much broader than just a relief problem. We realized that it was tied in with many other aspects of human life—education, employment, health, family welfare, and so forth. We saw that all phases of human existence were included in the whole problem of transiency and migration and, in an effort to veer away from just the relief aspects, we attempted to bring into our organization representatives of these other fields.

So they changed their name, opened their ranks, and continued to emphasize the broader aspects of transiency and migration until their final demise and absorption into Travelers Aid in the summer of 1939.[12]

While unqualified support for the Federal Transient Program had eroded significantly in the years since liquidation, there was still a virtual concensus on the need for some form of federal involvement in transient relief. The social work community, for one, had kept up the pressure for federal intervention by publicizing the plight of the transient and the chaotic and unacceptable conditions that had typified transient relief since the termination of the Federal Transient Program. *The Survey* and *Survey Graphic* carried regular notes about happenings in the states after the termination of FERA, while reporter Gertrude Springer brought the same to life with her sympathetic feature articles. *Social Work Today* contributed a series of articles and gave editorial support to the need for a resumption of federal responsibility. *The Transient*, of course, continued its advocacy role, providing its readers with updates on state legislation and information from the field, all directed once again to the need for a national solution. *Public Welfare News* offered the support of the public relief community by conducting its own surveys and reporting the results. In addition to the proliferation of literature, the social work community also convened a number of special conferences to discuss the transient's plight and formulate recommendations. In March 1936 representatives of twenty-two Eastern states met at the Trenton Conference on Transient and Settlement Laws. The following year fifteen states were represented at a regional Midwest conference on the same. Albany, New York was also host city to a one-day institute on transiency. In each case, the delegates called upon Washington to assume responsibility. Transiency and/or migrancy was, likewise, a frequent topic at the annual National Conference of Social Work. Groundwork laid there by McCall and Ryan, John Webb, Ruth Blakeslee, Nels Anderson, T. J. Woofter, Jr., and Robert Wilson resulted in a 1941 "Platform on Interstate Migration" that called for a non-discriminatory system of federal relief for all needy regardless of settlement or residence.[13]

The interest expressed in the field for a federal resumption of responsibility was reiterated throughout the Tolan Hearings. As the witnesses filed before the panel, they insisted that destitute persons crossing state borders constituted a national problem that demanded a national solution. On the opening day of the hearings, Mayor

LaGuardia explained: "Now, this question, gentlemen, under our form of government, is entirely a Federal question. There is no other way." New York State Assemblyman James J. Wadsworth added that, "the longer the States individually are expected to handle it, the more complicated and costly it will become, the more the rights of individuals will be jeopardized, and the more dangerous becomes the national situation." "The States simply cannot take care of it," explained Congresswoman Caroline O'Day of New York, "the Federal Government is responsible." Ruth Taylor, commissioner of welfare of Westchester County, concurred: "In our opinion the problem of the nonresident dependent can be handled justly and fairly only through Federal action. No state or locality will be willing or financially able for long to maintain adequate standards of relief." Social Welfare Commissioner Adie summarized what his fellow New Yorkers were saying. New York took immense pride in its State Charge Program, and "we want to continue this kind of care and see it extended in other States, but we doubt if the State of New York, unaided by the Federal authorities, can carry on such a program indefinitely, in its present form." Federal intervention was crucial. The committee, itself predisposed to agree, listened sympathetically.[14]

Impatient with the years of talk and no action, Philip Ryan challenged the witnesses to lay specific proposals before the committee. The time was now at hand. Congress was listening. "Advocates of federal responsiblity should be prepared to support that claim with a specific program. The shouting days are over; the time has come to get down to clear and definite proposals as to the way in which responsibility is to be exercised."[15] That was exactly what they did, as witness after witness gave his or her recommendations — from abolishing state settlement laws, to establishing a national employment service for migrant labor; from drastic economic readjustments to stop migration at its source, to resettlement schemes to remove persons from despressed areas and reestablish them on submarginal land elsewhere; from land reclamation and soil erosion projects to make "home" more livable to the migrant, to an aggressive expansion of educational and health services to meet the needs of a mobile people (One witness proposed stationing teachers at much-traveled intersections to intercept and teach students as they passed.); from rezoning to unionization, taxation, registration, and fingerprinting. These and other plans, some practical and some not, were carefully spelled out and argued before the committee.

The recommendaiton most frequently heard was for a system of federal grants-in-aid to the states that would bring federal dollars to the state and local levels to be expended on the general relief population, regardless of settlement, while providing uniform standards of relief through federal supervision. While some like Mayor LaGuardia and the Conference of Mayors continued to argue for a 100 percent federally financed and administered transient program, the majority of the witnesses agreed with Ryan, Adie, Wickenden, and a host of others who favored a permanent federal plan of general relief for the total relief population, settled and unsettled. Many suggested that this could best be done by adding a fourth category to the Social Security Act. Congress had already recognized its responsibility for the aged, the blind, and dependent children. Now, proponents argued, it was time to expand the federal umbrella to include general relief. Perhaps, some suggested, the government could establish a Social Security category for general relief, and, to guarantee that the states would not forget the transient, establish a separate division within that category for the unsettled. Others argued that the transient had too long been stigmatized by separation and should now be considered as part of the general relief population and treated accordingly. To guarantee that he would not be discriminated against at the local level, state participation in the scheme could be made contingent upon the inclusion of the nonresident needy in each state's general relief program.

Meanwhile back in New York, the state legislature and the Department of Social Welfare were dealing with the realities of which Commissioner Adie spoke. The State Charge Program was expensive, and it was growing more so each day. During the first year of operations, 1937–38, the state expended $1,709,637 on state charges. In fiscal year 1938–39 that figure escalated to $2,695,058. The estimates for the next two years were well over three million. Reaction was beginning to set in. Pressure was increasing to raise state settlement from one to five years. Additional counties were being allowed to increase their local requirements to five years for certain categories such as persons infected with tuberculosis. Concern was rising over the growing number of persons losing settlement due to the lack of conformity between state laws, or, in the case of women and dependent children, because of the absence of father or husband from the state. A full 52.9 percent of the nonsettled in the program derived their status in this manner. Forty percent of all state charges, furthermore, had at one time or another had New York State settlement. Many had resided in the state for as long as six years without ever qualifying for settlement. What all of this meant to the department was that the state charge population was largely stationary, growing, and costly, and, as Commissioner Adie explained to Tolan, the continuation of the program depended upon federal assistance.[16]

The department's position was articulated in the preliminary findings of an in-house, comprehensive review and analysis of the program that was conducted in March 1941. Consistent with prevailing throught, the resulting report asserted the value of migration as "an important, normal and vigorous phenomenon in national progress." Nearly all of those who migrate, it was noted, do so to improve their status, and most were successful. Those who were forced to resort ot public assistance represented a small percentage, yet "the basic method of treatment . . . has been to surround these non-settled persons with restrictions like settlement laws, inadequate care and prejudicial treatment, as to make it most difficult or impossible for them to establish themselves in the new community." To end this discrimination and admittedly inhumane treatment, the report recommended a federal grants-in-aid program for general relief, on a 50–50, state-federal, ratio, to be provided to all needy under the Social Security Act. It also called for a uniform settlement law and a rethinking of the policy of removal.[17]

Anticipating a significant change at the federal level as a result of the Tolan Hearings, the report recommended that no substantive legislation be enacted at that time. The legislature responded that same month with a new Social Welfare Law that consolidated and superseded the Public Welfare Law and State Charities Law, but made no substantive changes.[18] The legislature was waiting for action from Washington. But there was to be no return to federal responsibility.

The Tolan Committee had expected to finish its work and make its recommendations to Congress in early 1941; however, the deepening war in Europe and America's indirect role in it were having decided effects on the subject under study. A new, vigorous defense industry was changing the terms of migrancy. People were still migrating, but they were now focusing their sights on those cities and towns where a geared-up war industry was rapidly absorbing the unemployed. A new set of problems and concerns resulted.

Consequently, Congress changed the official name of the committee to the House Commiteee Investigating National Defense Migration and extended its term to January 3, 1943.[19]

The Tolan Committee had had every intention of recommending federal participation in transient relief. Social security representatives had expressed interest in the idea of a fourth category of general relief. The stage was set, but the war intervened, and the transient was once again all but forgotten. In the seven years that separated the Cuttings and Tolan Hearings, thought about transients had matured in many ways. In many other ways, however, things were unchanged.

The transient problem did not end simply because the government choose not to recognize it. Even World War II and the affluent 1950s did not finally absorb all of the needy. Shortly after the war, President Harry Truman found it necessary to establish a Commission on Migratory Labor to investigate the continuing problem. In the following decade, Congress took up the task again as it conducted hearings in 1963 and 1965 to gather testimony on the relative merits of a number of Senate bills designed to correct problems involving migratory labor. The problem gained a new urgency in the latter half of the decade as migratory workers rallied around union chief Cesar Chavez to demand their rights. Interest in migratory labor has continued through active studies of migration at Cornell University and the New York State Migrant Center at the State Univesity College at Geneseo.[20]

Concern over the injustice of residency laws also continued in the post-war period. In a 1956 symposium entitled "Residence Laws: Road Blocks to Human Welfare," Travelers Aid again raised the same questions about freedom of movement and citizenship that had been articulated three decades earlier.[21] In 1969 the Supreme Court finally put an end to the discussion in the case of *Shapiro vs. Thompson.* In the long overdue decision, the Court invalidated residency as a criterion for relief on the grounds that it represented an arbitrary restriction that violated the constitutional rights guaranteed the individual by both the Fifth and Fourteenth Amendments. In a majority opinion reminiscent of the arguments presented by defense counsel in the Chirillo case, the Court ruled that the use of residency requirements for the "purpose of inhibiting migration by needy persons into the State," was "constitutionally impermissible."[22]

With the question of residency decided, the issue of transiency became, for all intents and purposes, a moot point. The transient was now legally indistinguishable from the nation's homeless population, and it was to that classification of needy that attention turned in the seventies and eighties. Once again the terminology had been adjusted to accommodate the contemporary situation, and the transient was encompassed within the larger whole. Transiency did not, however, disappear. Among the nation's estimated 250,000 to 1,000,000 homeless there remains a significant population who continue to cross local and state boundaries indiscriminately in search of opportunity or adventure. In many ways their stories are similar to those of their depression predecessors. The temptation to make direct comparisons between the victims of the recession of the 1970s, today's homeless, and the unemployed of five decades earlier is especially compelling. There are, however, also very different aspects of the contemporary situation that qualify that comparison. The deinstitutionalization of many of the nation's mental hospitals, for example, has significantly affected the composition of the homeless population of the 1980s.[23] While the contemporary situation is intriguing, the story of the transient related within these pages closes with the end of the depression. Both that economic crisis and the migration it spawned were thought by contemporaries to be over as the war began.

The experiences related within these pages make it evident that even the Empire State, wealthy by comparison to its neighbors and sincerely trying to modernize its welfare laws, even to the point of including the stranger, could not assume the place that rightly belonged to the federal government. At first the failings of New York were due to the countervailing forces of competing traditions, yet, even when the state made a significant break from the stranglehold of the past, the financial burden was more than it could carry and checks to qualify the generous intent of the laws were applied. What was needed to relieve both the state and the transient was the long-overdue participation of the federal government in the public welfare system. The years between 1933 and 1935 provide only a glimpse of what might have been, but, impatient for results, the government retracted too quickly to ever realize a significant change. What does this tell us about the nature of the New Deal, and what does it tell us about that state of New York?

In his 1937 inaugural address Roosevelt moved the crowd with a ringing defense of the New Deal:

> It is not enough that wheels turn. They must carry us in the direction of a greater satisfaction in life for the average man. The deeper purpose of democratic government is to assist as many of its citizens as possible, especially those who need it most, to improve their conditions of life, to retain all personal liberty which does not adversely affect their neighbors, and to pursue the happiness which comes with security, and an opportunity for recreation and culture.[24]

But who was the "average man," and how many of them were actually reached? From what we know about the transient, the label average man is a neat fit, yet we also know that the numbers of them reached was minimal and the time short. Did those who "need it most" receive the help they needed? The need of the transient was well demonstrated. The inadequacy of the help they received has been equally demonstrated. Was the "personal liberty" of the transient retained? He was presumably at liberty to starve, but other constitutional guarantees, as we have seen, were in doubt. Did he indeed have the security necessary to "pursue happiness"? Hardly. The New Deal has been criticized by some historians as a middle class reform effort which, in fact, never did reach the "forgotten man." From the evidence of the foregoing pages, it would seem that such a judgment, in perhaps a qualified manner, is warranted. While the federal government did not discriminate directly against nonresidents, the apparatus of federal/state administration that was established in most New Deal programs allowed the local exclusion of the transient. The transient, in fact, had little part in the New Deal. As Dr. Ellen Potter once queried, "Where does the migratory worker get his 'security number'?"[25]

In the absence of federal responsibility how does the state fare? Was New York in fact more liberal in intent than the Roosevelt administration? The state did take full responsibility when the federal government renounced its obligation. It was the state that first broke with the idea of local responsibility when that idea did not fit the circumstances of the 1930s. The federal government, on the other hand, tested the waters but turned back. Granted that it was unable to fulfill the obligation it assumed, New York State did more to fully recognize the needs of "as many of its citizens . . . who need it most" than the federal government — in this category at least. FDR's New Deal did break precedent by assuming responsibility for the unemployed, but when it came to taking that one further step, the one that would have abandoned the poor law and aided the transient, Washington backed off. The federal government continued to explain, a lá Hoover, that it did not want to destroy personal initiative and encourage idleness by subsidizing the needy. Thus the state was left to assume the responsibility. To its credit, New York State, almost alone among its peers, made a valiant effort to be equal to the task.

Notes

INTRODUCTION

1. Victor Weybright, "Rolling Stones Gather No Sympathy," *Survey Graphic* (January, 1939), vol. 28, p. 29. Weybright also added that transients are penalized for showing the same spunk that their forefathers did. They would, therefore, be better to stay at home and go on welfare.

2. "Jobless Women in Parks," *The New York Times* (September 20, 1931), section II, p. 2N; "54 Men Hail Arrest in Subway Arcade," *ibid.* (October 7, 1932), p. 2.

3. "Flee Dustbowl for California," *Business Week* (July 3, 1937), p. 36.

4. National Association of Travelers Aid Societies, *A Community Plan for Service to Transients* (Washington, D.C., 1931), title page.

5. 48, *United States Statutes at Large*, p. 57.

6. Ellen C. Potter, *After Five Years* (New York, 1937), p. 5, roll 1, National Association of Travelers Aid Societies records, Social Welfare History Archives, University of Minnesota, microfilm collection.

7. James T. Patterson, *The New Deal and the States: Federalism in Transition* (New Jersey, 1969), p. vii.

CHAPTER ONE

1. C. J. Ribton-Turner, *A History of Vagrants and Vagrancy and Beggers and Begging* (Montclair, New Jersey, 1972 ed.), pp. 43–44.

2. *Ibid.*, pp. 67–90.

3. Ribton-Turner, pp. 132–33; Sidney and Beatrice Webb, *English Poor Law History* (11 vols., Hamden, Connecticut, 1963 ed.), vol. 7, part 1, p. 368.

4. Ribton-Turner, p. 52.

5. Karl de Schweinitz, *England's Road to Social Security* (New York, 1961 ed.), pp. 39–40.

6. Webb and Webb, vol. 7, p. 32.

7. Charles Dickens, *Bleak House* (New York, 1964 ed., originally 1852), p. 277. For additional critics of the poor law and passing-on system see also: Sir Thomas More, *Utopia* (London, 1956 ed.), p. 33; William Hay, *Remarks on the Laws Relating to the Poor with Proposals for Their Better Relief and Employment* (London, 1751), p. xi; George Coode, *Report of George Coode, Esq., to the Poor Law Board on the Law of Settlement and Removal of the Poor* (London, 1851).

8. John Cummings, *Poor Laws of Massachusetts and New York* (New York, 1895), pp. 21–22.

9. Douglas Jones, "The Strolling Poor: Transiency in Eighteenth Century Massachusetts," *Journal of Social History* (Spring, 1975), vol. 8, pp. 46–47.

10. Walter I. Trattner, *From Poor Law to Welfare State* (New York, 1974 ed.), p. 19; Josephine Chapin Brown, *Public Relief 1929–1939* (New York, 1941), p. 5.

11. *The Colonial Laws of New York* (5 vols., Albany, 1894), vol. 1, pp. 131–33.

12. June Axinn and Herman Levin, *Social Welfare: A History of the American Response to Need* (New York, 1975), p. 15.

13. *The Colonial Laws of New York*, pp. 131–33.

14. Harry Hirsch, *Our Settlement Laws* (Albany, 1933), pp. 8–10.

15. Brown, p. 5.

16. Benjamin Joseph Klebaner, *Public Poor Relief in America, 1790–1860* (New York, 1976), chapter 4 (pages are not numbered).

17. 394, *United States Reports*, p. 619.

18. Richard Hofstadter, *Social Darwinism in American Thought* (New York, 1959 ed.), p. 41.

19. Perry Miller, *The New England Mind: From Colony to Province* (Boston, 1961 ed.), pp. 40–41.

20. Hofstadter, p. 51.

21. Charles A. Beard and Mary R. Beard, *A Basic History of the United States* (New York, 1944), pp. 360–63.

CHAPTER TWO

1. E. B. O'Callagan, editor and translator, *Laws and Ordinances of New Netherland* (Albany, 1868), pp. 32, 155–58, 439–40.

2. David M. Schneider, *The History of Public Welfare in New York State, 1609–1866* (Chicago, 1938), p. 46.

3. *The Colonial Laws of New York* (5 vols., Albany, 1894), vol. 1, pp. 131–33, vol. 2, pp. 56–58.

4. *Ibid.*, vol. 5, pp. 513–17.

5. *Laws of New York, 1784*, 7th session, chapter 35 (Albany, 1886), pp. 651–59; *Laws of New York, 1788*, 11th session, chapter 62 (Albany, 1886), pp. 731–34.

6. *Laws of New York, 1801*, 24th session, chapter 184 (Albany, 1887), pp. 512–24.

7. "Report of the Secretary of State in 1824 on the Relief and Settlement of the Poor," *Assembly Journal* (February 9, 1824), reprinted in full in State Board of Charities, *Annual Report for the Year 1900* (3 vols., Albany, 1901), vol. 1, pp. 968, 978, 967, 984.

8. *Ibid.*, pp. 978–9, 1008.

9. *Laws of New York, 1824*, 47th session, chapter 331 (Albany, 1825), pp. 382–85.

10. *Revised Statutes of New York, 1827*, chapter 20 (Albany, 1829), pp. 621–22, 630.

11. Winfield and Another v. Mapes and Others, Superintendents of the Poor of the County of Orange, 4, *Denio's Reports* (Albany, 1849), pp. 571–73.

12. *Revised Statutes of New York, 1827*, pp. 632–33.

13. David M. Schneider and Albert Deutsch, *The History of Public Welfare in New York State 1867–1940* (Montclair, New Jersey, 1969 ed.), pp. 107–8.

14. New York Association for the Improvement of the Condition of the Poor, *The First Annual Report, for the Year 1845* (New York, 1845), pp. 19–21; *ibid.*, *The Seventh Annual Report, for the Year 1850* (New York, 1850), pp. 25, 27–29.

15. *Laws of New York, 1873*, 96th session, chapter 661 (Albany, 1873), pp. 1029–32.

16. "Report of Select Committee Appointed to Visit Charitable Institutions Supported by the State, and All City and County Poor and Work Houses and Jails," *New York State Documents*, 80th session, Doc. No. 8, pp. 6–7.

17. *Ibid.*, chapter 571, pp. 885–86. Reports were made each year to the legislature and are included in the legislative documents series.

18. State Board of Charities, *Annual Report for the Year 1900* (3 vols., Albany, 1901), vol. 2, p. 487; *ibid.*, *Annual Report . . . 1916* (3 vols., Albany, 1917), vol. 1, p. 364 (hereafter referred to as S.B.C.)

19. S.B.C., *Annual Report . . . 1899* (2 vols., Albany, 1900), vol. 1, p. 968; *ibid.*, *Annual Report . . . 1898* (2 vols., Albany, 1899), vol. 1, p. 113; *ibid.*, *Annual Report . . . 1897* (2 vols., Albany, 1898), vol. 1, p. 113.

20. Schneider and Deutsch, *The History of Public Welfare . . .*, *1867–1940*, p. 110.

21. Paul Ringenback, *Tramps and Reformers 1873–1916, The Discovery of Unemployment in New York* (Westport, Conn., 1973), pp. 191, 15.

22. Kennth Allsop, *Hard Travellin': The Hobo and His History* (New York, 1967), pp. 116–17.

23. *Laws of New York, 1896*, 119th session, chapter 225 (Albany, 1896).

24. *Ibid.*, pp. 140, 142, 144.

25. *Ibid.*, pp. 166, 150.

26. *Ibid.*, pp. 162, 155.

27. *Ibid.*, p. 169.

28. S.B.C., *Annual Report . . . 1896* (Albany, 1897), p. 89.

29. William Booth, *The Vagrant and the Unemployable, A Proposal Whereby Vagrants may be detained under suitable conditions and compelled to work* (London, 1909); *Laws of New York, 1911*, 134th session, pp. 2307–08; Schneider and Deutsch, p. 203.

30. Schneider and Deutsch, *The History of Public Welfare . . . , 1867–1940*, pp. 214–15, 274; Marsha Branscombe, *The Courts and the Poor Laws in New York State, 1784–1929* (Chicago, 1943), p. 270.

31. Belle Zeller, *Pressure Politics in New York* (New York, 1937), pp. 133–55.

32. State Charities Aid Association, Committee on Revision of the Poor Law, *Patchwork or Progress? Why a Public Welfare Law is Needed* (Albany, 1929).

33. *Laws of New York, 1929*, 152nd session, chapter 565 (Albany, 1929), pp. 1105–51.

34. S.B.C., "Annual Report for the Year 1929," *New York State Legislative Documents*, 153rd session (Albany, 1930), vol. 4, p. 5.

35. *Laws of New York, 1929*, pp. 1169–70.

36. *Ibid.*, pp. 1164–65.

37. Schneider and Deutsch, *The History of Public Welfare . . . 1867–1940*, pp. 286–88.

38. Edith Abbott, *Public Assistance* (2 vols., New York, 1966 ed.), vol. 1, p. 7.

39. *Laws of New York, 1929*, p. 1167.

40. *Ibid.*, p. 1168.

41. *Ibid.*, p. 1169.

CHAPTER THREE

1. United States Senate, 72d Congress, 2d session, *Hearings before a Subcommittee of the Committee on Manufactures, on S5121* (Washington, D. C., 1933), p. 23 (hereafter cited as S5121); "Report on Census of Transient and Homeless Persons for the United States for January 9, 10, and 11, 1933," folder Transient General Correspondence, NATA Prior to 9/1/33, box 83, FERA records, Record Group 69 (hereafter cited as RG 69), National Archives (hereafter cited as NA).

2. Carl A. Heisterman, Legal Research Division, U. S. Children's Bureau, "Statutory Provisions Relating to Legal Settlement for Purposes of Poor Relief," *Social Service Review* (1933), vol. 7, pp. 95–106.

3. John N. Webb, *The Transient Unemployed*, WPA research monograph (Washington, D. C., 1935), pp. 93–95.

4. John N. Webb, *Migrant Families*, WPA research monograph (Washington, D. C., 1938); *ibid.*, *The Migratory-Casual Worker*, WPA research monograph (Washington, D. C., 1937).

5. Nels Anderson, *Men on the Move* (Chicago, 1940).

6. Henry Hill Collins, Jr., *America's Own Refugees, Our 4,000,000 Homeless Migrants* (Princeton, New Jersey, 1941), p. 8.

7. S5121, p. 126.

8. Harry Hirsch, *Our Settlement Laws: Their Origin, Lack of Uniformity, and Proposed Remedies* (Albany, 1933), p. 30.

9. *Public Papers of the Presidents of the United States, Herbert Hoover* (4 vols., Washington, D.C., 1976), vol. 2, p. 511.

10. Josephine Chapin Brown, *Public Relief 1929-1939* (New York, 1940), p. 70.

11. National Association of Travelers Aid Societies, *A Community Plan for Service to Transients* (Washington, D. C., 1931), title page.

12. Robert S. Wilson, *Community Planning for Homeless Men and Boys* (New York, 1931), p. iii.

13. S5121, pp. 91–104.

14. *Public Papers . . . Herbert Hoover*, vol. 4, p. 853.

15. "Governor Emphasizes Social Welfare Legislation," *Social Welfare Bulletin* (February, 1930), p. 2.

16. David M. Ellis, et al., *A History of New York State* (Ithaca, New York, 1967), p. 416.

17. State of New York, *Public Papers of Governor Roosevelt* (4 vols., Albany, 1931-39), vol. 2, p. 173.

18. *Laws of New York, 1931*, 154th session, chapter 798 (Albany, 1932), pp. 2398, 2402.

19. New York State, Temporary Emergency Relief Administration, *Relief Today in New York State* (Albany, October 15, 1933), p. 7.

20. State Board of Social Welfare, *64th Annual Report . . . for the Year Ending June 30, 1930* (Albany, 1931), p. 29 (hereafter referred to as S.B.S.W.).

21. *Ibid.*, pp. 30–31; *ibid.*, *65th Annual Report*, pp. 186–87; *ibid.*, *66th Annual Report*, pp. 174–75; *ibid.*, *67th Annual Report*, p. 200; *ibid.*, *68th Annual Report*, p. 191.

22. S.B.S.W., *64th Annual Report*, p. 30; *ibid.*, *65th Annual Report*, p. 186.

23. S.B.S.W., *64th Annual Report*, p. 30; *ibid.*, *65th Annual Report*, p. 186; *ibid.*, *66th Annual Report*, p. 174; *ibid.*, *67th Annual Report*, p. 200; *ibid.*, *68th Annual Report*, p. 191.

24. S.B.S.W., *68th Annual Report*, p. 191.

25. *Ibid.*, *64th Annual Report*, p. 191.

26. *Ibid.*, *68th Annual Report*, p. 196.

27. *Ibid.*, *64th Annual Report*, p. 31; *ibid.*, *65th Annual Report*, p. 187; *ibid.*, *66th Annual Report*, p. 176; *ibid.*, *67th Annual Report*, p. 204; *ibid.*, *68th Annual Report*, p. 198.

28. *Laws of New York, 1933*, 156th session, chapter 449, p.986.

29. Wilson Messer, "Statement to Governor Herbert H. Lehman, Concerning, Assembly Bill Int. 1330, Print 2591, by Mr. Messer"; David Adie, "Memorandum to Governor Lehman Regarding Assembly Bill Int. 1330, Print 2591". Both located in *Bill Jacket Collection, 1933*.

30. Adie Memorandum.

31. *Constitution of the United States*, article IV, section 2, clause 1.

32. *Ibid.*, Fourteenth Amendment.

33. Onondaga County v. Town of Milo, 246, *The New York Supplemental* (St. Paul, Minnesota, 1931), p. 138; Town of Manlius v. Town of Pompey, 250, *ibid.*, p. 690.

34. New York Governor's Commission on Unemployment Relief, *Public Relief for Transient and Non-settled Persons in the State of New York (Albany, 1936), pp. 48–50*.

35. "Report on Census of Transient and Homeless Persons . . . ," n.p.

CHAPTER FOUR

1. Erie County, New York, Department of Charities and Correction, *Annual Report, 1930* (Buffalo, 1930), p. 41.

2. *Ibid.*, p. 45.

3. *Ibid.*

4. New York City, Department of Public Welfare, *1934 Annual Report* (New York, n. d.), p. 130.

5. *Ibid.*, *1930 Annual Report* (New York, n. d.), p. 61, 63.

6. *Ibid.*, "New York's Homeless Men," *Social Welfare Bulletin* (March, 1932), p. 3.

7. New York City, *1931 Annual Report* (New York, n. d.), pp. 78, 84, 8.

8. Matthew Josephson, "The Other Nation," *The New Republic* (May 15, 1933), vol. 75, pp. 14–16.

9. *Ibid.*, p. 15.

10. *Ibid.*, p. 16. For a similar inside view of the Buffalo Loding House and the resulting negativism that the experience generated see Donald Adams Clark, "Men on Relief in Lackawanna, NY, 1934–35;" reprinted in *The University of Buffalo Studies*, vol. 14. See also: Loula D. Lasker, "Rediscovered Men," *Survey Graphic* (July, 1933), vol. 22, p. 357, for a stark comparison of the sterile life of the NYC Municipal Lodging House and an experimental camp program sponsored by the New York Welfare Council.

11. New York Governor's Commission on Unemployment Relief, *Public Relief for Transient and Non-settled persons in the State of New York* (Albany, 1936), p. 48 (hereafter cited as Governor's Commission).

12. Erie County, *Annual Report, 1932* (Buffalo, 1932), p. 41; *Social Welfare Bulletin* (May, 1930), p. 5; Josephson, p. 15.

13. Josephson, p. 16.

14. Robert S. Wilson, *Community Planning for Homeless Men and Boys* (New York, 1931), pp. 24-28.

15. Syracuse Community Chest and Council, *Social and Health Programs in Syraucse* (Syracuse, May, 1934), pp. 66-72.

16. *Ibid.*, pp. 69, 71.

17. Owen R. Lovejoy, "Scores Camp Plan for Nomad Youth," *The New York Times* (February 16, 1933), p. 22.

18. "Travelers Aid — From Past into the Future" (paper presented at the annual Travelers Aid Convention, June 15, 1931), roll 36, National Association of Travelers Aid Societies records (hereafter referred to as NATAS), Social Welfare History Archives, University of Minnesota, microfilm collection (hereafter referred to as SWHA); NATAS, Travelers Aid (April, 1932), roll 25, *ibid.*

19. NATAS, *Service to Transients* (April, 1932), roll 25, NATAS records, SWHA.

20. NATAS, "Standards for the Care of Transients and Homeless," and "Men Off the Road," roll 36, NATAS records, SWHA; *ibid.*, "Early History of Selected Traveler's Aid Associations, 1917-1948," and "Children Under Sixteen Travelling Alone," roll 1, *ibid.*

21. Lieut. William C. Davis, "Nomads, The Salvation Army Method of Dealing with the Homeless Man Problem," *War Cry* (January 21, 1933), p. 4. The complete run of *War Cry* is available on microfilm at the Salvation Army Archives and Research Center, New York (hereafter cited as SAA).

22. "Bowery Breadline Longest Since 1914," *War Cry* (April 12, 1930), p. 11; "The Bowery Eats," *War Cry* (September 20, 1930), p. 4; *The Salvation Army and the Present Crisis, Report of Unemployment Emergency Work in Greater New York, October 1, 1930 - September 30, 1931* (New York, 1931), pamphlet found in SAA.

23. "Concerning the Homeless Man," *War Cry* (October 24, 1931), p. 10.

24. "The S. S. Broadway," *War Cry* (October 24, 1931), p. 7.

25. Edward H. McKinley, *Marching to Glory: The History of the Salvation Army in the United States of America, 1880-1980* (San Francisco, 1980), p. 165; *In the Front Line, An Account of the Unemployment Emergency Relief Work by the Salvation Army in Greater New York, October 1, 1931–September 30, 1932* (New York, 1932), pamphlet found in SAA; Esther H. Elias, "Gold Dust Lodge," *War Cry* (December 31, 1933), p. 3.

26. Jean Johnson, "Pure Gold at Gold Dust Lodge," *War Cry* (November 4, 1933), p. 3.

27. Josephson; National Committee on Care of Transient and Homeless (hereafter cited as NCCTH), minutes, March 29, 1933, folder 82, National Social Welfare Assembly records, supplement 1 (hereafter cited as NSWA), SWHA; Johnson, "Pure Gold at Gold Dust Lodge."

28. "Concerning the Homeless Man," p. 10.

29. NCCTH minutes, March 29, 1933, folder 82, National Social Welfare Assembly Records supplement 1, (hereafter referred to as NSWA), SWHA.

30. Syracuse Community Chest and Council, pp. 69–71; "The Army Meeting Mammoth Emergency Relief Situation," *War Cry* (December 6, 1930), p. 9; "Concerning the Homeless Man," p. 10; "Joe Wanderer Finds Friends," *War Cry* (March 25, 1933), p. 3.

31. Robert S. Wilson and Dorothy B. de la Pole, *Group Treatment for Transients* (New York, 1934), pp. 31–35.

32. *The Salvation Army and the Present Crisis*, p. 7.

33. "Women's Canteen and Rest Room," *War Cry* (January 31, 1931), pp. 9–10; *The Salvation Army and the Present Crisis*, pp. 14–15.

34. *The Salvation Army and the Present Crisis*, p. 13; "Women and Children First," *War Cry* (October 24, 1931), p. 6.

35. Ellen C. Potter, *After Five Years (New York, 1937)*, NATAS, roll 1, SWHA; *United States House of Representatives, 76th congress, 3rd session, Hearings before the Select Committee to Investigate the Interstate Migration of Destitute Citizens* (34 parts, Washington, D. C., 1940–44), part 10, pp. 4224–4226; NCCTH minutes, 1932–38, folders 82 and 83, roll 31, NSWA supplement 1, SWHA.

36. *Ibid.*

37. NCCTH minutes, March 29, 1933, folder 82, NSWA supplement 1, SWHA.

38. Governor's Commission, pp. 44–47.

39. United States Senate, 72d Congress, 2d session, *Hearings before a Subcommittee of the Committee on Manufactures on S5121* (Washington, D. C., 1933), pp. 196–97 (hereafter cited as S5121).

40. Governor's Commission, p. 43.

41. *Ibid.*, p. 148.

42 "37 Homeless Men Seized in Subway," *The New York Times* (October 2, 1933), p. 2; "23 Jobless Sent to Jail," *ibid.* (October 30, 1933), p. 8; *Laws of New York, 1931*, chapter 284.

43. S5121, p. 54.

44. Robert S. Wilson, "Transient Families," *The Family* (December, 1930), pp. 243–50; Jessanine S. Whitney, "The Tuberculous Migrant, a Family Problem," *Proceedings of the National Conference of Social Work, 56th Annual Session, 1929* (Chicago, 1930); *Laws of New York, 1929*, p. 1065.

45. "Finds Mental Ills Factor in Vagrancy," *The New York Times* (February 24, 1930), p. 24.

46. Niles Carpenter and William M. Haenzel, "Migratoriness and Criminality in Buffalo," *Social Forces* (December, 1930), vol. 9, pp. 254–55.

47. Ellen C. Potter, "Mustering Out the Migrants," *Survey* (December, 1933), vol. 69, pp. 411–12; J. Prentice Murphy, "America on the March," *Survey Graphic* (March, 1933), vol. 22, pp. 147–50; "Forgotten and Scrapped," *The New Republic* (June 21, 1933), vol. 75, pp. 141–42; "Vagabond Children," *Ladies' Home Journal* (November, 1932), vol. 49, p. 22.

CHAPTER FIVE

1. "Report on Census of Transient and Homeless Persons for the United States for January 9, 10, and 11, 1933," folder Transient General Correspondence, NATA Prior to 9/1/33, box 83, Record Group 69, National Archives; Nels Anderson, *Men on the Move* (Chicago, 1940), p. 18.

2. Anderson, p. 33; For the following description of those elements of the hobo's life that the transient shared, I am indebted to a variety of authors who tell basically the same story including Kenneth Allsop, *Hard Travellin': The Hobo and His History* (New York, 1969); Thomas Minehan, *Boy and Girl Tramps of America* (New York, 1934); Ben L. Reitman, *Sister of the Road, The Autobiography of Box-Car Bertha* (New York, 1937); Tom Kromer, *Waiting for Nothing* (New York, 1935); Nels Anderson, *The Hobo* (Chicago, 1923). Hereafter only direct reference from these sources will be cited.

3. Kromer, p. 153.

4. Allsop, p. 161.

5. United States Senate, 72d Congress, 2d session, *Hearings before a Subcommittee of the Committee on Manufactures, on S5121* (Washington, D. C. 1933), p. 114 (hereafter cited as S5121).

6. *Ibid.*, pp. 25–27.

7. *Ibid.*

8. Kromer, pp. 164, 167, 172–73.

9. Minehan, p. 265.

10. Gertrude Springer, "Well Advertised Breadlines," *The Survey* (February 15, 1931), vol. 65, p. 545.

11. S5121, p. 157.

12. National Committee on Care of Transient and Homeless minutes, March 29, 1933, folder 82, National Social Welfare Assembly Records supplement 1, Social Welfare History Archives, University of Minnesota, microfilm collection.

13. *Ibid.*

14. *Ibid.*

15. *Ibid.*

16. "Told at a Free Food Depot," *War Cry* (March 7, 1931), p. 9.

17. "Weary Wayfarer in a Jam Seeks Rest on Hudson Bridge," *The New York Times* (December 3, 1930), p. 3; "Court Aids Jobless Youth," *ibid.*, (December 1, 1930), p. 2.

18. S5121, pp. 56, 70, 144.

19. Kromer, pp. 17, 41, 53, 124, 72, 74.

20. *Ibid.*, pp. 187–88.

21. Frank Bunce, "I've Got to Take a Chance," *The Forum* (February, 1933), vol. 89, pp. 108–12.

22. *Ibid.*

23. *Ibid.*

24. *Ibid.*

25. "Wandering Women," *The Pittsburg Press* (July 30, 1933), p. 1.

26. Thomas Minehan, "Girls of the Road," *Independent Woman* (October, 1934), p. 316.

27. "Report on Census of Transient and Homeless Persons. . . ."

28. Anderson, *The Hobo*, p. 137.

29. S5121, p. 51.

30. Reitman, p. 16.

31. Walter C. Reckless, "Why Women Become Hoboes," *The American Mercury* (February, 1934), vol. 31, p. 175.

32. *Ibid.*

33. Agnes O'Shea, "Development of the Care of Transient Women," *The Transient*, vol. 1, pp. 1, 3, 6. The complete run of *The Transient* is available on microfilm at SWHA, Minnesota.

34. Reckless, p. 175.

35. Minehan, p. 110.

36. Reitman, p. 56.

37. Minehan, pp. 139–40.

38. J. R. Roberts, "Lesbian Hoboes, Their Lives and Times," *Dyke* (Fall, 1977), p. 40.

39. Roberts, p. 41.

40. Nan Cinnater, "Woman Hoboes of the Great Depression: Survival in Hard Times" (paper presented at the Sixth Berkshire Conference on the History of Women, June 1, 1984).

41. Reitman, p. 251.

42. Reckless.

43. *Ibid.*, p. 178.

44. *Ibid.*, p. 178, 177.

45. *Ibid.*, pp. 178, 176, 179.

46. *Ibid.*, p. 180.

47. "Report on Census of Transient and Homeless Persons . . .;" Minehan, pp. 256, 133.

48. Minehan, pp. 37, 42, 24, 48, 53.

49. *Ibid.*, p. 55, 117.

50. *Ibid.*, p. 54.
51. *Ibid.*, pp. 267-68.
52. *Ibid.*, pp. 76, 127, 128.
53. *Ibid.*, pp. 112-13.
54. *Ibid.*, pp. 27, 203, 204, 40, 116, 113.
55. S5121, p. 110.
56. *Ibid.*, p. 110-14.
57. Minehan, pp. 120-21.
58. William E. Leuchtenburg, *Franklin D. Roosevelt and the New Deal* (New York, 1963), pp. 52-53, 174; Minehan, p. 166.

CHAPTER SIX

1. United States Senate, 72d Congress, 2d session, *Hearings before a Subcommittee of the Committee on Manufactuers, on S5121* (Washington, D. C., 1933), p. 67 (hereafter cited as S5121).
2. *Ibid.*, pp. 2, 73, 104, 105, 121.
3. *Ibid.*, pp. 196-97.
4. *Ibid.*, pp. 41, 45, 46, 86.
5. *Ibid.*, pp. 78; A Wayne McMillen, "An Army of Boys on the Loose," *Survey Graphic* (September, 1932), vol. 21, p. 389; Towne Nylander, "Wandering Youth," *Sociology and Social Research* (July-August, 1933), pp. 560-68; "Uncle Sam's Runaway Boys," *Survey* (March, 1933), vol. 69, pp. 98-101; "200,000 Vagabond Children," *Ladies' Home Journal* (September, 1932), vol. 49, pp. 8-9.
6. S5121, p. 84.
7. David A. Shannon, *Twentieth Century America* (3 vols., Chicago, 1974), vol. 2, p. 151.
8. United States Senate, 72d Congress, 2d session, *Hearings before a Subcommittee of the Committee on Manufactures, on S5125* (Washington, D. C., 1933), p. 167 (hereafter cited as S5125).
9. *Ibid.*, p. 389.
10. 47, *United States Statutes at Large*, p. 709; Edith Abbott, "Falacy of Local Relief," *The New Republic* (November 9, 1932), vol. 72, pp. 348-50.
11. "Is It to Be Murder, Mr. Hoover?" *The Nation* (August 3, 1932), vol. 35, p. 96; "Shall America Starve?" *ibid.* (November 30, 1932), vol. 135, p. 518.
12. "Assert Only RFC Can Rescue Cities," *The New York Times* (February 19, 1933), section II, p. 9.
13. S5125, p. 1.
14. *Ibid.*, pp. 80, 87, 88, 69.
15. *Ibid.*, pp. 80, 81, 74, 75.
16. 48, *United States Statutes at Large*, p. 57.

17. "Direct Relief at Last," *The Nation* (April 5, 1933), vol. 136, p. 362; Gertrude Springer, "The New Deal and the Old Dole," *Survey Graphic* (July, 1933), vol. 22, pp. 347-52.

18. Jacob Fisher, *The Response of Social Work to the Depression* (Cambridge, Mass., 1980), pp. 47-49.

19. William W. Bremer, *Depression Winters: New York Social Workers and the New Deal* (Philadelphia, 1984).

20. Springer.

21. Bremer.

22. 48, *United States Statutes at Large*, p. 57.

23. Harry L. Hopkins, *Spending to Save* (Washington, D. C., 1936), p. 133; Ellery F. Reed, *An Evaluative Survey of the Federal Transient Program* (New York, 1934), p. 44; Theodore E. Whiting, *Final Statistical Report of the FERA*, WPA report (Washington, D.C., 1942), p. 74.

24. "Editorial," *The Transient* (March, 1934), p. 2.

25. Bertha McCall to C. M. Bookman, Federal Emergency Relief Administration, August 8, 1933, folder Transient General Correspondence, NATA, Prior to 9/1/33, box 83, Record Group 69 (hereafter cited as RG69), National Archives (hereafter cited as NA).

26. "Party Tidbits Feed Homeless in Jail," *The New York Times* (March 3, 1933), p. 19; "Asks Aid for Needy Boys," *ibid.* (March 5, 1933), p. 4.

27. Harry Hopkins to Alfred H. Schoellkopf, folder New York Transient, 1933, box 201, RG 69, NA.

28. *Ibid.*; New York State, Temporary Emergency Relief Administration (hereafter referred to as NYS, TERA), press release, November 27, 1933, folder 421 New York Transient, December, 1933, box 201, RG 69, NA.

29. FERA, *Rules and Regulations No. 3*, reprinted in Edith Abbott, *Public Assistance* (2 vols., New York, 1966), vol. 2, pp. 780-84.

30. Harry Hirsch, New York State Department of Social Welfare, *Compilation of Settlement Laws of all States in the United States* (Albany, April, 1935).

31. "Transients," *Social Welfare Bulletin* (December, 1933), pp. 2-4; New York State Governor's Commission on Unemployment Relief, *Public Relief for Transient and Non-Settled Persons in the State of New York* (Albany, 1936), p. 89 (hereafter referred to as Governor's Commission).

32. NYS, TERA, "Rules and Regulations on Care of Transients," bulletin #20, *TERA Official Bulletin* (January 20, 1934), p. 1.

33. Robert S. Wilson and Dorothy B. de la Pole, National Association of Travelers Aid Societies *Group Treatment for Transients* (New York, 1934), pp. 16-18.

34. NYS, TERA, *Manual of Procedure* (Albany, April, 1935), Item 707.

35. Thomas Minehan, "Boy and Girl Tramps of the Road," *The Clearing House* (November, 1936), p. 138.

36. E. J. W. to Franklin D. Roosevelt, April 26, 1934, folder, Transient General Correspondence, U-Z, box 82, RG 69, NA.

37. NYS, TERA, *Manual of Procedure*, Item 707.
38. Governor's Commission, p. 78.
39. Herman J. P. Schubert, *Twenty Thousand Transients* (Buffalo, 1935), p. 112; Governor's Commission, p. 106.
40. Schubert, pp. 111–12.
41. *Ibid.*
42. Folder 421 New York State Transient Complaint, A-F, box 201, RG 69, NA; folder 421 New York State Transient Complaint, G-M, *ibid.*; New York Transient Complaint, N-Z, *ibid.*
43. Schubert, p. 121; interview with Dr. Herman J. P. Schubert and his wife, Dr. Mazie Earle Wagner, June 14, 1985.
44. Schubert, p. 122.
45. Schubert, pp. 122–23; Schubert interview, June 14, 1985.
46. Schubert, p. 112; Governor's Commission, p. 106.
47. Governor's Cofmmission, p. 91.
48. *Ibid.*, pp. 81–82.
49. Schubert, pp. 35–36.
50. F. M. to Franklin D. Roosevelt, July 16, 1934, folder 420 New York Transient, August, September, 1934, box 200, RG 69, NA.
51. Hopkins, p. 133.
52. Robert S. Wilson, "Problems in Co-ordinating Service for Transient and Resident Unattached from the Point of View of Individualized Service," *Proceedings of the National Conference of Social Work, Sixty-Second Annual Meeting, Montreal, 1935* (Chicago, 1935), pp. 210–23.
53. J. K. to FERA, January 17, 1935, folder 420 New York Transient, January 1935, box 199, RG 69, NA.
54. Schubert, pp. 145, 124.
55. Gertrude Springer, "Men Off the Road," *Survey Graphic* (September, 1934), vol. 23, p. 422.
56. Alfred Friendly, "Transient," *Survey Graphic* (July, 1937), vol. 26, p. 402.
57. Schubert interview, June 14, 1985; Schubert, p. 145.
58. Governor's Commission, pp. 133–34.

CHAPTER SEVEN

1. William Booth, *The Vagrant and the Unemployable, A Proposal Whereby Vagrants may be detained under suitable conditions and compelled to work* (London, 1909); Edmund Kelly, *The Elimination of the Tramp* (New York, 1908).
2. Ellery F. Reed, *Federal Transient Program, An Evaluative Survey, May to June, 1934* (New York, 1934), pp. 58–60.
3. Gertrude Springer, "Men Off the Road," *Survey Graphic* (September, 1934), vol. 23, p. 422.

4. "To Establish Transient Camp at Saratoga for Work on Reservation," *The Saratogian* (March 20, 1935), p. 3.

5. Herman J. P. Schubert, *Twenty Thousand Transients* (Buffalo, 1935), pp. 125-26.

6. *Ibid.*, pp. 125-27.

7. New York State Governor's Commission on Unemployment Relief, *Public Relief for Transient and Non-Settled Persons in the State of New York* (Albany, 1936), p. 108 (hereafter referred to as Governor's Commission).

8. "Camp Saratoga," report, folder 420 New York Transient, April, May, 1936, box 199, Record Group 69 (hereafter referred to as RG69), National Archives (hereafter referred to as NA).

9. Governor's Commission, pp. 108-110.

10. Ruth A. Lerrigo, "On Every Town's Doorstep," *Survey Graphic* (June, 1936), vol. 25, p. 391.

11. "Camp Saratoga," report: "Transients Aid Toy Exchange Work Project," *Schenectady Gazette* (March 20, 1936).

12. Resolution of St. Johnsville, New York, Town Board, April 23, 1936, to FERA, submitted by Mr. Edward Davis, Town Clerk, folder 420 New York Transient, April, May 1936, box 199, RG 69, NA.

13. Springer, p. 423.

14. *Ibid.*, p. 422.

15. Transient complaints can be found in FERA records, RG 69, NA, on a state by state basis. Each state has specific transient division complaint files.

16. Springer, p. 424.

17. *Ibid.*, p. 423.

18. *Ibid.*

19. *Ibid.*, pp. 425-26.

20. Lerrigo, p. 364; Robert S. Wilson and Dorothy B. de la Pole, *Group Treatment for Transients* (New York, 1934), p. 73.

21. Springer, p. 427.

22. Ben L. Reitman, *Sister of the Road, The Autobiography of Box-Car Bertha* (New York, 1937); Tom Kromer, *Waiting for Nothing* (New York, 1935); Thomas Minehan, *Boy and Girl Tramps of America* (New York, 1934), p. 141; Kenneth Allsop, *Hard Travellin': The Hobo and His History* (New York, 1969), pp. 212-219.

23. Wilson, p. 70.

24. "2,500 Will Clear State Flood Area," *The New York Times* (August 2, 1935), p. 15.

25. Bert Lord to Franklin Roosevelt, August 2, 1935, folder 420 New York Transient, August, 1935, box 199, RG 69, NA; "Lord Berates Transient Use in Flood Area," *The Evening Tribune, Hornell* (August 2, 1933), p. 6; "Eaton Says State Botched Flood Aid," *The New York Times* (August 4, 1935), p. 6; "CCC Men Will Join Flood Relief Work, *The New York Times* (August 9, 1935), p. 17.

26. "Report of Progress, August 15, 1935, Flood Control Project for Southern Central New York State, Transient Division," folder 420 New York Transient, August 1935, box 199, RG 69, NA: Governor's Commission, p. 112–13.

27. "Floodlite," July 26, 1935, folder 420 New York Transient, June, July and August, box 199, RG 69, NA; Harry Hopkins to Franklin Roosevelt, August 13, 1935, folder 420 New York Transient, August 1935, *ibid.*

28. "Transients Services Volunteered On All Fronts During Disaster; Rescue, Free House Resident," *The Evening Tribune, Hornell* (July 25, 1935), p. 7; "Transient TERA Workers Helping Flooded Farmers," *Steuben Courier* (September 13, 1935), p. 1.

29. "Floodlite," p. 1.

30. "Report of Progress. . . ."

31. "Narrative Report of Activities of the National Park Service, Technical Agency of Elks Park Camp for the Month of March, 1936," report, folder 420 New York Transient, April, May 1936, box 199, RG 69, NA; "Works Progress Report, WPA Camp Marathon," March 20, 1936, *ibid.*; Mayor of Marathon to Director, Camp Marathon, April 7, 1936, *ibid.*

32. Boyden Sparkes, "The New Deal for Transients," *The Saturday Evening Post* (October 19, 1935), vol. 208, pp. 23ff. John Benton, "Rest for Weary Willie," *ibid.* (September 5, 1936), vol. 209, pp. 5ff., and (September 12, 1936), pp. 14ff.

33. Schubert, p. 140; Springer, p. 425; "Transient's Picture of Flood Scene is Gift for City," *The Evening Tribune, Hornell* (July 26, 1935), p. 9.

34. A. A. M. to FERA, May 23, 1935, folder 421 New York Transient Complaint, G–M, box 201, RG 69, NA; report of supervisors of Camp Greenhaven, June 11, 1935, *ibid.*

35. W. S. to Harry Hopkins, November, 1935, folder 421 New York Transient Complaint, N–Z, box 201, RG 69, NA; director of Stony Brook to FERA, *ibid.*

36. D. D. to Harry Hopkins, n.d., folder 421 New York Transient Complaint, A–F, box 201, RG 69, NA; Homer Borst to Elizabeth Wickenden, February 16, 1935, *ibid.*

37. J. H. M. to FERA, October 29, 1934, folder New York Transient, October 1934, box 200, RG 69, NA.

38. William Weatherby and Emily Smith, "Journalism in Transient Bureaus," *The Transient* (May, 1935), pp. 8–9.

39. "Makeshift Gong Summons 120 Camp Workers to Meals: Green Haven Project Finds Rehabilitation Beginning," *The Sunday Courier,* Poughkeepsie, New York (May, 1936), folder 420 New York Transient, April, May 1936, box 199, RG 69, NA.

40. Governor's Commission, p. 86.

41. Schubert, p. 125.

42. Springer, "Men Off the Road."

43. Wilson, p. 46; "Some Observations on the Transient Problem," *Public Welfare News* (January, 1936), p. 3.

44. Wilson, p. 45; "What's Next for Transients," *The Transient* (September, 1934), p. 2.

45. Harry L. Hopkins, *Spending to Save* (Washington, DC, 1936), p. 134.

46. New York State Temporary Emergency Relief Administration (hereafter cited as NYS, TERA), monthly bulletins of relief statistics, 1934 and 1935.

47. Hopkins, p. 134.

48. Governor's Commission, pp. 91–93, 88.

49. Springer, p. 428.

50. J. Paul McGirr to Charles Alspach, June 11, 1936, folder 420 New York Transient, June, July and August, 1936, box 199, RG 69, NA; J. Paul McGirr to Franklin Roosevelt, May 20, 1936, *ibid.*; T. Moore, President Skidmore College to Chamber of Commerce, Saratoga, May 8, 1936, *ibid*; Junior Civic League, Saratoga, to Chamber of Commerce, Saratoga, April 27, 1936, *ibid.*; Girl Scouts, Saratoga, to Chamber of Commerce, Saratoga, April 27, 1936, *ibid.*

51. James M. Meed to Harry Hopkins, folder New York Transient, March, April, 1934, box 201, RG 69, NA.

52. Wilson, p. 44.

53. "Hartford House Huddle," December, 1934, vol. 1, folder 420 New York Transient, December, 1934, box 199, RG 69, NA.

54. "Hartford House," *The Transient* (January, 1935), vol. 2, pp. 4ff.

55. "Hartford House Huddle," December, 1934.

56. *Ibid.*

57. *Ibid.*

58. "Hartford House;" Governor's Commission, p. 80; "Hartford House May Go," *The New York Times* (September 20, 1935), p. 10.

59. "Report of Proposal, Hartwick School for Transient Young Men and Boys Under the Auspices of the Transient Division of the New York State, Temporary Emergency Relief Administration," folder Camp Facilities, Minimum Requirements, box 40, RG 69, NA; "School for Transients," *The Survey* (August, 1935), vol. 71, p. 241.

60. Eleanor Roosevelt to Lester W. Herzog, WPA, May 21, 1936, folder 420 New York Transient, June, July, August, 1936, box 199, RG 69; NA; Governor's Commission, p. 80.

61. Thomas L. Cotton, Director, Division of Camp Management, WPA to Elizabeth Wickenden, Assistant to Administrator, FERA, May 12, 1936, folder 420 New York Transient, May, June 1936, box 199, RG 69, NA.

62. Hopkins, p. 132; Reed, p. 23.

63. Governor's Commission, pp. 164–68, 118.

64. Schubert, p. 97; Governor's Commission, pp. 143, 118.

65. S5121, pp. 67, 74; "Development of the Care of Women," *The Transient* (November, 1934), vol. 1, p. 7; NYS, TERA, *Five Million People, One Billion Dollars* (Albany, 1937), pp. 51–52; Governor's Commission, p. 168.

CHAPTER EIGHT

1. Theodore E. Whiting, *Final Statistical Report of the Federal Emergency Relief Administration*, WPA Report (Washington, D.C., 1942), p. 71.

2. John N. Webb, *The Transient Unemployed*, WPA research monograph (Washington, D.C., 1935) pp. 100, 20, 19.

3. *Ibid.*, p. 12; Harry L. Hopkins, *Spending to Save* (Washington, D.C., 1936), p. 129.

4. Whiting, p. 74.

5. New York State, TERA, "Relief and Emergency Employment in New York State, December, 1936," *Bulletin on Public Relief Statistics* (Albany, n.d.), p. 10.

6. Robert S. Wilson, *Individualized Service for Transients* (New York, 1935), pp. 2–3; Hopkins, p. 126.

7. Lucretia Penny, "Pea Picker's Child," *Survey Graphic* (July, 1935), vol. 24, pp. 352–53; Webb, pp. 94, 1,2.

8. New York Governor's Commission on Unemployment Relief, *Public Relief for Transient and Non-settled Persons in the State of New York* (Albany, 1936), pp. 54–63 (hereafter referred to as Governor's Commission).

9. Herman J. P. Schubert, *Twenty Thousand Transients* (Buffalo, 1935), pp. 13, 14, 23–43, 61–74.

10. *Ibid.*, pp. 142–43.

11. *Ibid.*, pp. 106–10.

12. Ben L. Reitman, *Sister of the Road, The Autobiography of Box-Car Bertha* (New York, 1975 ed., originally published in 1935), p. 251.

13. Schubert, p. 106.

14. Esther Hachtel, "A Study of One Hundred and Thirty-one Young Transient Women" (Masters thesis, University of Tulane, 1935).

15. Robert S. Wilson, "Transient Families," *The Family* (December, 1930), vol. 11, p. 245.

16. Schubert, pp. 96–103.

17. National Committee on Care of Transient and Homeless minutes, September 27, 1934, and March 20, 1934, folder 82, National Social Welfare Assembly Records, supplement 1, (hereafter referred to as NSWA), Social Welfare History Archives, University of Minnesota, microfilm collection (hereafter referred to as SWHA).

18. Ellery F. Reed, *Federal Transient Program, An Evaluative Survey, May to June, 1934* (New York, 1934).

19. Reed, pp. 35, 88, 110.

20. Harry L. Hoplins, *Spending to Save* (Washington, D. C., 1936), pp. 127-28.

21. Governor's Commission, p. 83; "Put Transient in County Jail as Shoplifter," *The Evening Tribune, Hornell* (August 8, 1935), p. 5; "Arrested for Car Theft After Race to Ballston Spa," local paper Saratoga Springs (June 5, 1936), folder 420 New York Transient, June 1936, box 199, Record Group 69, National Archives; "Train Hoboes Killed Murray for Pittance," *The Canisteo Times* (August 22, 1935), p. 1.

22. J. Arthur Flynn, "How do we Interpret 'Problems on March'" in MacEnnis Moore, "Collected Papers of Interpretation of 'Problems on the March,'" roll 1, National Association of Travelers Aid Societies records, SWHA.

23. "Resume of Federal Transient Program as Reported by Transient Director, FERA," *The Transient* (May, 1934), vol. 1, p. 4; "Relief Agencies Here Protest Liquidation of Federal Program for Transients," *The New York Times* (September 20, 1935), p. 10.

24. Hopkins, p. 132.

25. Reed, pp. 48, 50.

26. Governor's Commission, p. 93.

27. State Board of Social Welfare, *69th Annual Report* (Albany, 1936), p. 179; *ibid.*, *70th Annual Report* (Albany, 1937), p. 20.

28. *Ibid.*, *68th Annual Report* (Albany, 1935), pp. 193, 198.

29. *Ibid.*, *69th Annual Report*, pp. 181-186.

30. Nels Anderson, *Men on the Move* (Illinois, 1940), p. 307.

31. "Nomadic Boys in City Doubled in Year," *The New York Times* (July 15, 1934), secton II, p. 1.

32. "Army of Beggars Held a Menace to Health," *ibid.* (January 29, 1934), p. 17.

33. Schubert, p. 146.

34. "Relief Agencies Here . . . ," p. 10; Reed, p. 87; Hopkins, p. 138; "The Transient Emerges," *The Transient* (March, 1934), vol. 1, p. 2.

35. Ellen C. Potter, "Absorbing the Migrant," reprinted in *This Business of Relief, Proceedings of the Delegate Conference American Association of Social Workers, Washington, D. C., February 1936* (American Association of Social Workers, New York, n.d.), p. 48; Governor's Commission, pp. 151, 98; "Rate Lodging House High," *The New York Times* (April 21, 1935), p. 21.

36. Reed, p. 87.

CHAPTER NINE

1. "What About Transients?" *The Transient* (September, 1935), vol. 2, cover; "Transient Relief Cut to Begin Saturday," *The New York Times* (September 19, 1935), p. 21.

2. Gertrude Springer, "New Deal, Old Dole," *Survey Graphic* (July, 1933), vol. 22, p. 350.

3. Samuel I. Roseman, compiler, *The Public Papers and Addresses of Franklin D. Roosevelt* (5 vols., New York, 1938), vol. 4, pp. 19–20.

4. Jacob Fisher, *The Response of Social Work to the Depression* (Cambridge, Mass., 1980), pp. 56, 99, 122, 143; William W. Bremer, *Depression Winters: New York Social Workers and the New Deal* (Philadelphia, 1984), p. 141.

5. "No More Federal Relief?" *The Survey* (February, 1935), vol. 71, p. 35; "The Unsettled In the New Program," *The Transient* (June, 1936), p. 5.

6. Harry L. Hopkins, *Spending to Save* (New York, 1936), pp. 136–37.

7. "Recent Observations on the Transient Problem" *Public Welfare News* (January, 1936), vol. 4, p. 4.

8. "Relief for Transients," *The New York Times* (September 26, 1935), p. 22; Ellen C. Potter, "Absorbing the Migrant," reprinted in *This Business of Relief, Proceedings of the Delegate Conference American Association of Social Workers, Washington, D. C., February, 1936* (American Association of Social Workers, New York, n.d.), pp. 149–50.

9. "Relief Agencies Here Protest Liquidation of Federal Program for Transients," *The New York Times* (September 20, 1935), p. 10; "Chest Groups Ask Transient Care Extended," *Syracuse Post-Standard* (October 4, 1935), p. 10; "Take Care of Transient Poor Welfare Leaders Petition Governor," *Albany Evening News* (December 13, 1935), p. 3.

10. "When Winter Comes," *The New York Times* (October 12, 1935), p. 16; "Relief Agencies Here Protest Liquidation of Federal Program for Transients," *ibid.* (September 20, 1935), p. 10; "Homeless Men Ponder Latest Federal Order" *Syracuse Post-Standard* (September 22, 1935), p. 13.

11. "End of Federal Aid for Transients Scored," *The New York Times* (October 7, 1935), p. 2.

12. Robert Lane, New York City Welfare Council to Aubrey Williams, WPA, October 20, 1935; folder 420 New York Transient, October 1935, box 199, Record Group 69 (hereafter referred to as RG 69), National Archives (hereafter referred to as NA); Letter on Welfare Council letterhead, October 16, 1935, *ibid.*; Charity Organization Bulletin #906, October 14, 1935, *ibid.*

13. "US Transient Center to be Closed Dec. 1," *Syracuse Post-Standard* (November 2, 1935), p. 10; "Westchester Fights Closing TERA Camp," *The New York Times* (November 5, 1935), p. 30; "City Terminates Transient Relief," *ibid.* (November 9, 1935), p. 3.

14. New York State, Governor's Commission on Unemployment Relief, *Public Relief for Transient and Non-Settled Persons in the State of New York* (Albany, 1936), p. 26 (hereafter referred to as Governor's Commission).

15. "New Relief Cases Barred for Month," *The New York Times* (November 27, 1935), p. 7; "Transients Not a Local Burden," *ibid.* (December 30, 1935), p. 6.

16. "State Conferences Act on Transient Problem," *The Transient*

(November, 1935), vol. 2, p. 3; Donald S. Howard, *The WPA and Federal Relief Policy* (New York, 1943).

17. P. V. C. to Director of Transient Activities, June, 1936, folder 420 New York Transient, June 1936, box 199, RG 69, NA.

18. Mrs. A. D. to Franklin D. Roosevelt, January 13, 1936, folder 421 New York Transient Complaints, A-F, box 201, RG 69, NA; M.H. to Franklin D. Roosevelt, folder 421 New York Transient Complaint, G-M, *ibid.*

19. "State Conference Acts on Transient Problem," *The Transient* (November, 1935), vol. 2, p. 3.

20. Thomas Cotton to Harry Hopkins, June 5, 1936, folder 420 New York Transient, May, June, 1936, box 199, RG 69, NA; Thomas Cotton to Aubrey Williams, June 10, 1936, *ibid.*

21. Nels Anderson, *Men on the Move* (Illinois, 1940), pp. 177, 191–92, 144–45, 170–73.

22. David A. Shannon, *Twentieth Century America* (3 vols., Chicago, 1974), vol. 2, p. 216.

23. United States House of Representatives, 76th Congress, 3rd session, *Hearings before the Select Committee to Investigate the Interstate Migration of Destitute Citizens* (34 parts, Washington, D.C., 1940-1942), part I, pp. 216–17 (hereafter cited as Tolan Hearings).

24. William E. Leuchtenburg, *Franklin D. Roosevelt and the New Deal* (New York, 1963), pp. 243–56.

25. Fisher, p. 145.

26. Ellen C. Potter, *After Five Years* (New York, May 19, 1937), p. 10, roll 1, National Association of Travelers Aid Societies records, Social Welfare History Archives, University of Minnesota, microfirm collection.

27. Harry M. Hirsch, compiler, *Compilation of Settlement Laws of all States in the United States*, revised as of September, 1939 (Chiago, 1939).

28. *Ibid.*

29. *Ibid.*

30. *Laws of New Yrok, 1929*, 152nd session, chapter 365 (Albany, 1929), pp. 191–92; "Family's Plight Stirs Sympathy," *Buffalo Evening News* (November 1, 1938), p. 15.

31. *Statues of California, 1900 Extra Session* (Sacramento, 1900), pp. 636–38; Edwards v. California, 314, *United States Reports*, pp. 160–86.

32. Hirsch.

33. Tolan Hearings, pp. 48–49; "State Trends in Settlement Legislation," *The Transient* (April, 1940), vol. 7, p. 7.

34. Josephine C. Brown, *Public Relief, 1929–39* (New York, 1940), p. 325.

35. Anderson, p. 305.

36. Eric Beecroft and Seymour Janow, "Toward a National Policy for Migration," *Social Forces*, (May, 1938), vol 16, pp. 484–85.

37. Philip E. Ryan, *Migration and Social Welfare* (New York, 1940), pp. 60–61; Beecroft, p. 484.

38. Potter, p. 2.

39. Beecroft, p. 480, 491–2; *Congressional Record, 1938*, vol. 83, pp. 2018–19.

40. Tolan Hearings, p. 2236.

41. Carey McWilliams *Factories in the Field* (Boston, 1939), pp. 310–11.

42. "Here and There on the Transient Problem," *The Transient* (March, 1936), vol. 3, p. 16; "Border Ban," *Buffalo Evening News* (February 6, 1936), p. 22.

43. Beecroft, p. 480.

44. Robert S. Lynd and Helen Merrel Lynd, *Middletown in Transition* (New York, 1937), p. 112; Ryan, p. 49.

45. Tolan Hearings, p. 46; Lynd, pp. 7, 136.

46. "Attending Annual Meetings," *The Transients* (May, 1936), vol. 3, p. 9; Ruth A Lerrigo, "On Every Town's Doorstep," *Survey Graphic* (June, 1936), vol. 25, p. 364; Anderson, p. 100.

47. Anderson, pp. 122–23.

CHAPTER TEN

1. "Further Reports on Community Planning," *The Transient* (March, 1936), vol. 3, pp. 10–15; Ruth A. Lerrigo, "On Every Town's Doorstep," *Survey Graphic* (June, 1936), vol. 25, p. 364; "Holding the Line," *The Transient* (January, 1936), vol. 3, p. 4; "Take Care of Transient Poor Welfare Leader Petitions Governor," *Albany Evening News* (December 13, 1935), p. 3; "Homeless Are the 'Forgotten Men' in Relief Situation," *ibid.* (January 10, 1936), p. 4; "What of the Transient," *Social Welfare Bulletin* (September, 1936), p. 7.

2. New York State's Commission on Unemployment Relief, *Public Relief for Transient and Non-Settled Persons in the State of New York* (Albany, 1936), pp. 36–37 (hereafter cited as Governor's Commission).

3. G. J. M. to Harry Hopkins, n.d., folder 421 New York Transient Complaint, G–M, box 201, Record Group 69 (hereafter referred to as RG 69), National Archives (hereafter referred to as NA).

4. D. H. C. to Franklin D. Roosevelt, February 18, 1936, folder 421 New York Transient Complaint, A–F, *ibid.*

5. Mr. and Mrs. T. Q., n.d., folder 421 New York Transient Complaint, N–Z, *ibid.*

6. Mrs. A. S. to Franklin D. Roosevelt, April 15, 1936, *ibid.*

7. Harry Hirsch, Director of Public Assistance, State Charges, "Settlement with Definitions, Procedures, and Case Illustrations: Policies and

their Application to Problems Arising in Settlement Work," 2d ed., revised, September, 1940, mimeographed report.

8. Mrs. N. M. to Eleanor Roosevelt, April, 1936, folder 421 New York Transient Complaint, G–M, box 210, RG 69, NA; New York City Department of Public Welfare to New York State, Temporary Emergency Relief Administration, April 29, 1936, *ibid.*

9. R. W. W. to Franklin D. Roosevelt, March 1, 1936, folder 421 New York Transient Complaint, N–Z, box 201, RG 69, NA.

10. Mrs. A. J. J. to Mrs. Roosevelt, February 27, 1936, folder 421 New York Transient Complaint, G–M, *ibid.*

11. R. W. to FDR

12. Governor's Commission, pp. 127, 23, 26–27.

13. Janet V. Hirt, "The Transiency Problem as Reflected by a Study of Short Contact Cases in a Buffalo Agency" (Master's thesis, University of Buffalo, 1939), p. 43.

14. *Ibid.*, appendix B, pp. iv–xi.

15. *Ibid.*, pp. ix, x.

16. "Take Care of Transient Poor . . ." p. 3.

17. *Ibid.*, pp. 157, 158–61.

18. *Laws of New York, 1937*, 160th session, chapters 358, 73, 603, (Albany, 1937); "Lehman Signs Bill on School Degrees." *The New York Times* (May 8, 1935), p. 6.

19. *Laws of New York, 1937*, chapter 358, pp. 922–25; *Laws of New York, 1938*, 161st session, chapter 443, 447, 346, (Albany, 1938), pp. 1169–70, 1175, 986–87; *Laws of New York, 1939*, 162nd session, chapter 802 (Albany, 1938), pp. 1965–66.

20. New York State Department of Social Welfare, *Public Assistance Manual* (Albany, 1938), pp. 41–48.

21. Philip E. Ryan, *The New York State Program for Non-Settled Persons* (Albany, 1939), p. 20; United States House of Representatives, 76th Congress, 3rd session, *Hearings before the Select Committee to Investigate the Interstate Migration of Destitute Citizens* (34 parts, Washington, D. C., 1940–44), pp. 217–18 (hereafter cited as Tolan Hearings).

22. Ryan, *The New York State Program for Non-Settled Persons*, p. 46; Tolan Hearings, p. 218.

23. Ryan, *The New York State Program for Non-Settled Persons*, p. 48.

24. "Relief Family Faces Removal," *Buffalo Evening News* (April 24, 1937), p. 1; "Fight Carried Into Court by Relief Aide," *Rochester Democrat and Chronicle* (March 16, 1937); "Court Backs Welfare Law," *Rochester Times-Union* (March 17, 1937); "Aid Family Ordered to Leave Area," *Rochester Democrat and Chronicle* (April 7, 1937); "Relief Couple Banned Here Hike for Plea to President," *Rochester Democrat and Chronicle* (April 11, 1937); "Trio Missing, Lawyer Files Appeal Notice," *ibid.* (April 22, 1937); "Deportation Case Argued," *Rochester Times-Union* (May 17, 1937).

25. "Westchester Wars on Relief Floater," *The New York Times* (December 29, 1939), p. 1; "59 Relief Floaters Defy Westchester," *ibid.* (December 30, 1939), p. 5; "Chirillos Plead to Stay in State," *ibid.* (January 4, 1940), p. 25; "Westchestesr Acts to Evict Mother and Two in Widening Drive Against Relief Floaters," *ibid.* (January 6, 1940), p. 17; "Westchester Bans Relief 'Floaters,' County Judge Orders Widow and Two Children to Go Home to NJ," *ibid.* (January 9, 1940), p. 17; "Westchester Wins War on Floaters," *ibid.* (January 17, 1940), p. 23; "Relief Floaters Lose Removal Suit," *ibid.* (July 25, 1940), p. 19; "Federal Court Here Refuses to Interfere with State Order to Oust Indigent Family," *ibid.* (December 27, 1940), p. 12; "'Chirillos Must Go' Westchester Says," *ibid.* (May 9, 1941), p. 16; "Cobbler and Sons 'Deported' to Ohio from New York State," *ibid.* (May 20, 1941), p. 25.

26. Chirillos et al. v. Lehman, Governor, 38, *Federal Supplement*, p. 65; Matter of Chirillo, 283, *New York Reports*, pp. 417–18.

27. *Ibid.*, Tolan Hearings, p. 4000.

28. Tolan Hearings, pp. 3965–3982.

29. "High Court Bars Review of New York Relief Law," *The New York Times* (March 11, 1941), p. 26; "Westchester Meets New Complications as it Gets Right to Oust Chirillo Family," *The New York Times* (March 12, 1941), p. 23.

30. Tolan Hearings, p. 215.

31. Ryan, *The New York State Program for Non-Settled Persons*, pp. 48–49; Tolan Hearings, p. 202.

32. Ryan, *The New York State Program for Non-Settled Persons*, p. 61.

33. Tolan Hearings, p. 6.

34. Erie County, Department of Social Welfare, *Annual Report, for the Year Ending, December 31, 1939* (Buffalo, 1939), p. 27.

35. "Lodging House Brawl Sends 15 to Pen," *Buffalo Evening News* (January 16, 1937), p. 3; "Board Probes Quality of Lodging House Food," *ibid.* (January 29, 1937), p. 81; "Board is Asked to Shift Lodgers," *ibid.* (February 23, 1937), p. 13; "Adie Ends Feud Over Relief Here," *ibid.* (July 27, 1938), p. 3; "Seamen's Home Relief Plea up to State Jeacock Claims," *ibid.* (September 14, 1938), p. 21.

36. "County Halts Free Lodging to Transient," *Rochester Democrat and Chronicle* (October 4, 1939).

37. A. E. Kannwishcer, "People's Rescue Mission of Rochester, New York," January 20, 1938, mimeograph report located in Rochester Public Library, pp. 6–7, 32–34; People's Rescue Mission of Rochester, New York, *The Forty-eighth Annual Report, People's Rescue Mission* (Rochester, New York, 1937), p. 4.

38. Tolan Hearings, pp. 328–29; "A Refuge for 75,000 Men," *War Cry* (August 7, 1937), p. 8.

39. Tolan Hearings, part 1.

40. *Ibid.*, p. 4226.

41. *Ibid.*, p. 330.

42. *Ibid.*, p. 903.

43. John N. Webb, *The Migratory-Casual Worker*, WPA monograph (Washington, 1937), p. 69; United States House of Representatives, 77th Congress, 1st session, House Report #369, *Interstate Migration Report of the Select Committee to Investigate the Interstate Migration of Destitute Citizens* (Washington, 1941), pp. 561, 557 (hereafter referred to as Interstate Migration Report).

44. "Child Workers on Farms in Erie County, New York," *Monthly Labor Review* (April, 1941), vol. 52, pp. 864–65.

45. Interstate Migration Report, pp. 562–68.

46. "Child Labor on Truck Farms in New York State," *Monthly Labor Review* (February, 1941), vol. 52, pp. 391–92.

47. Interstate Migration Report, pp. 390, 577.

48. Tolan Hearings, pp. 252–54.

Chapter Eleven

1. Bertha McCall, "Migration Problems and the Federal Government, *Proceedings of the National Conference of Social Work,* 67th Annual Conference, 1940, p. 131.

2. *Ibid.*, pp. 138–39.

3. United States House of Representatives, 76th Congress, 3rd session, *Hearings before Select Committee to Investigate the Interstate Migration of Destitute Citizens* (34 Parts, Washington, 1940–44), pp. 1–2 (hereafter cited as Tolan Hearings); John J. Sparkman, "Two Years of Work by the Tolan Committee," *Proceedings of the National Conference of Social Work*, 69th Annual Conference, 1942, p. 176.

4. Tolan Hearings, p. 319.

5. Sparkman, p. 177.

6. Elizabeth Wickenden, "Transiency — Mobility in Trouble," *The Survey* (October, 1937), vol. 73, p. 307.

7. *Ibid.*, pp. 307–9.

8. *Ibid.*

9. Philip E. Ryan, "Relief for Transients," *Survey Midmonthly* (September, 1940), vol. 76, pp. 252–53.

10. Tolan Hearings, pp. 3329, 3336.

11. Nels Anderson, *Men on the Move* (Chicago, 1940), dedication page.

12. Tolan Hearings, p. 4226.

13. McCall, "Migrant Problems . . . "; Philip Ryan, "State and Local Organizations for Coping with Interstate Migration," *Proceedings of the National Conference of Social Work*, 67th Annual Conference, 1940; John Webb,

"Internal Migration: Asset or Liability," *ibid.*, 1939; Ruth Blakeslee, "Laws and Administrative Practices as Barriers to Mobility," *ibid.*; Nels Anderson, "Highlights of the Migrant Problem Today," *ibid.*, 1940; T. J. Woofter, Jr., "Possibilities of Future Migration," *ibid.*; Robert S. Wilson, "Problems in Coordinating Service for Transient and Resident Unattached from the Point of View of Individual Service," *ibid.*, 1935; "Platform on Interstate Migration," *ibid.*, 1941.

14. Tolan Hearings, pp. 7, 155, 319, 252, 226, 219, 220.

15. Ryan, "Relief for Transients," p. 251.

16. New York State Department of Social Welfare, "Settlement and Social Welfare in New York State," March 12, 1941, report, pp. 4, 3, 14, 15; Tolan Hearings, p. 254.

17. "Settlement and Social Welfare in New York State," pp. 8, 9, 17.

18. *Ibid.*, p. 19; *McKinney's Consolidated Laws of New York* (New York, 1941), vol. 52A, pp. 46–47.

19. Sparkman, pp. 179–85.

20. President's Commission on Migratory Labor, *Migratory Labor in American Agriculture* (Washington, 1951); United States Senate, 88th Congress, 1st session, *Hearings before the Subcommittee on Migratory Labor of the Committee on Labor and Public Welfare, on S521, S522, S523, S524, S525, S526* (Washington, 1963); United States Senate, 89th Congress, 2d session, *Hearings before the Subcommittee on Migratory Labor of the Committee on Labor and Public Welfare, on S1864, S1866, S1867, S1868* (Washington, D.C., 1966).

21. National Travelers Aid Association, *Residence Laws: Road Block to Human Welfare* (New York, 1956).

22. Shapiro v. Thompson, 394, *United States Reports*, p. 617.

23. Testimony of Kim Hopper and Ellen Baxter, National Coalition for the Homeless, before the House Committee on Banking, Finance and Urban Affairs, December 15, 1982, provided to the writer by Ellen Baxter.

24. David M. Schneider and Albert Deutsch, *The History of Public Welfare in New York State, 1867–1940* (Montclair, New Jersey, 1969 ed.), p. 380.

25. Ellen C. Potter, *After Five Years* (New York, May 19, 1937), p. 10.

Bibliography

I. ARCHIVAL RESOURCES

Federal Emergency Relief Administration. Records. Record Group 69, National Archives, Washington, D.C.
National Association of Travelers Aid Societies. Records. Social Welfare History Archives, University of Minnesota, Minneapolis, Minnesota.
National Committee on Care of Transient and Homeless. Records. Social Welfare History Archives, University of Minnesota, Minneapolis, Minnesota.
New York State, Temporary Emergency Relief Administration. Records and Reports. New York State Library, Albany, New York.

II. OFFICIAL UNITED STATES PUBLICATIONS

Congressional Record. 75th Congress, 3d session. Washington, D.C. 1939,
Federal Supplement. Vol. 38. St. Paul, Minneapolis: West Publishing Co., 1941.
President's Commission on Migratory Labor. *Migratory Labor in American Agriculture.* Washington, D.C., 1951.
Public Papers of the Presidents of the United States, Herbert Hoover. 4 vols. Washington, D.C., 1976.
United States, House of Representatives, 76th Congress, 3rd session. *Hearings before the Select Committee to Investigate the Interstate Migration of Destitute Citizens.* 34 parts. Washington, D.C., 1940–44.
United States National Resources Committee. *The Problems of a Changing Population.* Washington, D.C., 1938.
United States Reports. Vol. 314. Washington, D.C., 1941.
United States Reports. Vol. 394. Washington, D.C., 1969.

·United States Senate. 72d Congress, 2d session. *Hearings before a Subcommittee of the Committee on Manufactures, on S5121.* Washington, D.C., 1933.
————. 72d Congress, 2d session. *Hearings before a Subcommittee of the Committee on Manufactures, on S5125.* 2 parts. Washington, D.C., 1933.
————. 88th Congress, 1st session. *Hearings before the Subcommittee on Migratory Labor of the Committee on Labor and Public Welfare, on S521, S522, S523, S524, S525, S526.* Washington, D.C., 1963.
————. 89th Congress, 2nd session. *Hearings before the Subcommittee on Migratory Labor of the Committee on Labor and Public Welfare, on S1864, S1866, S1867, S1868.* Washington, D.C., 1966.
United States Statutes at Large. Vol. 47. 72d Congress, 1st session.
United States Statutes at Large, Vol. 48. 73d Congress, 1st session.
Webb, John N. *Migratory Families.* Works Progress Administration monograph. Washington, D.C., 1938.
————. *The Migratory-Casual Worker.* Works Progress Administration monograph. Washington, D.C., 1937.
————. *The Transient Unemployed.* Works Progress Administration monograph. Washington, D.C., 1935.
Whiting, Theodore E. *Final Statistical Report of the Federal Emergency Relief Administration.* Works Progress Administration report. Washington, D.C., 1942.

III. OFFICIAL NEW YORK STATE PUBLICATIONS

The Colonial Laws of New York. 5 vols. Albany, 1894.
Cowen's Report. Vol. 5. Albany, 1827.
Denio's Report. Vol. 4, Albany, 1849.
Department of Social Welfare. *Public Assistance Manual.* Albany, 1938.
————. *Social Welfare Bulletin.* Albany, January 1930 to February 1937.
Governor's Commission on Unemployment Relief, *Public Relief for Transient and Non-Settled Persons in the State of New York: A Study of the Nature and Administration of the Care Extended Destitute Persons Not Having Legal Settlement in the Community Where They Receive Aid.* Albany, 1936.
Hirsch, Harry M. *Our Settlement Laws: Their Origins, Their Lack of Uniformity, Proposed Measures of Reform.* Albany, 1933.
Johnson's Supreme Court Cases. Vol. 17. Albany, 1820.
Laws of New York: 1788, 1801, 1817, 1824, 1873, 1896, 1929, 1931, 1933, 1937–39. Albany, 1788–1939.
New York Reports. Vol. 283. Albany, 1940.
New York Supplement. Vols. 246 and 250. St. Paul, Minnesota, 1931.
Public Papers of Governor Roosevelt, Forty-eighth Governor of the State of New York. 4 Vols. Albany, 1931–39.
Revised Statutes of New York, 1827. Albany, 1829.

Ryan, Philip E. *The New York State Program for Non-Settled Persons.* Albany, January 31, 1939.

State Board of Charities. *Annual Reports:* 1895–1900, 1916.

State Board of Social Welfare. *Annual Reports:* 1929–36.

Temporary Emergency Relief Administration. *Bulletin on Public Relief Statistics.* Albany, 1934–36, Vols. 3–5.

————. *Manual of Procedure.* Albany, April 1935.

————. *TERA Official Bulletins.* Albany, July 11, 1933 to June 13, 1936.

IV. MISCELLANEOUS OFFICIAL DOCUMENTS

Erie County, New York, Department of Social Welfare. *Annual Reports:* 1930–40. Buffalo, 1931–41.

New York City, New York, Department of Public Welfare. *Annual Reports:* 1930–40. New York, 1931–41.

Statutes of California, 1900 Extra Session. Sacramento, 1900.

V. MISCELLANEOUS UNOFFICIAL DOCUMENTS

Hirsch, Harry M., comp. *Compilation of Settlement Laws of all States in the United States, revised as of September 1939.* Chicago: American Public Welfare Association, 1939.

New York State, Bill Jacket Collection, 1933. Microfilm collection of materials forwarded to the Governor with each bill for his consideration.

O'Callaghan, E. B., trans. and comp. *Laws and Ordinances of New Netherland, 1638–1674.* Albany: Weed, Parsons and Company, 1868.

Roseman, Samuel I., comp. *The Public Papers and Addresses of Franklin D. Roosevelt.* 5 Vols. New York: Random House, 1938.

VI. PAMPHLETS

Coyle, David Cushman. *Depression Pioneers.* Washington, D. C., 1939.

National Association of Travelers Aid Socieities. *A Community Plan for Service to Transients.* Washington, D. C., 1931.

New York State, Temporary Emergency Relief Administration. *Five Million People, One Billion Dollars,* Albany, 1937.

————. *Relief Today in New York State, A Summary of the Activities of the Temporary Emergency Relief Administration of New York State Pertaining to the Period, November 1, 1931 to September 1, 1933.* Albany, 1933.

————. *Three Years of Public Unemployment Relief in New York, The Need and How it Has Been Met, 1931–34.* Albany, October 15, 1934.

People's Rescue Mission. *The Forty-Eighth Annual Report of the People's Rescue Mission.* Rochester, New York, 1937.

Potter, Ellen C., M.D. *Ater Five Years.* New York: Committee on Care of Transient and Homeless, May, 1937.

Public Affairs Committee. *Restless Americans.* Washington, D.C., 1936.

The Salvation Army. *In the Front Line, An Account of the Unemployment Emergency Relief Work by the Salvation Army in Greater New York, October 1, 1931 - September 30, 1932.* New York, 1932.

———. *The Salvation Army in the Present Crisis, Report of Unemployment Emergency Relief Work in Greater New York, October 1, 1930–September 10, 1931.* New York, 1931.

State Charities Aid Association, Committee on Revision of the Poor Law. *Patchwork or Progress? Why a Public Welfare Law is Needed.* Albany, 1929.

VII. MISCELLANEOUS UNPUBLISHED MATERIAL

Cinnater, Nan. "Women Hoboes of the Great Depression: Survival in Hard Times." Paper presented at the Sixth Berkshire Conference on the History of Women, June 1, 1984.

Coalition for the Homeless. "Cruel Brinkmanship: Planning for the Homeless—1983." New York, August 16, 1982.

Coalition for the Homeless. "Federal Housing Programs and Their Impact on Homelessness." New York, October, 1982.

Hachtel, Esther. "A Study of One Hundred and Thirty-one Young Transient Women." Master's thesis, University of Tulane, 1935.

Hirsch, Harry M. "Settlement With Definitions, Procedures and Case Illustrations: Policies and Their Application to Problems Arising in Settlement Work." 2nd edition, revised. Report for New York State Department of Social Welfare found in New York State Library, Albany, New York. Mimeo.

Hirt, Janet V. "The Transient Problem as Reflected by a Study of Short Contact Cases in a Buffalo Agency." Master's thesis, University of Buffalo, 1939.

Hopper, Kim, and Baxter, Ellen. National Coalition for the Homeless, New York City. Testimony Before The House Committee on Banking, Finance and Urban Afairs, Subcommittee on Housing and Community Development. December 15, 1982, Washington, D. C.

Kannwischer, A. E. "People's Rescue Mission of Rochester, New York." January 20, 1938. Ms. located in the Rochester Public Library.

McCall, Bertha. "Early History of Selected Travelers Aid Associations, 1917–1948." Paper located in NATAS microfilm collection, University of Minnesota.

National Association of Travelers Aid Societies. "Children Under Sixteen Traveling Alone." Paper located in National Association of Travelers Aid Societies microfilm collection, University of Minnesota.

————. "Homeless and Transient Persons Reported by Social Agencies in the United States, January 9, 10, 11, 1933." Report prepared by the Committee on Care of Transient Persons, dated February 21, 1933. Located in National Association of Travelers Aid Societies microfilm collection, Social Welfare History Archives, University of Minnesota.

————. "Standards for the Care of Transient and Homeless." Paper located in National Association of Travelers Aid Societies microfilm collection, Social Welfare History Archives, University of Minnesota.

————. "Travelers Aid—From Past into the Future." Paper presented at the annual Travelers Aid Convention, June 15, 1931. Located in National Association of Travelers Aid Societies microfilm collection, Social Welfare History Archives, University of Minnesota.

National Committee on Care of Transient and Homeless. "Report on Census of Transient and Homeless Persons of the United States for January 9, 10, and 11, 1933." February 21, 1933. Report located in Record Group 69, National Archives. Mimeo.

New York State Department of Social Welfare. "Settlement and Social Welfare in New York State, Preliminary Report." Albany: 1941. Report found in New York State Library. Mimeo.

Schubert, Herman J. P., and Wagner, Mazi Earle. Interview with author. Buffalo, New York, June 14, 1985.

VIII. Newspapers

Albany *Evening News*. 1930–1940.
Buffalo *Evening News*. 1930–1940.
Rochester *Democrat and Chronicle*. 1936–1939.
New York *Times*. 1929–1940.
New York *The Village Voice*. 1982.
Saratoga Springs *The Saratogian*. 1934.
Syracuse *Post-Standard*. 1935.
Rochester *Times-Union*. 1937.
New York *The Wall Street Journal*. 1982.
Pittsburg *The Pittsburg Press*. 1933.

IX. General Literature

Abbott, Edith. *Public Assistance*. 2 vols. New York: Russell and Russell, 1966 ed.

Allsop, Kenneth. *Hard Travellin': The Hobo and His History*. New York: The New American Library, Inc., 1967.

Anderson, Nels. *The Hobo, The Sociology of the Homeless Man*. Chicago: The University of Chicago Press, 1923.

———. *Men on the Move*. Chicago: The University of Chicago Press, 1940.

Axinn, June, and Levin, Herman. *Social Welfare: A History of the American Response to the Need*. (New York: Dodd, Mead and Co., 1975).

Baxter, Ellen, and Hopper, Kim. *Private Lives/Public Spaces: Homeless Adults on the Streets of New York City*. New York: Community Service Society, February, 1981.

Beard, Charles A., and Beard, Mary R. *The Basic History of the United States*. New York: Doubleday, Doran and Co., 1944.

Booth, William. *The Vagrant and the Unemployable, A Proposal Whereby Vagrants may be detained under suitable conditions and compelled to work*. London: Simpkin, Marshall, Hamilton, Kent and Co., Ltd., 1909.

Branscombe, Martha. *The Courts and the Poor Laws in New York State, 1784-1929*. Chicago: The University of Chicago Press, 1943.

Bremer, William W. *Depression Winters: New York Social Workers and the New Deal*. Phildelphia: Temple University Press, 1984.

Brown, Josephine Chapin. *Public Relief 1929-1939*. New York: Henry Holt and Co., 1940.

Bruns, Roger A. *Knights of the Road, A Hobo History*. New York: Methuen, Inc., 1980.

The Business of Relief, Proceedings of the Delegate Conference, American Association of Social Workers, Washington, D. C., February 14-16, 1936. New York: American Association of Social Workers, 1936.

Collins, Henry Hill, Jr. *America's Own Refugees, Our 4,000,000 Homeless Migrants*. Princeton, New Jersey: Princeton University Press, 1941.

Coode, George. *Report of George Coode, Esq. to the Poor Law Board on the Law of Settlement and Removal of the Poor*. London: 1851.

Cummings, John. *Poor Laws in Massachusetts and New York*. New York: MacMillan and Co., 1895.

de Schweinitz, Karl. *England's Road to Social Security*. New York: A. S. Barnes and Co., Inc., 1961 ed.

Fisher, Jacob. *The Response of Social Work to the Depression*. Cambridge, Massachusetts: Schenkman Publishing Co., 1980.

Hofstadter, Richard. *Social Darwinism in American Thought*. New York: George Braziller, Inc., 1959 ed.

Hopper, Kim, et al. *One Year Later: The Homeless Poor in New York City, 1982*. New York: Community Service Society, June, 1982.

Hopkins, Harry L. *Spending to Save*. New York: W. W. Norton and Co., 1936.

Kelly, Edmund. *The Elimination of the Tramp*. New York: G. P. Putnam's Sons, 1908.

Kimble, Grace Eleanor. *Social Work with Travelers and Transients, A Study of*

Travelers Aid Work in the United States. Chicago: University of Chicago Libraries, 1935.

Klebaner, Benjamin Joseph. *Public Poor Relief in America, 1790–1860.* New York: Arno Press, A New York Times Co., 1976.

Kromer, Tom. *Waiting for Nothing.* New York: Hill and Wang, 1968 ed. Originally published in 1935 by Alfred A. Knopf, Inc.

Leuchtenburg, William E. *Franklin D. Roosevelt and the New Deal.* New York: Harper and Row, 1963.

Link, Arthur S. *American Epoch, A History of the United States Since the 1890's.* New York: Alfred A. Knopf, 1963.

Lynd, Robert S., and Helen M. *Middletown.* New York: Harcourt, Brace and World, Inc., 1956 ed.

———. *Middletown in Transition.* New York: Harcourt, Brace and World, Inc., 1937.

McKinley, Edward H. *Marching to Glory: The History of the Salvation Army in the United States of America, 1880–1980.* San Francisco: Harper and Row, 1980.

McKinney's Consolidated Laws of New York. Vol. 52A. New York: Edward Thompson Co., 1941.

McWilliams, Carey. *Factories in the Field.* Boston: Little, Brown and Co., 1939.

Minehan, Thomas. *Boy and Girl Tramps of America.* New York: Farrar and Rinehart, 1934.

National Travelers Aid Association. *Residence Laws: Road Blocks to Human Welfare.* New York: National Travelers Aid Association, 1956.

Patterson, James T. *The New Deal and the States: Federalism in Transition.* Princeton, New Jersey: Princeton University Press, 1969.

Proceedings of the National Conference of Social Work, 1929–41. (Chicago: The University of Chicago Press, 1930–41).

Reed, Ellery F. *Federal Transient Program, An Evaluative Survey, May to June, 1934.* (New York: The Committee on Care of Transient and Homeless, 1934).

Reitman, Ben L. *Sister of the Road, The Autobiography of Box-Car Bertha.* (New York: Harper and Row, 1975 ed.). Originally published in 1937 by Macaulay Co.

Ribton-Turner, C. J. *A History of Vagrants and Vagrancy and Beggars and Begging.* Montclair, New Jersey: Patterson Smith Publishing Corporation, 1972 ed.

Ringenback, Paul. *Tramps and Reformers 1873–1916, The Discovery of Unemployment in New York.* Westport, Connecticut: Greenwood Press, 1973.

Romasco, Albert. *The Poverty of Abundance.* New York: Oxford University Press, 1956.

Ryan, Philip. *Migration and Social Welfare.* New York: Russell Sage Foundation, 1940.

Schneider, David M. *The History of Public Welfare in New York State, 1606*-1866. Chicago: The University of Chicago Press, 1938.

Schneider, David M., and Deutsch, Albert. *The History of Public Welfare in New York State, 1867-1940*. Montclair, New Jersey: Patterson Smith, 1959 ed.

Schubert, Herman J. P. *Twenty Thousand Transients*. Buffalo, New York: Emergency Relief Bureau, 1935.

Shannon, David A. *Twentieth Century America*. 3 vols. Chicago: Rand McNally College Publishing Co., 1974, 3rd. ed.

Smith, Adam. *Wealth of Nations*. New York: P. F. Collier and Son, 1909 ed.

Stein, Walter J. *California and the Dust Bowl Migration*. Westport, Connecticut: Greenwood Press, Inc., 1973.

Steinbeck, John. *The Grapes of Wrath*. New York: Viking Press, Inc., 1958 ed.

Trattner, Walter I. *From Poor Law to Welfare State, A History of Social Welfare in the United States*. New York: Free Press, 1974.

Webb, Sidney, and Webb, Beatrice. *English Poor Law History*. 11 vols. Hamden, Connecticut: Archon Books, 1963 ed. Vol 7.

Wilson, Robert S. *Community Planning for Homeless Men and Boys*. New York: Family Welfare Association of America, 1931.

————. *Individualized Service for Transients*. New York: National Association of Travelers Aid Societies, 1935.

Wilson, Robert S., and de la Pole, Dorothy B. *Group Treatment for Transients*. New York: National Association for Travelers Aid and Transient Services, 1934.

Zeller, Belle. *Pressure Politics in New York*. New York: Prentice-Hall Inc., 1937.

X. ARTICLES

Abbott, Edith. "The Fallacy of Local Relief." *The New Republic* (November 9, 1932).

"Aiding the Woman." *The War Cry* (December 17, 1932).

Alspach, Charles H. "The National Situation." *The Transient* (January 1936).

"The Army Meeting Mammoth Emergency Relief Situation." *The War Cry* (December 6, 1930).

"Attending Annual Meetings." *The Transient* (May 1936).

Beecroft, Eric, and Janow, Seymour. "Toward a National Policy for Migration. *Social Forces* (May 1938).

Benton, John. "Rest for Weary Willie." *The Saturday Evening Post* (September 5, 1936 and September 12, 1936).

Bookman, C. M. "FERA Yesterday—Today—Tomorrow." *The Survey* (June 1934).

———. "The Federal Transient Program." *The Survey* (April 1935).

"The Bowery Eats," *The War Cry* (September 20, 1930).

"Braking the Transient Treadmill." *The Survey* (January 1933).

"The Business of Federal Relief." *The Survey* (January 1935).

Bunce, Frank. "I've Got to Take a Chance." *The Forum* (February 1933).

Carpenter, Niles, and Haenszel, William M. "Migratoriness and Criminality in Buffalo." *Social Forces* (December 1930).

"The Case of the Transients." *The Survey* (October 1935).

"Child Labor on Truck Farms in New York State." *Monthly Labor Review* (February 1941).

"Child Workers on Farms in Erie County, New York." *Monthly Labor Review* (April 1941).

"A Clearing House for Women." *The War Cry* (November 14, 1931).

Colcord, Joanna C., and Kurtz, Russell H. "1932—Relief Policies and Practices—1935." *The Survey* (December 1935).

"The Committee Looks to the Future of the Federal Program in its Evaluative Survey and Recommendations." *The Transient* (January 1935).

"Concerning the Homeless Man." *The War Cry* (October 24, 1931).

Davis, William C., Lieut. "Nomads, The Salvation Army Method of Dealing With the Homeless Man Problem." *The War Cry* (January 21, 1933).

"Development of the Care of Transient Women." *The Transient* (November 1934).

"Direct Relief at Last." *The Nation* (April 5, 1933).

"The E. F. Hutton Free Food Depot." *The War Cry* (January 3, 1931).

"Editorial." *The Transient* (March 1934).

"Editorial Paragraphs." *The Nation* (August 9, 1933).

Elias, Esther H. "Gold Dust Lodge." *The War Cry* (December 31, 1933).

Ellis, William J. "Interstate Cooperation—Viewed by the Public Administration." *The Transient* (March 1936).

"Findings of Survey Conducted by U.S. Department of Labor." *The Transient* (July 1937).

"The First Inter-State Commission Conference on Transient Relief." *The Transient* (March 1936).

"Flee Dustbowl for California." *Business Week* (July 3, 1937).

"Floating Hotel for Destitute Mariners." *The War Cry* (January 3, 1931).

"Forgotten—and Scrapped." *The New Republic* (June 21, 1933).

"Further Reports on Community Planning." *The Transient* (March 1936).

"Hartford House." *The Transient* (January 1935).

"Here and There on the Transient Problem." *The Transient* (March 1936).

"Holding the Lines." *The Transient* (January 1936).

"Is It to Be Murder, Mr. Hoover?" *The Nation* (August 3, 1932).

Jackson, Glenn E. "New York State's Settlement Laws." *Social Work Today* (June-July, 1941).

Jacobs, Haskell. "The Lawyer Looks at Inter-State Cooperation." *The Transient* (March 1936).

"John Wanderer Finds Friends." *The War Cry (March 25, 1933).*

Johnson, Jean. *"Pure Gold at the Gold Dust Lodge." The War Cry* (November 4, 1933).

Jones, Douglas. "The Strolling Poor: Transiency in Eighteenth Century Massachusetts." *Journal of Social History* (Spring 1975).

Josephson, Matthew. "The Other Nation." *The New Republic* (May 17, 1933).

Kurtz, Russell H. "No More Federal Relief?" *The Survey* (February 1935).

Lerrigo, Ruth A. "On Every Town's Doorstep." *Survey Graphic* (June 1936).

LeSueur, Meridel. "Women are Hungry." *The American Mercury* (March 1934).

McIntyre, William A., Commissioner. "The Homeless and Transient Problem in the United States." *The War Cry* (July 15, 1933).

McMillen, A. Wayne. "An Army of Boys on the Loose." *Survey Graphic* (September 1932).

Minehan, Thomas. "Girls of the Road." *Independent Woman* (October 1934).

Murphy, J. Prentice, "America on the March," *Survey Graphics* (March 1933).

"Nationwide Protest Against Liquidation of the Federal Transient Service." *The Transient* (November 1935).

"New Hope for Depression Youth." *The Transient* (January 1935).

O'Shea, Agnes V. "Development of the Care of Transient Women." *The Transient* (November 1934).

Outland, George. "Is it Worth While Returning Transient Boys to Their Homes?" *The Transient* (January 1935).

Penny, Lucretia. "Pea Picker's Child." *Survey Graphic* (July 1935).

"Planks Go into the Platform." *The Transient* (January 1936).

Potter, Ellen C., M.D. "Mustering Out the Migrants." *The Survey* (December 1933).

"Questions You Must Answer!" *The Transient* (September 1935).

"Rallying to Aid the Army's Emergency Relief Activities." *The War Cry* (November 21, 1931).

"Recent Observations on the Transient Problem." *Public Welfare News* (January 1936).

Reckless, Walter C. "Why Women Become Hoboes." *The American Mercury* (February 1934).

"A Refuge for 75,000 Men." *The War Cry* (August 7, 1937).

"Resume of Federal Transient Program as Reported by Transient Director, FERA." *The Transient* (May 1934).

Roberts, J. R. "Lesbian Hoboes, Their Lives and Times." *Dyke* (Fall 1977).

Ryan, Philip E. "Relief for Transients." *Survey Midmonthly* (September 1940).

"School for Young Transients." *The Survey* (August 1935).

"The S. S. Broadway." *The War Cry* (October 24, 1931).

Sartain, Geraldine. "Bowery Breadlines Longest Since 1914." *The War Cry* (April 12, 1930).

"Shall America Starve?" *The Nation* (November 30, 1932).

"Shakedowns and Pressures." *The Survey* (August 1935).

Smith, Dorothy Wysor. "California Liquidates the Transient." *Social Work Today* (April 1936).

"The Social Front." *The Survey* (February 1936).

Sparkes, Boyden. "New Deal for Transients." *The Saturday Evening Post* (October 19, 1935).

Springer, Gertrude. "Men Off the Road." *Survey Graphic* (September 1934).

———. "The New Deal and the Old Dole." *Survey Graphic* (July 1933.)

———. "Send 'em Back Home." *The Survey* (December 1935).

———. "Transients in No-Man's-Lane." *The Survey* (January 1936).

———. "Well Advertised Breadlines." *The Survey* (January 1931).

"State Conferences Act on Transient Problem." *The Transient* (November 1935).

"State Trends in Settlement Legislation." *The Transient* (April 1940).

"Steps Ahead." *The Transient* (November 1935).

"A Survey of Labor Migration Between States." *The Transient* (September 1937).

"Survey of Transient Boys in the United States." *Monthly Labor Review* (July 12, 1932).

"Told at a Free Food Depot." *The War Cry* (March 7, 1933).

"The Transient Boy—Who and Why." *The Transient* (January 1935).

"The Transient Emerges." *The Transient* (March 1934).

"And There is the Problem of Settlement Laws." *The Transient* (November 1936).

"Transient Order Arouses Protest." *The Survey* (October 1935).

"Transients and Settlement Laws." *The Transient* (March 1936).

"200,000 Vagabond Children." *Ladies' Home Journal* (September 1932).

"The Unattached in the New Program." *The Transient* (June 1936).

"Uncle Sam's Runaway Boys." *Survey* (March 1933).

"Vagabond Children." *Ladies' Home Journal* (November 1932).

Weathersby, William, and Smith, Emily. "Journalism in Transient Bureaus." *The Transient* (May 1935).

Weybright, Victor. "Rolling Stones Gather No Sympathy." *Survey Graphic* (January 1939).

"What About Transients?" *The Transient* (September 1935).

"What Next for Transients?" *The Transient* (September 1934).

Wickenden, Elizabeth. "Transiency = Mobility in Trouble." *The Survey* (October 1937).

"Who are These Migrants?" *The Survey* (October 1933).

"Women and Children First." *The War Cry* (October 24, 1931).

"Women's Canteen and Rest Room." *The War Cry* (January 31, 1931).

Index